Jeannie Won't Mind

Alicia Bailey

Alicia Bailey

Published in 2021 by FeedARead.com Publishing

First Edition

A CIP catalogue record for this title is available from the British
Library.

Dedicated to my daughter Andrea
whose support, love and advice enhanced every word.
Without her my story would have remained untold.

INTRODUCTION

I slid back the glass door and marvelled at the sun in all its glory. It wasn't a cruel burning sun but a gentle warmth which tempted me outside. I made my way to the cane armchair at the far end of the verandah. Although it was shabby, the chair was a comfortable friend to me, where I spent much of my time reading and dozing off in the heat.

My life was relaxed and my health good. I had no debts and the cost of living in Cyprus was favourable. I was blessed with particularly good friends and neighbours and supported in my faith. Through the wonders of modern technology my three precious children were in daily contact with me.

Once I had settled into my chair, I looked at the glorious blossom on the citrus trees and optimistically predicted a heavy fruit crop. The verandah framed a tall Tecoma stans tree resplendent with clusters of bright yellow trumpet flowers, its boughs bowed low with the weight of its blossom. Nestling beneath was a small lime tree. When it was in blossom its beauty and perfume were so attractive, but its branches were lethal, covered with vicious thorns. In the corner of the garden stood an arched arbour where I often sat quietly lost in my thoughts. Jasmin trailed over it onto the boundary fences. Its fragrance filled the house. Orange and grapefruit trees concealed the back fences.

In the centre of the garden curved stone paths radiated out from a fountain. I loved the sound of its running water. It was a popular watering hole for the birds. I always placed crumbs and seeds at its base which gave them permanent food and me great pleasure. I spent hours observing them feed and bathe in the water as it splashed over the three cascades. Beneath the verandah were rockeries with succulents and various roses and miniature chrysanthemums, planted to remind me of home.

The garden to the side of the house was accessed by two steps with a small kidney shaped swimming pool dominating the area. It shimmered some days, was turquoise on other occasions and often reflected the sky, the deepest of blues. The pool was surrounded by large tubs, planted with tall vegetation to shield the pool from the harsh rays of the sun. Honeysuckle covered the fences and screened the remaining area.

My next-door neighbour was a mountain. It was quite stark, and remarkably high. It was mainly covered with shrubs with various trees dotted here and there. The trees were a haven for roosting birds. At around four in the afternoon, I would see massive black clouds of birds descend. The noise was deafening.

At night, a visiting owl used to sit on the top of a telegraph pole. As darkness fell it would stare down at me. Fireflies often encircled the pole and looked like they were paying homage to the owl. It was spectacular to watch.

I felt Peyia was a wonderful place to live. I remember thinking one day, *'Am I really living here? How did I end up in this paradise?'* I had travelled such a long way for a docker's daughter from the East End of London.

CHAPTER ONE

The combination of strangers, coupled with lots of noise frightened me. Two unsmiling women I had never seen before were talking to two very stern looking men. One woman was in a navy dress, the other wore a skirt, blouse and cardigan. The buttons on her cardigan caught my eye because none of them were missing. In 1934 it wasn't uncommon, in West Ham, to see children and sometimes adults with garments devoid of buttons.

I was crying and no one was paying any attention to me. The men, dressed in dark suits were looking down at the floor. Not a word was said to me. I was unaware that my mother was in the bedroom and had just delivered a still born baby girl. It was all very confusing and frightening. I was only four years old.

My fears vanished as soon as Auntie Pat walked through the door. She was my favourite aunt and I loved her dearly. She always cuddled me and made things all right.

My sister Bette and my brother Horace must have been at school as they were nowhere to be seen. My elder brother Bob worked with my father in the Royal Albert Docks. My sister Eileen, the eldest of my siblings was fourteen years older than me, and was already living away from home, employed as a cocktail waitress in a hotel in the West End.

Auntie Pat reassured me, and I stopped crying. She spoke with all the adults in the room then they went into my mother's bedroom to speak in private. She re-emerged with the two women and gave me my warm Sunday clothing to put on. My baby brother Alan was lifted out of his highchair, dressed and strapped into his pushchair. Our lovely auntie was taking us home with her. One of the women accompanied us which puzzled me. I wondered why she was coming.

Auntie suddenly stopped. "We are walking too fast for the little one." She then turned to me. "Get under the handle and stand on the axle Jeannie."

I recall being so happy because no one had ever allowed me to do such a thing before. I always had to run to keep up.

Milner Road was my first home. It was in a block of flats known as 'the buildings'. It had a balcony that overlooked a courtyard surrounded by identical blocks with lots of washing blowing on the lines. Some of the women used to call to each other or holler to their children but my mother didn't call out to us or shout to other people.

We were not allowed to play in the courtyard with the other children. Bette and I were allowed to talk to them in passing but we were taken straight to the park to play. We accepted these boundaries without question. My mother was different from the other mothers. She was considered by her neighbours a snob but as an adult I realised that all she wanted was a better life for us.

My memory of what happened next is very hazy. I suspect that I was traumatised by the day's events. I have no recall of leaving Auntie Pat's house or how I was transported to Fyfield Open Air School, near Ongar in Essex. It was only on researching Fyfield for this book that I discovered it was a residential school for malnourished or sick children from West Ham.

I liked Fyfield and felt happy there. I clearly remember being in a large white iron cot which was pushed onto a lawn. I kept walking around the cot holding onto its top bar. I enjoyed feeling the warm sunshine on my back. I don't know how long I stayed but it could only have been months.

Bette informed me years later that I was in the nursery with the young babies. Eventually it was time for us to return home. We travelled by car. When I climbed into the vehicle my sister Bette was already sitting on the back seat. I was pleased to see her, but she wouldn't look at me. We were not told where we were going. A gentleman was behind the steering wheel with a woman sitting beside him. They spoke in very low voices. The number two-nine-two was mentioned a couple of times.

"Here it is," the woman said finally. "292 Beckton Road. Children this is where you are going to live." The street comprised rows of houses interspersed with blocks of flats. My heart beat so rapidly that I felt sick as we approached. I had wanted to stay in the security of Fyfield. Thoughts about my parents didn't cross my mind. We entered the block, climbed the first staircase when the door on the left was flung open. It was my mother, but it was too late. I had wet myself and soaked the new doormat. "Don't worry Jeannie. It doesn't matter. I will soon find you some dry knickers." This was my mother's first greeting to me. It was very reassuring.

My mother washed me, made me comfortable then signed some papers before bidding the couple farewell. When mother closed the door, I felt all was right with the world. We were given homemade lemonade and biscuits then my mother showed us around and we saw where we would be sleeping.

The furniture in the living room was all new and very pleasant and had a strange smell. I didn't know at the time that it was the smell of leather. A sideboard stood against the wall with some china ornaments displayed on the top. We had similar furniture to this in our previous home, but they were very old pieces that Gran had given to us. The big bedroom next to the living room was for our brothers Bob, Horace and baby Alan. Next to that was a small room that had a bath and a basin. I couldn't see a lavatory. To the right was another big L shaped bedroom that was for my parents plus Bette and me. There were two double beds in the room. Our bed was tucked away round the corner, almost out of sight. We had a pretty little cabinet next to our bed. Mum showed us underneath its cover. It was made from a wooden orange crate. I thought how clever she was and that probably no one else's mother would know how to make such an ingenious thing.

The kitchen was a generous size and our old kitchen table with all its chairs stood centre place. I was so pleased to see it again. I thought the outsized sink was a bath, but my mother explained it was called a Butler sink. It stood next to a gas cooker. A door opened onto a small balcony. I discovered the door leading off to the left housed the lavatory and another to the right was the coal cupboard. The area was enclosed with fancy ironwork to prevent any accidental falls.

We followed Mum down the flight of stairs outside the flat. It led to a large, grassed area which was marked out into four sections, one of which was ours. It was our very own garden, our first. Mum said it was for tenants to either grow vegetables or it could be made into a play area for their children. Beckton Road was such an improvement on our previous home. It was all so wonderful, and I couldn't believe that we were going to live there as a family. Mum told us it was forever, and we would never move again.

We trooped back upstairs into the flat, all smiles then Mum asked us to sit down on the settee as she had to explain something important to us. "You must listen to me properly because what I have to say is especially important. Daddy isn't going to live with us anymore."

Bette spoke for the first time. "Why?"

"Because some very important people have said he mustn't. Daddy will come to the recreation field on certain days to see you and to talk to you. He will want to see if you are all right and well and perhaps play some games with you. Maybe he will play on the see-saw or push you on the swings. You must not ask Daddy to come back here."

"Won't he ever come back to live with us?" I asked.

"We shall have to wait and see." Mum replied.

I was to find out when I was older that my mother had gained a legal separation which was a rarity in those days, especially in the East End of London.

Now I was back to an uneasy and uncomfortable place. It was such a rollercoaster ride. I became fearful again. Nothing ever seemed to stay the same.

"Where is the baby's cot?" I asked anxiously.

Mum said, "He will be sleeping in my bed with me so that I can keep an eye on him. At the moment he is in hospital at Great Ormond Street recovering from a very big operation. Alan had to have a damaged kidney removed. He is getting much better and will soon be home with us."

Years later I was told by my mother that it was the result of my father lashing out. His blow to her abdomen had had dire consequences.

"Can we go to see Alan?" I asked my mother.

"No because little children are not allowed to visit. They could pass on nasty germs to the sick children."

We met our father regularly in the recreational park. We crossed Beckton Road and were able to enter via the rear gate of the park. Mum would see us across the road and when we reached the gate dad would always be there. We did this every day after we had lunch then Bette had to return for afternoon school. On reflection I realise that it must have been quite a task for my father to fit the daily visit in with his work routine. Dad would always relate some story to us or sing. He had a very good voice and sang in clubs or at functions during the weekends. On one occasion he was practising a new song for the coming weekend. He requested that we listened to the words carefully and the first one of us to learn the song would get a penny. I was the first. I never received the penny. I was hurt that this promise was not kept. The song was called "It's a Sin to Tell a Lie," and starts with the line, "Be sure it's true when you say I love you." My mother heard me singing it over and over again. I wonder now, was my father sending my mother a message?

Winter was upon us, and it was getting far too cold to sit in the park which meant another way of meeting Dad had to be arranged. Every Sunday we visited Gran, my mother's mother. It was always a time that I looked forward to. I loved her so much, as did all her other grandchildren. When it was time to leave Gran's house, she used to give us one penny each. A halfpenny was for the Sunday school collection and a halfpenny to spend as we wished which was usually in Larkins, the corner sweet shop. Dad waited for us outside or if it was raining, he would be in the sweetshop. After we had spent our money, he walked us to the entrance of our block of flats. Mum agreed to this arrangement in the colder weather but as soon as the weather improved, we resumed our visits to the park. Our little brother Alan had recovered from his operation and accompanied us. Bette pushed him there and then returned to school. Dad would see both Alan and me back across the road whilst Mum came to collect us. Neither she nor Dad ever looked or spoke to

11

each other. Even at that tender age it made me sad. This routine went on for some time. Summer was much better as we were able to run and play on the swings. I must have been very observant as a child because I knew that when other children's parents chatted to Dad, they always felt sorry for him. They started to call him Harry. I didn't like them chatting with him because they used our special time.

Another winter was upon us and the routine of the previous one was adhered to. On two occasions Dad failed to appear. Mum made enquiries and was told that he was ill with pneumonia, confined to his rented room not very far from where my grandmother lived. My mother made hot lemon drinks for him. Bette and I were delegated to deliver these to his lodgings. We did this repeatedly. On several occasions we took hot soup and bread and butter pudding. These visits were the spur for Dad returning to the flat to live with us. We were back as a family again.

We were given no explanation, but children of that time wouldn't have expected one. We just accepted that Dad was back in charge again. We started to see our eldest sister Eileen far more frequently. She visited us on her days off, usually accompanied by her current boyfriend. My favourite boyfriend of Eileen's was a chap called Stan. He drove an M.G. sports car and was always kind to us and sometimes drove us to the end of the road. We always hoped that the other children playing in the road would see us showing off.

Life was about to change for me. I was now five years of age and school was beckoning. For years we had attended a Methodist Sunday school. I treasured every moment spent there. I was totally absorbed by the story telling and we were allowed to borrow books to take home. What a privilege this was. I loved Hans Christian Anderson and Grimm's fairy tales. I remember these books being so heavy for me to carry but no one prevented me from borrowing them even though I was so young and unable to read. My mother said I used to just sit for hours turning the pages and absorbing the illustrations. I knew, even at that tender age, that you must take care of books. I still wonder how a child acquires the desire for knowledge in a household devoid of books or discussions.

I felt such a grown-up girl on my first day of school. Crying or clinging to my mother's skirt was not for me. I wanted to be there. Mothers seemed to be everywhere. Prams and pushchairs looked like an army of invaders. At last, my name was called, and Mum was given my class number. It was a huge school called Holborn Road with all the classrooms flanking its large hall. The classroom doors were all numbered. I didn't feel fearful as I had been inside many times. There were special little chairs awaiting us. Our teacher called out our names and we were told to raise an arm when we heard our own. I didn't have to wait long as they were called out in alphabetical order.

Shortly afterwards our teacher placed some large pictures upon an easel. We had to raise our hands if we could identify the animals in the pictures. I thought, *"Everybody knows what cows and horses, or lambs look like. This is a silly game."* After I answered by calling out a couple of times the teacher covered the pictures and asked me what word matched which animal. I managed to tell her, and she took me to another class. I somehow had slipped into reading gradually and no one could understand how. I saw words as pictures. I was a very ordinary pupil for the rest of my days, but my love of reading is a constant pleasure still.

I stayed at that infant school until I became a junior. They were happy days until my last week. Our infant school was next door to the senior school with adjacent playgrounds. Both schools conformed to the rule of having pupils standing in line before being called in one line at a time. On this occasion I caught sight of Horace, my gentle brother, as I had done many times before. I waved to him, and he reacted as usual by ignoring me but would smile and then look down at his feet. Suddenly a commotion erupted behind him in the line. Six boys who were last in the line were called to the front. A cane was brought out and my lovely brother who was not even talking was caned along with the rest. When he was caned, he dropped to the ground. The teacher shouted at him. "Bailey, get up!" We were always addressed by our surnames in those days even the infants. When Horace arrived home my parents were horrified. His hand was cut to the bone on his palm. It was the only time that my parents visited the school to complain. The injury was so bad because the cane that had been used was split. If this was not terrible enough, one of the caned boy's parents came to our home later that evening. They related to my parents that their son had told the teacher concerned that Bailey was not part of the skirmish. The teacher had responded by saying, "It's his bad luck for being in front of you." That incident spoiled my lovely memories of Holborn Road School where I spent all my formative days. As an adult I was able to let it go, remembering instead all the gentle and kind teachers that touched my life.

A lasting memory of my infant school is the afternoon naps in the little camp beds covered with hand knitted blankets and the bottles of milk, freely given, which were enjoyed by us all. Children in that school were never made to feel inferior or unimportant. All the children were valued and sent home with smiles and in many cases with a clean, dry pair of knickers or fresh pants.

Our family life was very disturbed. As children we lived each day and accepted whatever life had to bring us. I think that is probably how we survived. In our family the elder siblings were remote. It was as though we were two families. To us they were adults with busy working lives. On arriving home from work my older brothers would spend most evenings and weekends out socialising. Sometimes we would be in bed by the time they came home from work. I know that they were always kind to us 'little ones,' as they called us. On one of Eileen's visits, we overheard talks of a party. Eileen's twenty first birthday was coming up. During the following weeks Mum seemed to always be bringing in parcels and finding places to put them. To us little ones we didn't realise that this party would be different from those we usually had when people came back from the pub and had a sing song around the piano. Lots of the organising must have taken place whilst we were in bed. All we were told was that we were going to be looked after at Auntie Pat's house with our cousins. We children didn't like the thought but were consoled by the promise that when the day arrived, we would be off to Auntie Pat's with bags of special goodies - chocolate, crisps, lemonade and Tizer. Such luxuries had rarely been seen or enjoyed by us before. All our cousins would be at the Gainsborough

14

Road house. We were told we could go to bed when we liked or sleep on the floor. We thought this was wonderful. When the time came, I can recall one or two little fights but only amongst the bigger cousins, all of whom wanted to be the boss.

We returned home the next day to the party still going on. Some people were asleep, others sitting on the stairs outside the flats. Smoke from their cigarettes and cigars filled the stairwells. The party lasted two days. I asked my mother in later years how they afforded it. Apparently, Eileen paid for all the food and the various young men paid for the drinks. We were never to see another party such as that again.

All too soon our home life reverted to how it was before with my father being aggressive and abusive to my mother. It had resumed soon after his return. I never saw my father drunk but I have no doubt that drink fuelled the demons within him. My mother's face was never marked, and she would remain the same with never a reference to even a row. I am sure she must have known that we could hear all the shouting and insults that occurred. Hearing the pleas of my mother has never left me. I can hear her plea of, "Don't Harry," and the sound of furniture crashing to this day. The pain is etched in my heart and mind and now well into my eighties I know it never will leave me. To the world at large Dad was a kind, loving and generous man. We children never experienced his wrath. He always made sure all was well with us. Every night he would see us bathed and ready for bed and tell funny stories to make us laugh. I always had a serious face, but Bette would laugh at his jokes and the tricks he played to amuse us. When I told my sister Bette that I could not forget or forgive his treatment of our loving gentle mother she said, "When you get older you will know adults always make up in the end." I know as an adult that is not true.

Mother appeared to be the same as usual after one of these sessions but only to protect the happiness of her children. I used to watch Dad every night as he polished our shoes for school. He would have a gentle loving smile on his face as though he was polishing love into every pair he shone. Mum's shoes were polished with the same lovely smile, even the arches received the same care as the uppers and would gleam. Mum used to place our school clothes in our allotted place and

15

Dad would place the polished shoes beneath. This routine was adhered to daily. What happened to make this seemingly caring husband and father turn into this violent husband? On reflection as an adult, I feel he was trying to break my mother's spirit. She was refined. She never raised her voice and never revealed how she was suffering. I am sure that the neighbours must have heard some commotion and noise, but my mother used to go about her normal life as though there was not a cloud upon the horizon. I knew even at that young age that she was different from a lot of other women. She was always immaculate, as was the house. All the neighbours would get a smile and a 'good morning' as she passed by. Thank goodness she had a very loving mother, brother and sisters. These were her only contacts with the outside world. Every Wednesday the siblings would meet at their mother's house to catch up with family news. They were aware of what was going on between my parents and would pass their opinions as to what Mum should do. However, for all their knowledge and opinions my mother stayed with my father.

It was extremely hard for anyone to believe that this was all going on behind the scenes. To the outside world we looked like a family that people envied. Dad was someone who could walk into a room and the whole place would light up. Should anyone be in trouble or want advice, 'Ask Harry,' he always knew the right person or where to go if one needed help. As well as being a docker Dad was chauffeur to the boss of the renown P&O Line. He was on hand for whenever the boss needed driving around the docks. This gave Dad extra money and certainly some prestige. On the sporadic weekend, when the boss wanted an early pick up my father would bring the car home. As children we looked forward to these occasions because we knew that maybe we would have a treat in store. Sometimes Dad would take us to the docks. We three children would sit in the back of this beautiful car with our knees covered up under a thick, soft car blanket. Either my sister Bette or I would be delegated to hold father's pipe under the blanket as smoking was forbidden in the docks. On approaching the gates Dad would roll down the car window to be recognised. His charisma, and the fact it was the boss's car ensured that we were waved on with a "Good morning, Harry" and a "Hello children." The docks were an enthralling world and whilst we were there all the unpleasantness in our lives was put on hold. To see the big liners of the trading world moored side by side and stern to stern was awesome. I can still feel the wonder of this spectacle.

Dad also had the use of the boss's motor launch. We were told never to attempt to move around whilst on board. We were warned that should we do so we would never be allowed aboard again. Three little faces with necks stretched to their limit gazed out at the sights. We were just a mere speck against these giants of ships. We saw monkeys on the shoulders of some of the Lascars who were manning the ships. Their English was extremely limited, but they threw bananas and oranges down to the launch calling to Dad. " 'Arry dees for childer to eat." We thought we were so lucky to have this treat.

It is so hard to believe now in this present day that liners filled the London docks with trade. One of my memories of that time was seeing large heaps of fruit lying rotting, waiting to be dumped out at sea. The fruit were slightly too ripe to get to the shops in time and would be taken out along the Thames and dumped overboard. This was a disgrace when so many people were hungry and without jobs. Nobody cared or wanted to think of the needs of these people, and it was long before the Welfare State. It was a much-divided society between the haves and the have nots. For all the sadness and stress within the four walls of our home we knew as children how fortunate we were compared to many others. Life was extremely tough for many.

In the 1930s Soup Kitchens were set up in the East End, one of which was not far from our home. If a family's income was below a certain means, they were allowed free meals. Hundreds of people of all ages needed this service. My mother's sister, my auntie Lizzie, was one of the senior cooks at the kitchen. We used to traipse along very reluctantly at 7.30 before school and sit on a little bench that auntie fitted into a corner by the servery. "Here comes Lizzie's children," was the cry when we arrived. "Sit down and get warm." I hated it. The food was basic but good. My pride was the problem. I didn't think we were poor. My mother paid into an insurance organisation called the H.S.A. It was for health cover. The premium was one shilling per week for the whole

17

family. She paid this right up to the time that Dad got injured in the first blitz on the docks.

We didn't play in the streets very often because our mother always made suggestions to us of things we could do. One of which we really loved and didn't cost a penny. Bette and I would walk to the entrance of the Blackwell Tunnel. It wasn't too far, and we used to take our little brother with us. On arrival my sister would decide if we would walk through the tunnel to the other side first and come back by the ferry or do the reverse. We didn't mind the walk and what excitement there was when we boarded the ferry. We pretended we were paying passengers going on a holiday. We were so fortunate to always be allowed, by the crew, to stay on board. Many children had the same idea but didn't behave themselves and the crew used to turf them off. We didn't run around. We pretended we were going to Australia or sometimes America. Bette always chose the country we were travelling to. If we had decided to walk the outgoing journey, we returned by ship stopping off at the little park that was at the start of the Blackwell Tunnel. Joy of joys it had a sand pit. We arrived home with our socks and knickers stained orange. We were then forbidden to go to the sand pit in the park.

On our very next trip I thought I would be so smart and take my knickers off. My sister was horrified but I went into the shrubs and removed them, tucking them into my liberty bodice. I thought I had solved the problem of being caught out. Bath time came and all was well, and nothing was said to the others except Mum asked me what my knickers were doing in my bodice. "I don't know," I answered. Before long we made a further exciting journey to an unknown destination. As Mum gave us our sandwiches and a bottle of homemade lemonade she said, "You are not to play in Blackwell Tunnel Park or to ever take your knickers off to deceive me. I know everything that you do, every moment of the day." I was amazed that our mother had such magical powers. As an adult and a mother, I shudder to think of the hundreds of risks that we were liable to encounter. We could have drowned if we had not obeyed the rules or come across undesirable people. None of these things were explained to us. We were just taught not to talk to strangers or accept sweets or treats from anybody. That was the golden rule which protected us.

One of our other make-believe outings was going to the allotments. Once again, a picnic was packed. Bette was always in charge of everything, even the two sweets each, that was the allocation for the day. We would set up camp in my father's allotment. Bette would always choose my father's shed as her house because she knew where the key was hidden. I chose a stranger's and that was my pretend house. I always took my doll on those trips because we were playing families and having the doll made it more real to me. Whilst we were there we weeded and watered the plants. I remember one allotment keeper telling us what good children we were because we didn't walk over the dug ground.

Another of my favourite outings was to the churchyard. I could have spent every day there and I still find graveyards fascinating. I used to read the tombs and headstones and work out the family relationships. I felt so sorry and sad if someone was young when they died. I wandered around the plots and refilled all the vases if the flowers needed water. It seems strange to me now, but it didn't then. I was never conscious of the cemetery's relationship with death. It was the innocence of childhood. You all think you are going to live for ever.

A special time for us was the yearly visit to Bertram Mills Circus. My father would contact the Star newspaper each year and request tickets for the dress rehearsal. It was an exciting time for all the little children in our area. The day the tickets were due to arrive the door knocker was constantly banged and my mother would bind a towel around it to deaden the sound. It was such a thrill to be amongst the hustle and bustle of the organisation. Father had a difficult job as he had to allocate tickets fairly. Lists were consulted so that the same children didn't go every year. Tickets were finally allocated and then all the fortunate children chosen were on countdown for the big day. Three coaches always parked outside our block of flats. Parents often brought the children far too early but once aboard the fun would begin. My father always started a singsong and all the children joined in and were happy but when we arrived at Olympia the excitement was at its highest. We all knew what was to come. Each child was given a carrier bag full of

19

treats. It contained bars of chocolate, biscuits, fruit plus a funny hat. We now know the rights and wrongs of circuses but in those days, we thought they were so magical, full of colour and sound. So much was going on within the enormous ring whist everyone was settling into their seats. Clowns rolled about whilst others threw balloons into the audience. The arena was one noisy but joyful place. When we departed at the end of the show, we were given another little bag containing things to eat on the journey home. The circus was the highlight of my year.

My father had some arrangement with the organisers. He was always given all the bags from the unattended seats. He would later give these to the children that were unsuccessful in obtaining tickets.

All too soon our lives were to be shattered again. Both Mum and Dad requested that they wanted to talk to us after our baths before we went to bed. We were puzzled. Never had they both wanted to talk to us. Some six months previously Bette, Alan and I were shown small suitcases. We had one each. Mum had bought us new clothes to pack in them and toothbrushes with proper toothpaste. We usually cleaned our teeth with bicarbonate of soda. The cases had labels tied onto their handles. Our father had written our name and address on the front and a large number on the back. That night Mum and Dad told us that sometime soon we were all going on a holiday to the country, but we must not tell anybody our secret. I remember being told the name of this holiday. It was called The Crisis. At that time, we were excited because people in the East End didn't go on planned holidays. Not one of us told anybody because we had been told that it was a family secret. We obeyed our parents who at the time thought it was the best way to stop us worrying.

A strange incident happened not only to our family but to our neighbours and the children from school. Everyone was asked to congregate at a local hall. There was a real hullabaloo as many things were happening all at once. We were given horrible black rubber masks and asked to try them on. Many children started screaming. Parents with babies were given a different type of mask. Babies were lain inside with a clear window for them to see out. The babies didn't seem to like theirs either. We all went home with masks that supposedly fitted us. Mother wrote our names on the rubber as soon as we arrived home and then placed them on top of the wardrobe with our little suitcases.

So many things were happening in our lives that it got to the stage that nothing could surprise us. We got up the following day and life carried on as usual. Gradually people's conversations about this thing called 'war' seemed to diminish as did the mention from our parents about the special holiday. Life carried on as usual. We played, ate and slept with no thoughts about our lives changing in any way and the secret holiday was soon pushed to the back of our minds. I had also worked out that the bad things in our house with Daddy only happened at weekends but not each one. It was only when Daddy was singing at the clubs.

CHAPTER TWO

Friday 1st September 1939 is a day etched upon my mind and on the minds of many other children called evacuees - the name designated for us, the children with the labels and little suitcases. The government decided to evacuate children, mothers with babies and the infirm from major towns and cities because they feared many civilian deaths from German bombing. It took place in several waves, the first being on 1st September 1939 – the day Germany invaded Poland and two days before the British Declaration of war. Over the course of three days 1.5 million evacuees were sent to locations considered safe.

We got up very early, much earlier than usual and Dad was there as he hadn't gone to work. We thought we were going on this secret holiday called The Crisis - how wonderful. The little cases were lifted from the top of the wardrobe and placed by the door in readiness and by their sides were the gas masks. There was a strange atmosphere. No one was talking and our parents were looking at each other but without smiling. Dad often winked at one of us but not on this day. Out of the blue we were informed by our parents, "We are not going with you children. Some kind people are going to look after you." We were so frightened. Alan started to sob. I couldn't understand why Mum was crying as she hugged him. It was a very traumatic start to a never to be forgotten day. I was nine, Bette eleven and Alan nearly seven years old.

We left the flat in silence and I was shaking with fear of the unknown. As we reached the street outside there were hundreds of crying children and sobbing parents. All the children were carrying the same sized suitcases. We progressed along the street with the sheer force of numbers. We had no choice but to go with the flow of the crowd.

Buses were lined up in rows upon row, teachers were yelling through megaphones to their own pupils, "Read your labels, they will match your school number to a particular bus." Mothers were screaming as were most of the children. We were silent but somehow amidst the chaotic frenzy Mum and Dad found our bus by its number. It was packed. Some parents wouldn't get off, some were trying to leave their children and most of the children were hysterical. We eventually found that there were many buses with the same number, and we boarded another one. Mum hugged us and then suddenly she was not there. She told me years later that the sheer volume of people pushed her back. She was heartbroken and we were desolate and petrified. My little brother was shaking so much that his teeth were chattering, and he was soaking wet. As the bus started up there were screams from all the children inside with the two adult marshals on the bus platform trying their best to console their little passengers and contain them. I learned later that they were teachers who also didn't know what was going on and how to handle the situation. To a frightened child who had been brought up to be cautious of strangers the world had turned into a black and frightening place of unknown horrors.

The bus arrived at its destination of Paddington station and joined masses of other buses. All the buses and coaches were being directed by loud hailers as they had to wait for their turn to off load. We all became noticeably quiet, and the teachers were still manning the platform awaiting instructions on how to disembark. Hundreds and hundreds of crying children were marshalled into crocodile queues. On reaching the station you could not distinguish the railway lines or the platforms. Every available space was jam-packed with children and officials. To me this exercise rates as one of the most horrific blunders of the 1930s. That one journey alone was horrifying enough to create so many psychological instabilities and disorders for my generation.

Railway carriages seemed to go as far as the eye could see. There was pandemonium and the noise of thousands of children coupled with the blare from inadequate megaphones. Some mothers had had second thoughts about leaving their children and were shouting their names out loud in a vain hope of finding them. It was utterly terrifying for us.

Numbered seats proved to be of no use. It was a free for all. My sister went ahead of us and found herself a seat by a window. I found a seat in the middle of another row and held Alan on my knee. We couldn't see anyone because people were standing crammed into every available space. The children standing immediately in front of us must have been from a senior school as they seemed so very tall.

It felt as though we had been travelling for hours but of course we had not. I think the anxiety of waiting and the fear of the unknown had distorted our perception of time. The first glimpse of what was to become of us became apparent when the senior children moved away from us. I caught sight of a big sign - Slough. I remember I said to my little brother, "Don't worry. It's Sloff." I never see the word Slough now without mentally calling it Sloff. We had arrived at our destination, and I had the added burden of a very wet lap.

It took quite a while to unload the train because for the first time that day it wasn't chaotic. Men with clipboards entered every child's name and their school as they disembarked. Women greeted us with brown carrier bags which contained something, but we were told not to look inside until instructed. We all had our little cases to contend with, plus our gas masks around our necks. Someone carried Alan's for me. Bette was nowhere to be seen at this stage. We were marched off again still in crocodile formation. It seemed such a long way. Alan was crying for Mummy, and I couldn't see my sister. It was all extremely traumatic for us.

As we marched, we were all silent. There was no chattering or murmuring. Suddenly we were told to halt before a large block of flats on the corner of Stoke Poges Lane and Carmarthen Road.

It was a very hot day, and we were told to sit down on the grass. It was only a couple of minutes later when Bette found us, and we were able to sit together. We were then told we could look in the carrier bags and found to our delight it contained various sweets, chocolate biscuits and a drink. It was now lunch time, and we were very hungry. Alan had a little something to eat and promptly fell asleep on the grass. I said to my sister, "The sun is too hot on his little head." She promptly tore up one of the carrier bags and made him a shelter which covered his head

24

and his shoulders. I sat with my back shielding his legs. This gave us a little respite from our immediate worries.

As the afternoon wore on, we could see the officials were in a state of panic. People were coming onto the lawn and picking children out willy-nilly; children that they liked the look of or perhaps those they considered were better dressed. We felt very vulnerable. People were surrounding us and discussing the fact that we were from the East End of London. They spoke about us as though we were not there and warned one another that we were children that would swear and spit. How ignorant those adults were.

One hour turned into another and as the hours went on, we became exhausted and were so hot. It was evident that nobody was going to take on three children. I thought this was a good thing as they would have to take us home again. We could hear talk of an overnight stay in a hall if the remaining children were not housed. That didn't sound so good. Bette said, "I am not having that." I was pleased because I knew she would have the strength to carry out any decision that she made on behalf of us. We were very thin in number by now and Bette was ready to do battle and waiting to talk to the man with a clipboard. However, he turned his attention to a lady who said to him, "I cannot stand by and do nothing for these children." Her name was Mrs Nunn. She had seen the plight and distress of the children. She informed the man that she would double up her own daughters to make room for at least two children and volunteered to take Bette and me. For us it was a no, no. We had our little brother.

The billeting officer was empowered to place children in houses that were under occupied. A couple with no children lived two doors from Mr and Mrs Nunn and they had three empty bedrooms, so the billeting officer made the decision to billet Alan with them. This meant he would be as close as possible to us. We were extremely stressed by this decision but were comforted by Mrs Nunn who tried to reassure us by telling us that Alan could come every morning and stay with us for the whole day. He would only have to sleep at the other address. Alan was distraught and desolated once again. It made no difference when we tried to console him by telling him it was only for one night. We had to

25

let him go. I started to cry and then couldn't stop. We were shown the bedroom we were going to use. It had a double bed but was very nice and Mrs Nunn got Molly, her eldest daughter, to empty a drawer for us. When our cases were opened a surprised look passed from one adult to the other. Our clothes were all pristine and there was two of everything we needed. Many people assumed that anyone from the East End of London would be the dregs of society.

It was soon time for the evening meal. So far everyone in the household had spoken kindly to us. We were called to sit up at the table and as each plate of food was brought to the table Bette and I looked at each other puzzled. Every plate was the same with only meat and gravy on it. The family started to eat, and Mr Nunn said, "It's all right children, it is your food, and you can eat it." We were dumbfounded. Betty replied to Mr Nunn, "We like it, but we are waiting to say grace." We found out over the course of time that we stayed there, that some Yorkshire people ate the meat and gravy first. The vegetables followed the main course. The Nunn family ate all their courses in a different order to us.

We in turn continued to surprise the Nunn family. We informed them that our hair had to be tooth combed every evening. Once the Nunns realised that we had a routine and it wasn't because we were rebels or unhappy, everything was fine. Our last surprise for them came at the end of that very long day. Mrs Nunn pulled the covers back on the bed for us to jump in, but we just stood there. Bless her, she looked perplexed and then said, "Do you want me to decide what side you sleep on?" We were waiting to kneel by our beds to say our prayers before getting in and settling down. We certainly had a lot of prayers to say that night and we were used to saying them out loud. I remember Mrs Nunn left our bedroom with tears in her eyes.

Saturday started with the sound of very heavy knocking. We children were heavily asleep. The front door was being knocked as though something terrible had happened or was about to. Everyone in the household was up and at various stages of undress with their eyes fixed firmly upon the door. Mr Nunn opened the door to find a small boy sobbing. He was standing crying and saying he wanted his mummy.

It was Alan and it was only 7.30 a.m. The couple who he had been billeted with were post office workers and were leaving for work. What a start to our first day. Alan was seven years old and what made it worse for him was the fact that he had heard them say, "We don't want him, and we know nothing about children." He was taken in by the Nunns who gave us all cuddles and a nice breakfast. Alan had to stay with those people the following week until other arrangements were made for him. It was hard but we had him every second that he was awake. That first Saturday we just sat in the garden and played ball feeling frightened and uneasy and wondered what was to come next.

Mr Nunn said he would put our cases in the loft and asked if we would like to help him. Before handing him mine, I looked inside, and my label wasn't there. I cried out and sobbed and no one could console me. Eventually in between sobs I said, "My label has gone, and no one will know who I am or where my parents live." That label, in my child's mind, was the only thing that was constant. Mrs Nunn ran outside and searched their dustbin and retrieved the precious label. She wiped it clean and said, "There you are Jeannie. I will put it into your case, and it will always be there, and you can look at it whenever you wish." It was my most valued possession at that very painful time. It was my identity.

On the Sunday we arose as usual and went down to breakfast. Mr Nunn said, "Before you start breakfast, I want to show you something in the front room." We trooped into the parlour with both Patsy and Dodds, the name they called Dorothy. We were shown three of the largest bars of chocolate that you can imagine. "Now," he said, "If you can guess who gave them to you, they will be yours." We all know that amazing things and coincidences arise in life, and this was one of them. The previous day Mr Nunn, who worked in London, missed his train home to Slough. He decided to have a beer and walked to the nearest hotel. The hotel was full of people talking about the terrible evacuation of the children. Mr Nunn joined in and told the story of how he had witnessed the children being treated like cattle and although his family didn't have any spare room, they had taken in two little girls. The barmaid said, "My mother is demented with worry. My

27

two sisters and little brother went on Friday, and we don't know which part of England they have been taken to." Mr Nun said to her, "Our two little girls are called Bette and Jeannie and their little brother is called Alan."

The bar maid was our big sister Eileen. What was the probability of that chance meeting? A missed train had brought our sister and our new foster parent together. Eileen was able to inform our parents of our whereabouts and they in turn passed the information on to all the Tollgate School parents. When we were told the chocolate bars were from our big sister we were overjoyed. We also knew our parents would be relieved.

CHAPTER THREE

I was so unsettled. Auntie Nunn said I could go outside to play but only as far as the end of the drive. I enjoyed seeing passers-by and always said hello. Most people usually responded. A lady caught my eye as she turned the corner. She looked smartly dressed in a stylish suit, had highly polished shoes and was carrying a new baby swathed in a white shawl. As she approached, I realised this elegant lady was my mother, she was carrying my beautiful doll resplendent in real baby clothes. I was jubilant and promptly wet my knickers. I was mortified. Auntie Nunn was so kind and comforted me, "Quick let's get a dry pair of knickers before your mummy knows, otherwise it will worry her." She completely took my shame away at doing such a thing at nine years of age. It was proved later that anxiety was the cause of my wetting problem.

I cuddled Mum and she handed over my big doll. I now had something of my own. Mum's first words were, "You have grown taller, and you need a haircut. We will sort that out when I talk to your new auntie."

In the next hour, my confidence and security was challenged again. Mum informed me that Bette was returning to London with her. I screamed out immediately, "Not me or Alan?" I was traumatised again. Alan was listening and thought his mummy had come to take him home. We both started crying uncontrollably. My mother tried to calm us down and told us the reason for all this upheaval. Bette had passed the scholarship and our London high school was being evacuated to Weymouth and she would be joining them. Bette didn't seem at all surprised by this. Apparently, she already knew but was told to keep it from us until Mum could tell us herself. We were told one particularly good piece of news. Alan was going to join our cousin Tony at his billet which was in another part of Slough. The family had two sons and decided that they could accommodate Alan as well as our cousin. It was a happy household and Alan's foster carer Mrs Simmons was a kind and very loving lady. This left me on my own with the Nunns. I was sort of reassured by this but at nine years old I was expected to have no feelings of being abandoned again. I was carted off to get my hair cut with all this anguish inside me. The hairdresser was given the usual instruction of a bob cut to the ears and a fringe cut straight above the eyebrows. My hair was cut short because the haircut had to last but I only appreciate the need for that now. At the time I felt embarrassed and inferior because I thought people would think I had lice or fleas. What a day that was. I now had no sister, no little brother and had to say goodbye to Mum again, not knowing when or if I'd see her again.

Before too long I settled into a routine. My schooling was not full time as we evacuees and our teachers had to share existing classrooms which were already at capacity. Sometimes we would start school at 9 o'clock, on another day we would go in for the afternoon only. We were always told at the end of the session what time we had to be in school the next day. Fortunately, Alan was living quite close to my school which meant that occasionally I was able to visit after school, but I always had to have permission from the Nunns. Alan's billet was such a lovely household. They were always laughing and playing jokes on each other. Mrs Simmonds would often take her family on picnics to Burnham Beeches and sometimes I was allowed to go with them.

I remember one day particularly well. Mrs Simmonds took Alan, my cousin Tony and me along with her own children on a visit to her relatives in Stoke Poges. Their house was rather like a barn. It had a ladder to access the upper part where they all slept. There was no furniture, only straw filled palliasses. We thought that wonderful, rolling about and shrieking with laughter. Everything in the cottage was basic and seemed handmade. It felt a happy and welcoming home.

We were allowed to wander in the garden and the orchard beyond. I soon made my way, on my own, down a rough, overgrown path. I felt it magical. Apple trees heavy with apples were in abundance. I picked a large ripe one, not really believing it possible and that I was not dreaming. A deckchair was placed under one of the trees. It was shiny new; this was a favourite spot for somebody. Overwhelming joy filled me, and I thought, *'This is my wonderful present from God.'* Only he knew how sad and unwanted I felt. *'Perhaps he will allow me to live here forever'.* My thoughts were interrupted by the lady of the house. "Lift your dress up Jeannie and fill it with as many apples as you want. Pick the biggest you can reach." This was the first time I could recall feeling my heart pulsate with contentment. I was in such a dark place, and nobody seemed to notice or care. A stranger had lifted my spirits with her kindness. She didn't say, "Jeannie won't mind." Those words were repeated constantly throughout my childhood. "Jeannie will do it." "Jeannie won't mind." I wanted to shout to the world that Jeannie did mind.

I had become a happy child again. I was settling down and getting used to my new life when another bombshell was dropped on me - a decision that I found awfully hard to accept. I was to be moved again. *'Why me? I say my prayers each night and I thank God. I know he sees everything so why do these things keep on happening to me? Alan is at a lovely billet where he is loved and looked after. What have I done?'*

I gave God the credit for Bette's transfer. I believed she was moved because he knew I was a little frightened of my sister. She had such an explosive temper which used to alarm me.

I thought that perhaps I had committed some unspeakable crime, which I could not atone for because I didn't know what the misdemeanour was. I had told lots of people that I hated Hitler because he had sent planes to bomb Weymouth which had resulted in all the children being sent back to London to await further evacuation. Bette's school was quickly re-evacuated to Newquay in Cornwall, and this was the reason that I too would soon be re-evacuated. I was horrified but it was both our parents' wishes that we sisters should stay in the same area. My little brother was going to stay in Slough for the time being and a final decision would be made about him once we girls were settled in Cornwall. I was afraid and very apprehensive.

Weeks passed and then colossal events overwhelmed us all. One night in September 1940 the sound of repeated loud explosions could be heard and shortly afterwards the sky turned bright red. London was on fire and we could see it in Slough. It was the beginning of the Blitz. Hitler and Goring sent the Luftwaffe to systematically bomb London and other major industrial sites. Everybody stood outside in their gardens looking skywards monitoring the horrors. One of the neighbours called across the garden to Uncle Nunn.

"Isn't that where the children's parents live?" I started to shake. Auntie Nunn put a blanket around my shoulders and cuddled me. "The fire is not in London Jeannie, it's another part of England." I wasn't convinced and started to vomit. Patricia, their daughter, called out, "Stop being such a baby. You just want to get special attention."

The fires continued to rage; we could smell the smoke even though we were twenty odd miles away. In the days which followed we felt the presence of uneasiness in and around the home. The adults that surrounded us were whispering incessantly. Within a few days Auntie came into my bedroom and announced, "Today's the day Jeannie. You are going to join your sister in Newquay." I was heartbroken.

My case, now with the important label tied securely to its handle, was brought down from the loft to be packed once more. It didn't take Auntie long to pack the few possessions that I had. Sadly, I discovered the evening before my departure that my doll's head had been smashed. She was left under my bed. I never found out who had broken her. Auntie Nunn promised me that she would see if her damaged head could be repaired and if it were possible, she would have it mended and keep her safe for me. A little piece of my heart stayed with my doll.

A lady came to the house and took me home to London. I was so happy when I discovered that I was going to stay with my lovely Auntie Pat. I didn't question why I wasn't going to see my mother. I was much older when I found out that she had been urgently summoned to go and see my second eldest brother, Horrie, who was extremely ill with pleurisy and on the danger list.

What a welcome I got from Auntie Pat. She pulled me onto her lap and cuddled me. I was in heaven. Whilst snuggling up to her she told me that I was going to stay the night with her and that she had the most wonderful surprise for me. We were going to see The Wizard of Oz at the Gaumont Cinema in Stratford.

I had never known such joy. I asked Auntie, "Should I unpack my clothes?"

"Just leave them for now Jeannie." In my excitement I didn't realise the significance of her reply.

Off I set with my most favourite person in the world. Auntie Pat spoiled me and bought me sweets. We had wonderful seats and Auntie folded her coat to make a booster cushion for my seat. I felt as tall as she was. The organ came out of the orchestra pit playing wonderful music and then the magic began. I was lost in the wonder of what was on the screen. No occasion in my childhood ever surpassed that day. I didn't realise it at the time, but it was to sustain me for a long time – years in fact.

It was bedtime by the time we arrived back at Auntie Pat's house. "Sleep in your vest and knickers Jeannie. We don't need to unpack your case." My anxiety returned immediately on hearing those words. I knew something was about to happen, but I didn't know what. I promptly wet my knickers which then made me cry. Auntie just cuddled me and said, "It doesn't matter Jeannie."

The following morning, I was taken to London by an escort and put on a train called the Cornish Riviera. The journey seemed never ending. In the carriage were several other children who were being reunited with their siblings plus a lady minder. She had given each of us a lunch bag before we got on the train. I cannot remember what was in it now, but I recall it was very pleasant and there was plenty in it. If we wanted to go to the toilet we had to wait until the lady minder found the ticket collector who would watch us in her place. It was well organised. At one point we were told that if we looked out of the window, we would see both ends of the train at the same time. We thought it was an amazing sight. What a responsibility it must have been for the woman who had to keep a watchful eye on all of us.

In due course she announced in a loud voice, "Children put on your coats we are nearly there." I was disappointed as I really had enjoyed all the scenery. I had never been on a long-distance train journey before.

The guardsman called out, "Padstow Station." A name I had not heard of before. We alighted only to catch another train, on a local line, to our destination. It was a short journey and we soon disembarked and saw Newquay for the first time.

We stood in a group awaiting yet another official. We didn't have to wait for long. A couple of cars were waiting outside the station ready to deliver us to our billets. Quite a few stops were made. Each time one of the carers took a child to the front door, introduced them to the foster parents, and then quickly returned to the car ready for the next drop off. I was the last to be dropped off, but I had the benefit of seeing the sea as we drove through the town centre. Eventually we stopped at the top of a very steep hill. I looked at the house and thought it was very grand. It stood on the right-hand side of Tower Road. I imagine that it would have employed servants in its hey-day.

We were greeted by a pleasant lady who had a beautiful smile and enveloped me in her arms and gave me a cuddle. As I was the last to be dropped off, the carer decided to accept the invitation to have a cup of tea. We sat in the very warm kitchen. I was offered warm milk or fruit juice with Cornish scones layered with cream and topped with jam. I was delighted. I knew I was going to love staying there. After the carer said her goodbyes, I was taken by the lady to my bedroom. I was spellbound. It had lovely wallpaper and the most beautiful eiderdown. I was told to come down after I had unpacked my case. Mrs Stone had allocated a chest of drawers for my clothes. I had heard the carer say, "Hello Mrs Stone," when we arrived. I had had a teacher with the same name, so it made it easy for me to remember.

My days there were absolutely wonderful. There were no other children and Mrs Stone was like my gran. I was taken to school on the following Monday. It was so close to the house that we didn't have to allow any significant time to get there. My world had been put to right.

It seems strange now, but I didn't ask Mrs Stone where my sister was. I did ask when my little brother was coming and was informed that he would be arriving the following week. A billet had been found for Alan across the road with a lady called Mrs Lane. I thought it peculiar because there was room in the house for lots of people. I eagerly awaited Alan's arrival.

Before Alan's expected arrival time, Mrs Green, a billeting officer, said, "I have a surprise for you." I thought Alan had arrived early but no, it was to tell me that I would be joining my sister at the other side of Newquay in a road called Arundel Way.

'Oh no. Moving again!' I was shocked and cried, begging Mrs Stone to keep me. She cuddled me and said, "Jeannie I would if I could, but this is what is called a transit house and people only stay for a short time. We have been waiting for someone who can take two sisters. The authorities have a placement with a lady called Mrs Beaman who is willing to take you both as she has a large house."

Alan arrived and was placed in Mrs Lane's care. He loved Mrs Lane and her family. Two days passed before a car came to collect me. Once more complete strangers took me to a new location. We stopped en-route at the house where Bette had been staying and collected her. Our new home in Arundel Way was large.

Mrs Beaman greeted us, but she was very brusque and distant and told us to wait in the hall whilst she showed the billeting officer our bedroom. We could both hear the conversation from the room above us. The officer was questioning the size of the bed and the room. Next, we heard Mrs Beaman reply, "It is only for this weekend and then my sister will be leaving which will free the double room."

After the billeting officer left, we were taken upstairs to our bedroom. It was the smallest bedroom imaginable. The bed was a single, rather like a hospital bed with two pillows and a single eiderdown. There was a tug of war contest every night between Bette and me. The eiderdown was always being grabbed by one of us. We didn't get another bedroom or a different bed. The house was a boarding house. Mrs Beaman had one son who was my age. He was very sly and devious. He always told lies. It soon became apparent that this was not going to be a homely home for us. In fact, on reflection, I can say it never was a loving home to anybody.

We settled into yet another routine. We got up, had breakfast and went to school. At home time we ate supper then did our homework and went to bed. It didn't take long for Mrs Beaman to suggest to Bette that she could help with some housework, and I could walk Chinkie, their Pekinese dog. I hated and worried about this chore because he was such a nasty dog and would growl if you went near him. I was shown a set route that I had to take. To my horror the walk included a stile which had to be climbed over. Chinkie would go to bite me every time I had to lift him up. He was small enough to crawl under the bottom bar so I would try to cajole him to shimmy underneath, but it was always to no avail. That was one of my crosses to bear. Another was doing my homework.

Jack, the Beamans' son, would slyly push his books across the table to either make mine fall on the floor or spoil my writing. I was too nervous to say anything to stop him, but my sister would do her best to put him in his place. Very often they had physical fights. One day he unscrewed the lid on my bottle of ink and started to push his books across the table so that the ink would topple over onto my work and the carpet. Bette's reaction was quicker than Jack's and she reversed the position. He called out to his mother in the other room. "Look what that Jeannie is trying to do. She's trying to spoil my homework." It's all amusing now, and I can smile as I write these words but a part of me still feels my childhood anguish.

Staying at the house was an elderly couple called the Mr and Mrs Linton. They were paying guests and stayed for the duration of the war. Mrs Linton asked me one day, "Do you know who built St Paul's Cathedral?"

"Yes," I replied. "It was Sir Christopher Wren."

Mrs Linton went on to tell me that she was his descendent. A granddaughter about eight times removed. I could tell that she was pleased that I knew of Sir Christopher Wren.

Bette was really mistreated regarding housework. She was asked to scrub floors and was given other household chores. My new task was the clearing and re-laying of the tables. Mrs Beaman gave Bette some pocket money and thought that this gesture would make the everyday jobs tolerable but really, we were treated harshly. Evacuation was a huge logistical exercise and billets had limited inspection and in some locations no vetting at all. Some girls and boys had terrible experiences.

At this time, I was revising for the scholarship, and it was proving a strain. My school was the other side of town, a long way from Mrs Beaman's house. We were expected to go home for lunch. Bette was fortunate because her school paid for a bus pass. She was able to get to and from school easily as it was situated in the middle of Newquay. My school being at the far end of Newquay made each journey exhausting. I always had to run one way to enable me to get back on time to join the playground lines and not be late.

I had been feeling ill for some time and eventually I collapsed. I had contracted measles. I was put into bed and a doctor was summoned because there was the worry of other children becoming infected. This proved to be fortuitous for me. The doctor carried out a thorough examination. "Mrs Beaman, this child not only has measles but is very depleted and malnourished. How has this happened?"

"I don't know," replied Mrs Beaman.

He questioned her further. "How many children sleep in this bed?"

"Only this one."

"Then why are there two pillows with different head shapes in them?" He didn't pursue the enquiry any further.

The following week was the scholarship examination. I was too unwell to return to school to sit the exam. I didn't give any thought as to how it could affect my future. I just stayed in bed and felt sorry for myself.

The following week I was told I had to get dressed and wait for someone to take me to school. It turned out to be a teacher who placed a huge fluffy blanket around me and took me to a huge black car which was parked outside the house. A gentleman inside the car smiled at me. "Don't worry, everything is all right. We are taking you to school and you will be put in a classroom on your own with me and another gentleman. We are called adjudicators and we shall both be sitting in the classroom whilst you sit the scholarship paper."

I found this revelation hard to take on board.

On my arrival at school, I was taken into a classroom, seated next to a hot radiator and given the exam papers. I was still covered in my warm blanket. I was told to put my hand up if I felt ill and the examiners would stop the timer. I didn't raise my hand once and I didn't feel at all nervous. I was treated so kindly. On completion of the examination, I was given a mug of hot Horlicks. I felt like one of the royal princesses returning home in such a grand car.

We received the incredibly good news that our mother was coming for a visit. All three of us were so excited. We really had something to look forward to. Apparently, our family had moved from the flat to a house quite near to Auntie Pat and Mum was going to tell us all about it. She eventually told us that Bette and I would share a big bedroom. This was wonderful news to me as I really believed that it meant we would be going home one day soon.

Parents or guardians were only allowed to visit every six months. This required a written permit as Newquay was a restricted zone. Only the armed forces, evacuees and residents were allowed freedom of movement within the area. Check points manned by police both civil and military were set up on all roads leading into the zone.

It was a strange situation, we evacuees gathered in a hotel on the sea front to meet and greet our families. It was decided by the powers that be that it was not prudent for parents to inspect where their children were staying. It saved the authorities from any confrontations that could have ensued had they done so. It was an overnight visit. Most visitors were boarded for the one night at the same hotel.

Mother revealed so much family news. Our father was in hospital having been severely injured in the first bombing raid on the London docks. We didn't realise or think to ask the extent of his injuries. We were assured by Mum that Dad would write to us as soon as he was better. Our eldest brother Bob was in the Airforce and Horrie our second brother was doing war work and living in the country somewhere secret. Eileen had trained in bookkeeping and was working at High Duty Alloys in Slough. The family was scattered far and wide.

We sat on the promenade at Towan Beach eating our sandwiches and drinking lemonade whilst Mum related all the family news. We discovered that all our furniture was in storage because Mum could not afford to pay the council rent as well as rent rooms to be near Dad in hospital. It was a lot of news for the three of us to take in.

That day sped by so quickly. It was soon time to walk to the station to see Mum off. As we walked along, I told Mum how I had been looked after when I sat the scholarship.

"Mum have you received the results?" She informed me that she had not. "That means I have not passed."

37

She responded with, "Never mind Jeannie you can go to work when you are fourteen and earn some pennies for me."

We were almost at the station when Mum discovered she could not find her purse. Panic stations ensued. One of us had to return to where we had bought the sandwiches. Bette refused and said it was too far. Alan was too young so that only left me. I ran as fast as I could from one end of the town to the other but could not find the purse. When I ran back towards the station Bette and Alan were walking towards me. I felt utterly despondent, I had missed saying goodbye to my mother. My own common sense should have told me not to make the return journey. Bette informed me that Mum had found her purse in her pocket just after I had left.

Life's routine resumed and living with the Beamans didn't change. We had an occasional treat. Mr Beaman had an incredibly important job. It was all kept hush hush and had something to do with designing planes. This important position allowed him to have the use of a large car. Sometimes on a Sunday the family used to go for a drive. I had to sit in the back on Bette's lap. She hated it and so did I. There were always conversations flying back and forth between the Beaman family. They chatted away as if we were not present. They used to say what a nuisance it was, to have to put up with carting around evacuees. At one time I recall them telling us that our parents were having a good time without us and wouldn't want us back when the war was over. When we arrived at wherever they had decided to take us we were told where to sit, which inevitably was away from them on their lovely rugs. Even our sandwiches were wrapped differently and not included in the contents of their wicker basket. These were educated people who should have known better. East End children were portrayed as not knowing any better or not having any sensitivity.

Within a few days of my mother returning to London, I cannot remember the exact date, but I know it was a Monday, I received some news. I was standing at the end of the line having run back to school after lunch. I was breathless yet glad that I had made it to the line on time. The Headmistress stood at the front of the lines and called out, " I have an announcement to make. Where are you Bailey?" I raised my hand nervously and she announced, "I have received your results from London County Council. You have passed the scholarship with high marks." There was spontaneous clapping, it was the first time in my life that the applause was for me. I had to go and stand outside her study.

When she called me in she asked, "Have you a second name?"

38

"Yes, it is Alicia."

"You refrained from using it on your scholarship entry and it caused a delay. Your papers were returned to London, you caused problems for the examination board."

I really find that hard to believe as I was the only one sitting the exam on a different day. However, that didn't matter. I was on cloud nine. I was then told I could have the afternoon off to post the acceptance letter in the main post office. I left school on top of the world, running to the main post office, making sure that I could hear the letter drop into the box. I didn't find the walk home lengthy. I was ecstatic for the whole of the journey. I reached the kitchen door, turned the handle and found Mrs Beaman staring at me. "What are you doing home?"

I gave a big, excited smile, "I've been given the afternoon off because I have passed the scholarship."

Her face had a look of thunder, and she almost spat out the words, "You can't have done. If my Jack failed, then you can't have passed. He is much more intelligent than you. I will wait until your sister comes home and she will know the truth. Now take Chinkie out for a long walk."

I did take Chinkie out but for some reason I decided not to take the precious dog for a long walk. I sat on the grass smiling and feeling better. I must have been feeling very brave that day. Bette had already been told by her school that I would be joining them soon. For me that was a most wonderful day not only had I passed but I would also get a bus pass, no more running at lunch times. It did prompt some action from the Beamans. They applied and paid for their son to go to Newquay Grammar School. It didn't improve Jack's manners. He was still like a weasel and very deceitful.

Jack's hobby was making planes from kits of balsa wood. He had a real passion for this and was very skilled. These kits cost a fortune and he was always acquiring them from kind friends who didn't want to finish their models or could not understand the instructions. It dawned on Bette and me that these were in fact new kits that he had bought. It all came to light one day when I was asked by Mrs Beaman to account for the shilling that was in the fingertip of my glove. The Beamans had been searching through our possessions which included our clothing. Both Bette and I were perplexed as to why they did this. It transpired that money had gone missing from the house on more than one occasion and the Beamans had concluded that it just had to be the evacuees. Of course, they didn't find anything, only that shilling. I was able to tell them that the shilling belonged to Mrs Lane who had been trying to find some suet for her baking. I had told Mrs Lane that I would try and ask at our local shop. The Beamans didn't believe me and put me in their car and drove me to Mrs Lane's. I felt humiliated. I was told very sharply to stay in the car whilst they went to speak to her. They returned to the car with incredibly annoyed faces and spoke angrily to me. "Why did you think you would find suet in our shop? I cannot buy it for myself," shouted Mrs Beaman. There was no apology to either Bette or me. We never heard another word about missing money. I rather feel they found the culprit much closer to home. I hoped they carried a guilty conscience when they realised that their son was the guilty party.

It was such a miserable existence living in the Beaman household. Almost every other day I would go to see my brother Alan. Mrs Lane and her little children were always happy. It seemed idyllic to me and how I thought every home should be. Mrs Lane baked twice a week and when I used to visit, I could smell the cakes from outside the front door. The family were Salvationists but her husband, like so many others, was away serving in the armed forces. That special lady was always so kind to me. If the weather was suitable when it was time for me to return to Arundel Way, Mrs Lane used to put her baby in the pram and the whole family would walk halfway home with me. I loved that because I was allowed to push the pram and we walked through Penzance Gardens. When I was on my own, I was not allowed to do that short cut for safety reasons. These are my happiest memories of Newquay. That lovely lady will not have realised how her kindness has stayed with me all my life.

Life was becoming difficult at the B & B. It was obvious that we were never going to be given a bigger room or bed. Mrs Beaman approached her sister with an offer she could not decline. Should she choose not to return to her home in Yorkshire she could become the housekeeper of the B & B. She wouldn't have to vacate her double bedroom and she would be given the little bedroom, our bedroom, for her sitting room.

We were delighted with the news as we realised that we would be relocated in a new billet. Bette and I could not stop smiling and we couldn't wait for the billeting officer to visit. It took about two weeks but what a different atmosphere there was in the house. The household had happy smiling faces, little harmless jokes were played on us, but it was all one big act, probably because the Beamans' conscience got the better of them. If only that atmosphere had existed from the time of our arrival, our lives would have been so different. The Beamans' joy at getting rid of nuisance evacuees was very apparent.

Our small cases were packed, we were off once again. I thought Bette might have had some information about what was happening to us but she, like me, knew nothing. We were only in the car for a short time as we had only travelled to the centre of Newquay. As the car drew up, we could see it was a very long bungalow. Bette looked at me and shrugged her shoulders. It was again the unknown. Lanherne was the name on the plate fixed to the wall. Two incredibly small rotund ladies answered the door. Both their eyes and ours met and we appraised each other. We were invited into their private sitting room for the usual signing of documents. That is all we were really – statistics, numbers on pieces of paper.

My first impression of Lanherne was based on the small sitting room. It was cosy, furnished with old furniture but felt homely. My immediate judgement was that everything was going to be fine. Both sisters saw the official off and requested that we remain in our seats as the rules of the establishment needed to be explained to us. Our first revelation was to discover that lots of children boarded there. We were then given our table number which we had to always adhere to. We were informed that we had to queue with the other children in an orderly fashion in the rear kitchen where we would hold up our plates for the food to be served by the maid. She would serve the correct amount to us, and it would be sufficient. There must be no attempt to ask for more. My emotions began to take a downward spiral. This didn't sound so homely after all. The rules continued. Baths were once a week under supervision, and I was expected to use the same water as my sister. The baths would be in the stipulated four inches of water that the whole country had been asked to abide by.

Our bedroom was a pleasant surprise because of its size. We were allocated a large old-fashioned bed which looked spacious. There were also two single beds at the far end of the room. We were thrilled because we were used to our previous bedroom being so small. In addition, the bedroom had a hand basin. We could wash in our own bedroom. This was luxury. Sharing a bed was second nature to us both as we had done so since our days in cots. This was going to be a wonderful billet.

We both had smiles on our faces whilst we unpacked. Two girls came into the bedroom after school and said hello as they flung their satchels onto their beds. We now knew who we were sharing our room

41

with. Suddenly the sound of a ringing school bell shattered our peace. "It's the tea bell," said our roommates.

We followed them into a queue towards the front of the building which proved to be the dining room and lounge combined. "Bailey," was shouted out and our table was allocated to us. We joined two girls who were already seated. Six to a table was the system. The amount of food given to each table at teatime, and all other meals, was strictly allocated and that was it. It didn't take long to realise that it was never enough for six growing girls but like Oliver Twist it was pointless to ask for more. One girl told us that before our arrival somebody had asked for more food and been told, "Don't you know there is a war on."

We queued for all our meals, including breakfast, in the same fashion. We always had the same amount - one level tablespoon of each vegetable, three in all, and some brown liquid which was supposedly gravy. After the main meal one of the older children handed you a pudding dish containing semolina or sometimes rice or tapioca. All the puddings were the same, a white runny liquid. Tea consisted of two pieces of bread with jam plus one scone. You could not help yourself to more bread as you knew you would be depriving someone else. The rationing system was in full swing and was a means of ensuring the fair distribution of food. However, fruit and vegetables were not rationed and the food we received was too meagre for growing children and nothing like the food or amount our mothers would have served. One privilege was accorded to us on our birthday. The child whose birthday it was, was called five minutes earlier than the rest of the children and allowed to ring the bell to warn the rest of the household it was time to arise. Everybody seemed to enjoy this. Maybe it was the sense of power it created, if only for a short time.

It didn't take long to realise what living at Lanherne truly meant. I was about to embark upon a change of school. There was no mother figure to check up on our school uniform or our needs in general. If we had socks with holes in, there were no repair kits to mend them. All we did was turn our socks around, but then they became too small because we were growing. Our knickers were too small and also wearing out, but no one enquired. Some schools had stalls with cast-off clothes. However, the best had usually been picked out by the people who were distributing them. I was very worried as to how I would manage to obtain my new uniform. Most of my clothes were far too small. Bette had acquired a newer satchel from somebody that was returning home and she gave me her old one. That pleased me and was one worry off my mind. Bette was already at the school and got advanced notice of what day the High School were putting out their second-hand clothing stall. I was first in line when they opened the after-school sale. I managed to get all the uniform even the horrible dark knickers. I was on cloud nine. I look back now and think I was only eleven years old the previous March. What a burden it placed on our young shoulders and yet I, along with many others, accepted it all as though it was the norm.

I began to look forward to my first term at my new school. I had already decided that when asked I would take French and not German. I did consider German because my sister was good at it, and she would be able to help me if I got into difficulty. In the end I requested French in my pre-school interview.

You need to have lived in a Cornish seaside haven during the winter months to appreciate the severity of the weather. Some children had warmer clothing than others to cope with these conditions. As a parent I made sure my children were warm, safe and protected. We didn't have that love and protection as evacuees. Our mother was frantic with worry about my father as she had been told he was dying from his injuries. She cried many years later when she recounted what had happen. She really thought the people who we were billeted with would oversee things and care for us.

Winter in Lanherne was unbearable. The rooms in the bungalow were freezing cold. We had to keep warming our hands so that we could hold our pens to do our homework. There were three paraffin oil heaters in the whole of that room. We did our homework at the table where we ate, and we kept to the same chair. That way no child could select a chair near the heaters. It certainly was not conducive to serious study. In the coldest winter months, we could not wait to get into our beds to keep warm. Quarrels used to break out occasionally when one girl accused another of copying her homework or perhaps of having her pencils or pens. It was a challenging time. We were all growing and at the start of puberty with a need for more food and warmth. I was too young to have started my periods but the poor girls who were menstruating, had no guidance from any person and just had to deal with the problem as best as they could.

Some parts of the lounge were declared 'no go' areas and we soon got to know these forbidden zones. These spaces were covered with large old carpets and hid the floorboards which needed to be replaced. Before the war the bungalow had been the Newquay Museum. It became compulsory for homes to host assigned evacuees and the Hank sisters were given the choice to either have soldiers or children. The whole of Lanherne needed to be repaired. Other than the Hank's private lounge the bungalow looked as though they had just moved in. It lacked the love and care most people bestow upon a home.

On Saturdays we could do or go where we wanted. Much of Newquay was out of bounds with restricted areas so our choice was limited. Lots of men from the Royal Air Force were around and they used to smile at us and sometimes have a little chat. They asked us where we came from and if we liked it in Cornwall and often told us that they had little children themselves. Mostly, we walked on the various beaches or along the little alleys around the town. Bette pointed out where her best friend from school lived. It was a delightful house and remarkably close to the harbour and where Alan lived. If we called at Mrs Lane's, she would give us a drink and one of her homemade Cornish pasties. It was always such a disappointment when we found her out. We used to spend hours beachcombing, never finding much, only different shaped pebbles and rocks.

When we sat on Towan beach I used to look up at the suspension footbridge that spanned the sea from the mainland to a tiny island. I thought it mysterious and imagined somebody extraordinarily rich lived there. I was not sure that I would like to live there myself. We children all knew that the ghosts of sailors who had been shipwrecked came ashore in the winds and haunted the town. Bette and I really did believe that if they caught us, we would become ghosts too. I thought I would rather face the devil I knew such as Lanherne. All the children at Lanherne thought the bungalow was haunted. It certainly could have challenged any record for the most creaking floorboards in one house.

On Sundays after church, we had lunch on the beach. We were allowed to request a picnic on Sundays, so long as we asked at breakfast time and gave our names. A jam sandwich would be wrapped up with a fruit scone and placed in a paper bag with our name on.

The Cornish winters were so cold. We used to cover our mouths with our collars or hands. We certainly didn't take leisurely strolls along the beach. We were all expected to gather and bring back as much driftwood that we could find. This task was not easy as every beach in Newquay is far below the cliffs which meant that every piece of wood had to be carried up the very steep cliff paths. This chore was made far more challenging by the fierce winds. We had no roaring fire to greet us on our return home, only the paltry heat produced by oil heaters. The wood was used to fire the boiler for hot water. However hard it was for us young children, was never taken into consideration. The system worked for the Lanherne household.

I settled into my new school. I was fortunate to have my sister Bette there already. As I had witnessed her dealing with the school routine it was easier for me. I felt I looked good in my school uniform although it was noticeably second-hand. Some items could have been third or even fourth hand.

How hard it must have been for the teachers who had to still teach us to a certain standard. Our classrooms were in different locations around the town. My registration class occupied two rooms in the back of Woolworths in Newquay High Street. It was quite a distance away from Lanherne. Another set of lessons were in a church hall which was even further away by the harbour. At the beginning of each term, we copied a timetable that had been given to us. It covered all our lessons but every Monday we were given amendments. There were always unforeseen things occurring.

We soon got into an established routine that our school had devised. Piles of incredibly old looking textbooks were set out on tables, and we had to take the relevant books that we required for the week ahead. Sometimes the piles were depleted, and we had to accept that we would have to share with the person sitting next to us. However, this caused great problems for homework because we often didn't have the correct books. It was frustrating but something we grew to accept as the norm. I was fortunate because should I not have the relevant book, my sister would be able to recall the subject or know a girl who would have a copy. If needed Bette was able to support me in my lessons. I was soon to realise just how much she influenced my future in Newquay.

I have, over the years, remarked to many people about teachers being the unsung heroes of that time. A lot of teachers were single, young and inexperienced and they too were billeted in unfamiliar domestic settings. To teach without classrooms and equipment and impart lessons to children who were stressed must have taken its toll. Not only did they teach, but some also had the extra responsibly of being an overseer of children and their billets, plus all complaints whether from children or foster parents were channelled through them. What an extra burden it must have been for them.

On reflection I am always amazed that more children didn't play truant, especially when the whistle was blown to change lessons. Often the next lesson was at another building in town. Our books were quickly picked up, placed in our satchels and then we rushed off to the next venue in haste. I cannot recall any occasion when a child went missing during the exchange or protested at the speed with which we were expected to accomplish the changeover.

When my mother made her last visit to Cornwall, she informed Bette that she had requested that my younger brother Alan be returned home. She told Bette that she would be his escort. This was kept a secret from me until the day that my sister packed her case.

We were getting ready for school and Bette started to pack her suitcase which filled me with alarm. It was then that she told me that she was taking Alan back to Mum and would be away for two weeks. I was only consoled when she said, "On my honour, I am coming back." I accepted that but felt very unhappy as I had not said goodbye to Alan or to Mrs Lane. I was never to see Mrs Lane again. I cannot think why I didn't call in so see her, perhaps I was too full of my own concerns.

What started out as an ordinary day at school changed dramatically into something nightmarish. I was called out of class by a young man who had been in discussion with my teacher. My heart raced in anticipation of what was ahead. He smiled at me and said, "We are just going to your billet. There is nothing to worry about." I was truly petrified. He was so tall that I had a job to keep up with his long strides as we headed to Lanherne. I think he could see how frightened I was and held my hand. He tried to allay my fears and chatted about the sea and asked if I liked to go on the beach and generally tried to occupy my thoughts. All too soon we were on the doorstep of Lanherne, and he was ringing the bell. One of the Hank sisters answered the door and didn't say anything to him other than, "Do come in. Jeannie will show you to their room." It was obvious that something had been pre-arranged. I felt very uneasy. The fact that Miss Hanks allowed this young man to go into our bedroom added to my apprehension. His first question to me was, "Where do you and your sister keep your cases?"

I remember blurting out, "My sister is away, and I cannot go anywhere without her."

He was exceedingly kind-hearted and kept repeating, "You will be all right." He then asked me to pack all my clothing. He assisted me with the packing and Miss Hanks came in to check that I had taken everything. She then saw us off at the door.

As young as I was, the realisation that this situation was all pre-planned hit me like a ton of bricks. I sobbed and sobbed and in between sobs kept spurting out, "My sister will be so worried when she gets back."

After around ten minutes of pleading, whilst walking, the young man stopped and wiped my eyes and face with his handkerchief. He said, "Let's just stop for a minute and you can have a little rest. I think I am walking too fast for you." To this day I can see his kind face as he bent down to me and said, "You poor thing, you really don't know what is going on do you?" I didn't respond and he continued, "Your sister requested a transfer for you. She said you were always fighting with her and caused trouble between her and her friends." I could not believe his words. It was the final betrayal. I never answered Bette back. As for her friends, I never spoke to them as I always had to walk behind them, never by their side. It was all untrue and most people would have known that. The kind stranger also imparted that when my sister returned, she too would be going to a new billet. I didn't know it then, but I never saw my sister again in Newquay, apart from at a distance in the playground when the school congregated for a joint assembly, this was only a brief glimpse.

This wasn't the only time my sister was cruel to me. In my first year at school Bette confided in me and said she knew a terrible secret. It was the more worrying for me because for days she had said, "I want to tell you, but I have promised Mum and Dad that I won't." I did pester her to reveal the secret and eventually she told me that I was adopted and that if my parents found out that I knew they would send me back to the children's home. It was such a shock, I was traumatised. I promised that I would never tell anyone and asked Bette not to tell anybody else. I totally believed that story until I was about nine years old, even as an evacuee. I cannot recall now how it came about but I related the story to Auntie Nunn at my first billet in Slough. I do remember vividly that she cuddled me instantly and said, "Jeannie your mummy and daddy have enough children of their own without adopting anymore." I knew that she was right and was consoled by her explanation.

My new billet was tough for me. I had to share a double bed with another girl who I didn't like. I remembered her from Tollgate, my junior school. She used to live behind our flat in London. I do not know why but we both kept our distance from each other. I was only at my new billet for a few weeks when I started to feel ill and developed a terrible cough. Our foster carer kept me home from school which didn't make me feel happy, however I soon became joyous when I was told it was my time to go home to my parents, who were now living in St Albans. For the first time that I could remember I was over the moon.

I kept pretending I was well because I had been told that if I didn't improve, I wouldn't be allowed to travel. The pretence of being well was a burden. The night before my scheduled journey home I smothered my head under the blankets to cover the sound of my cough. The night was long, morning eventually dawned. I was on my way home to my parents. I was incredibly quiet on the journey home. I only moved to go to the toilet, I didn't want to eat my packed lunch.

My mother was at the station looking out for me. I could see her before she saw me. It felt like a dream. As I reached her, I collapsed with her first hug. "Are you ill Jeannie?" I was cuddled by her for the next part of our journey to St Albans. As I was being hugged, I remember thinking, *'thank goodness my mother is my real mother and not an adoptive one.'*

CHAPTER FOUR

I cannot remember much of the bus journey home from Paddington station, only the anxiety of feeling nauseous. It was the combination of tiredness and excitement. We arrived in St Albans, and I soon discovered the family home was just one room. I had expected a nice house. The room contained a double bed and a small canvas camp bed which I presumed was for me. My father was there but my little brother was nowhere to be seen. Mum undressed me and put my pyjamas on and then gave me hot bread and milk with plenty of sugar. It was a favourite of mine. In winter, after our baths, Mum would let us choose either a hot Marmite drink or hot bread and milk before going to bed. This comforting sustenance was my first reminder of family life.

I soon snuggled down and fell fast asleep. However, as the night wore on, I kept tossing and turning over and over and became very agitated until finally I started to scream out in pain. The pain was radiating from my chest and back. Mum took me into the double bed and my father made room for me, but I was fighting for my breath.

First thing in the morning my mother took me to a doctor in Latimore Road. We sat in the waiting room with my mother cuddling me. I was shivering with nerves and cold. The doctor was both kind and very gentle and repeatedly told me not to be afraid and that I would soon feel better. After a very thorough examination I was requested to wait outside as the doctor wanted to talk to my mother in private. I heard raised voices emanating from the room and the conversation seemed to go on for such a long time. Eventually Mum came out accompanied by the doctor who just ruffled my hair and patted my head. I was told by my mother years afterwards that when I left the room the doctor informed her that I was suffering from pneumonia and malnutrition. He was furious and wanted to know how this was possible. My chest had visibly caved in on the left-hand side. He was so angry and told my mother that he was going to report her to the authorities. My mother was

49

outraged and able to account for her actions. She informed the doctor that the apparent neglect was down to other people.

On leaving the surgery Mum took me to the British Home Stores restaurant. She said, "You can choose anything you want." I didn't want a thing, only to sit there with my mother. That was enough for me and wonderful. We chatted for a while but as soon as Mum said, "I have to talk to you," my heart sank. I had heard that sentence many times before and events never concluded happily. This proved no exception to the rule. Mum told me that she had to take me straight to a St Albans Hospital called Oster House.

The doctors at the hospital concurred with the GP's diagnosis. I had pneumonia and was malnourished. I was admitted straight away. As soon as I thought everything was changing for the better, something to the contrary happened. I truly felt that this was my lot in life. I had been so overjoyed to have 'my turn' with my parents and now it was the children's ward for me.

I was treated very sympathetically by the doctors and the staff in general. Little did I know on that day that my stay in hospital would last for two months. The authorities concerned had been informed that I would no longer be returning as an evacuee, but no one thought to tell me. Had they done so I am sure it would have hastened my recovery.

As I convalesced, I was concerned about my little brother as I had not seen him at the room in St Albans. On one of my parents' visits I remembered to ask about Alan. My parents' reply was reassuring. Alan had been placed at an infant school quite near to Latimore Road.

The school wasn't too far from our lodgings, but Alan kept arriving home with very dirty shoes. Mum asked him to stop playing football in muddy areas as she knew his walk to and from school was along good pavements. Eventually the real reason behind the muddy shoes came to light. Mum and Dad, used to buy savings stamps to help the war effort. The National Savings Movement was instrumental during World War II in raising funds. Mum had been giving Alan sixpence a week to buy stamps, but he kept forgetting to bring the completed book of stamps home. This resulted in Mum going to speak to his teacher at school to find out what the problem was. The teacher announced that she was surprised to see my mother as she thought the family had left and returned to London. Alan had not been to school for weeks.

My parents waited for Alan to arrive home. He had such an innocent face as he recounted to my parents that he knew our cousin

Tony was in a town called Hemel Hempstead and that he was boarding at a boys' school called Pixies Hill. He went on to tell them that he thought it would be good to visit him.

My nine-year-old brother not only worked out which buses he had to catch from St Albans to Hemel Hempstead but navigated his way to the boarding school from the bus stop. On the first occasion the school seemed quite a distance from where he exited the bus. He told me years afterwards that the bus conductors very often didn't take his fare. He had told them his story but not the fact that he was playing truant. My cousin supplied Alan with food on these excursions and there were always heaps of it, as all the boys in Tony's dormitory were in on the story and pinched food to keep him going.

After his ticking off and his apparent remorse the powers that be found Alan a place with his cousin where he stayed, with my parents' consent, until it was time for him to leave for senior school.

My days in hospital seemed lengthy but I remember feeling very secure and happy. I had to have one or two unpleasant medical procedures but apart from dealing with those I used to spend the day reading. Mum had to stop visiting me every day as she had found a job in Ryder's seed factory. It was sited in Holywell Hill, close enough to home for Mum to walk to work. This was a good opportunity as it not only gave her a much-needed income but also provided her with the companionship of other women. My mother had to contend with her small children being evacuated and an injured husband. Alan had always been a constant concern. In the early days of the evacuation, he needed to have a special eye kept on him, as his health was so precarious.

Dad was injured during the first bombing raid. He was working in the East India Docks. His injuries were so severe that he was left for two days in a corridor with lots of other men. Many dockers were injured and died. The persistent German Luftwaffe attacks on London during the war brought destruction on a scale never known before. 40,000 lives were lost and something like a million homes were destroyed by the bombardment. Many of the injured, like my father, were placed on trolleys and left in corridors, lain on floors, some even on old doors. The patients' injuries were assessed and prioritised. The 'hopeless' cases were left and just given minimal treatment to ease their passing.

My father was left, and my mother stayed by his side. After two days of being given fluids and morphine one of the doctors said, "Well old chap you are still with us, so I think we will take you into the theatre and see what we can do. We'll start by getting these clothes cut off." As my father was pushed into the theatre the doctor continued, "I have to prepare you for the loss of both your legs." My father was scared and horrified at the prospect of losing his legs and called out "'Please sir, I beg you not to take my legs off." Whether the doctor took note of Dad's plea we will never know but to Dad's great relief when he came around from the anaesthetic, he found that his legs had been saved. However, it was at a great cost. He was in constant pain and stayed in hospital for two years followed by a long convalescence. He never made a fuss about the pain and relentless treatment. He just said how lucky he was to survive. Leg callipers and crutches enabled Dad to have a quality of life that he had thought was lost for ever.

Eventually my father was found a job as a watchman in a buffer depot near to their room. The government stored food here in preparation for an invasion or the destruction of the food convoys.

All the fear and horror associated with Dad's violence became a thing of the past. His rages disappeared completely and never returned and were not alluded to. He spent the rest of his life spoiling my mother whenever possible.

It was time for me to be discharged from hospital. We had moved to a new home which I was unaware of. It was in Wiltshire Avenue quite near to a school. Our new home was in an ordinary council house. My parents rented a room and shared the communal facilities with the tenant and his pregnant daughter, who was the wife of a serving soldier. We were there for a couple of months before I was allowed to go to Cotton Mill Lane School. This decision was a directive from the medical team at the hospital.

I found my first weeks daunting. I was so behind with my schoolwork and the curriculum was completely different from the one I had been used to. On my first day I sat at the back of the class. I unexpectedly felt very sick and shot my hand up, but the teacher just looked at me and carried on with the lesson. I knew I could not hold on for much longer so semi stood and shook my arm for all it was worth. Suddenly it happened, I vomited. Unfortunately, the classroom seating was tiered, and sick went everywhere. I felt awful. The teacher's fury knew no bounds and she made me clear it up with the consequence that I was sick again. Most of the children started laughing which made me feel even more wretched. Fortunately for me, the headmistress came into the classroom shortly afterwards. She observed the situation and sent me to wait outside her study. On her return she invited me into her room and asked me to sit down. I was extremely apprehensive but to my relief and surprise she washed my face and patted it dry then shook talcum powder over my blouse and skirt. The talc obviously made everything white but covered up the smell. She finished by combing my hair and I was given a glass of water which she told me not to rush drinking. Whilst I sipped the water the head wrote a letter to my mother. I was sent home and told if my mother or any member of the family was not in, I was to return to school. I still remember her great kindness to me and the rather cruel attitude of my classroom teacher. Thankfully, I returned to find my mother at home and our circumstances were such that I never returned to that school.

It was quite close to this time that we had to leave our rooms again. I was sorry to leave as I liked our gentleman landlord very much. He was always so lovely to me. Every Saturday he gave me a sixpence. I found it unbelievable that someone could be so generous to me. On every occasion he would always say the same thing, "Don't spend it all at once. Save some for in the week."

Each day my mother asked anyone who would listen to her if they knew of anywhere that we could live. No one had any suggestions. It seemed an impossible undertaking. On one of her reconnoitres she found an advert offering two rooms for rent in a house in the countryside. Although this was a bus journey from the city centre both my parents went to view the accommodation in Colney Heath to get an idea of the distance from St Albans. The decision to rent these rooms was made from desperation. The accommodation really was too far away and too costly on the bus fares, however, there was no alternative, so we moved.

The landlady was young and very agreeable. Her husband was in the army, and she didn't like being in the house on her own. We had only been in Colney Heath for a short while when the weather turned very cold and eventually the snow came. It was severe and the snow became quite deep. It was a Herculean effort for my father to get off the bus and walk, with his legs in callipers, down the snow-covered lane. Both my parents knew this would have to be a temporary residence as it was neither affordable nor desirable. Mum had given up her job up as her wages didn't cover the bus fare. It was a worrying time for them and me.

I had not yet started school again and there was no mention of me registering. Weeks passed by and Mum and Dad showed no concern whatsoever that I was not at school. Eventually I approached my father and explained my unease at not being at school. Dad's only reply was, "You are company for your mother." They both perceived my role as companion not scholar.

One day in March we got up as usual and I discovered Dad had already left for work. Nothing much happened that day. Mum and I went for a walk and made sure we were at home for when Dad returned from work. He came back at his usual time and related to Mum his efforts of trying to find better accommodation. It was all so frustrating and very demanding for him as this had to be accomplished during his lunch time. This particular day Dad had seen one of the supervisors from Ryder's and she had asked him if Mum wanted to return to the company. The supervisor explained that the company would consider re-employing her. They spent the whole evening discussing the pros and cons of the situation and whether Mum should give it another try and work a couple of hours extra to pay for the bus fare. It was eight o'clock and we had the radio on and were listening to Ann Shelton, one of our favourite singers. She was singing requests for the Armed Forces.

Dad suddenly announced, "Bedtime Jeannie."

I replied, "Can't I stay up a little longer as it's my birthday?"

Neither of my parents had realised it was my special day. I was twelve years old. Mum said, "Oh I am so sorry. I have a lot on my mind." My father agreed to my request and said, "You can stay up an extra hour,"

Mum added, "You can play shops with the things in the sideboard if you like."

'For goodness' sake,' I thought. I was twelve going on fifteen. My life's experiences had matured me beyond my years. I think that after I went to bed both their consciences were pricked a little. The next morning, I was overjoyed to hear that Mum was going by Greenline bus to see Gran and was taking me with her. My fare was my birthday treat. This was joyous news. I was going to see my beloved Gran.

It was such a happy journey. Changing buses and travelling on a trolleybus was magical to me. I thought it amazing that the conductor had to jump off at various junctions and use a long pole to reconnect the current when changing direction. Everything was so special. I walked with noticeably light feet to 32 New Barn Street, my childhood haven.

We knocked on the door. It was opened by Auntie Lizzie. I was so excited I rushed straight into Gran's arms for a lovely cuddle. "Hello my little Jeannie." My joy knew no bounds but much more was to come. A lovely young couple came out from their hiding place. It was my beautiful cousin Dorothy. She was one of life's beauties with a gentle persona and voice to match. Standing by her side was a Canadian Officer looking like a film star. He was well over six feet tall, very handsome and with a delightful accent. We were all spellbound. Dorothy had brought Cal Forward to meet Gran, as he had asked her to marry him. This meant that Dorothy would eventually go to live in Canada. Dorothy and Cal were seeking approval. Gran and Dorothy were remarkably close because Gran, with Auntie Lizzie's help, had raised Dorothy from a little baby. Her mother tragically died during the Spanish Flu pandemic of 1918/1919. Over 50 million people died worldwide, and a quarter of the British population were affected. Well over 200,000 people died in Britain alone - if only antibiotics had been discovered earlier.

This was an incredibly happy and romantic day for us all. I remember seeing Dorothy and Cal's faces so full of love. We had spent a delightful few hours with the family. I was so happy, all our own troubles faded away for that short time. It was fate that our unexpected visit to Gran's coincided with Dorothy and Cal's announcement.

We still have the love and connection with the Forward family today. Dorothy continued to write to my mother for years and when Mum was no longer able to keep up the correspondence I took over and continue to remain in contact with my cousin's family. Since the invention of Skype and FaceTime we are in contact with several other cousins and their children in New Zealand and Australia. Online video calls really are one of the benefits of modern technology.

My mother returned to work and there was still no talk of me returning to school. It was only a couple of weeks after our wonderful day's outing to Gran's that we received another shock. Our landlady wanted us to leave our rooms in Colney Heath as she was going to take in somebody from her family who wanted to get out of London. Mum went to work as usual but started to cry during the lunch break. Many of her work friends were sympathetic as they knew of her predicament but when Mum told everyone that we had to be out within two weeks they felt even sorrier for her.

One co-worker said, "I have an idea. I am going to speak to my friend and suggest she meets with you." The friend agreed to meet with Mum and told her that she was going to stay with her mother for the rest of the war and therefore intended to give up her tenancy. "I am giving notice on Monday, and I haven't told the agent of my intention. Come with me and see if the estate agent will consider you for the tenancy."

Monday came and Mum was in a state of excitement as she accompanied her friend's friend to the agent's. At first the estate agent declared that he had loads of people that would like to rent the house. My mother then explained her circumstances and how desperate she was to find accommodation. The agent conceded and said, "Fine," granting Mum the tenancy. Hemel Hempstead was soon to have some new residents.

When Mum got back to Colney Heath and related the news. Dad cried and so did I, then Mum joined in. She threw the keys to the house up in the air. The tenancy had been accepted and we could move in. It was December and our intension was to have the best Christmas ever in our new home.

Our furniture was still stored in the old skating rink at the bottom of Holywell Hill in St Albans. I went with Mum to the store, and we spent the next few days sorting it out. Mice had gnawed their way into some of the boxes but fortunately not into any of the bigger pieces of furniture. Dad spoke to his welfare officer and one of the work's trucks from the Buffet Depot was made available to him. We had an address of our own at last. Our family could be reunited as soon as possible. Dad's job remained in St Albans, but he thought that he would be able to cope with the daily bus journey. Finally, all was well with the Bailey's world.

CHAPTER FIVE

It was a euphoric moment when we finally packed the last of our bits and bobs onto the truck at Colney Heath. Our landlady waved goodbye and gave us a cheerful send off. Mum and I had to travel by bus to our new residence. Dad travelled in the truck and directed his colleague to the location of the house. It was sited at one end of the town and was on the St Albans bus route. The bus stopped at the bottom of the road which eventually led to our house at 2 Pamela Avenue. How convenient that would prove for Dad.

Dad remarked, "At last we shall be a family again." One of his first tasks the following week was to put those words, 'At Last' onto a house plaque which he screwed to the front gate. I always felt very embarrassed by it. It seemed such a stupid name for a house. However, there it remained, the words a constant reminder of the incredible exploits we had undertaken to achieve a home of our own.

Constant discussions took place, mainly about which members of the family would return first, and planning began in earnest. My parents soon realised that much had changed since the start of the war. I had grown and matured. I knew I would still have to share a room with Bette, if necessary, but my eldest sister Eileen would expect a room of her own. Prior to the war her accommodation was always included with her job.

Bette was still in Newquay, but it was hoped that by the time she was due home things would be organised. The house really was a little small for the size of our family. My parents decided to just deal with their present brood, one bedroom for them, one for me and one ready for Alan. His room would be the priority. However, much to our astonishment he didn't want to leave Pixies Hill School as he was so happy.

After much deliberating with both Alan and the authorities it was decided that he could stay at the school until he sat the scholarship. My brother Horrie, who had now been nicknamed Sandy by all his friends, wanted to come home as soon as he was released from his war work. My eldest brother Bob was still in the Airforce and stationed in Lahore, India. Prior to his posting he had fallen in love with a girl from Ipswich and they had married and were now expecting their first child. I can recall my mother saying that the little one was an embarkation baby. When I talked about the forthcoming birth of my first little nephew, I included that he was an embarkation baby into the conversation. I had no idea what the word embarkation meant only that my mother used to say it in hushed tones when talking to her friends. I realise now that it was to confirm that he was not born 'the wrong side of the sheets'. The world was at war, people were being killed by the thousands but nonetheless proprieties had to be observed.

Christmas 1942 was almost upon us; my parents were excited by the family being back together again. Mum and Dad wanted Christmas to be the most special of times, especially after what we had all been through. They started making plans and invited many of our extended family to our home. They gave no thought as to where they would sleep. Many people during the war seemed to adopt a laissez-faire attitude and let things take their own course.

I was so excited and was comforted by the surrounding warmth of my family. I finally felt secure. It had taken years and so many tears to reach this stage in my life. It was years later, as an adult, that I realised just how traumatic those war years had been. The shocking revelation of discovering what evacuation truly meant, being passed from pillar to post plus the misery of living in six different homes with some very uncaring hosts and a sister who constantly undermined me. Finally, there was the injustice of arriving home malnourished and with pneumonia when someone had been paid by the authorities to care for me. These sentiments live in my heart to this day.

In September 2019, the seventieth anniversary of the outbreak of the war was commemorated. Alexander Chancellor wrote in the Guardian newspaper, "It's time to explode the myth that all children evacuated from the blitz were well treated." The article goes on to describe some evacuees as forgotten victims. I don't feel a victim, but the experience has certainly coloured my existence and influenced me greatly in the upbringing of my children.

By the time we moved to Hemel Hempstead my parents' relationship was more stable. My father did everything possible to make my mother happy and there was never a sign of his previous aggression or impatience. If he could do anything to make Mum's life easier, he would do it. My siblings were still away, spread out across the country. I was an only child for that short period, and I relished it. I believe that it gave me the stability that I had yearned and longed for.

Christmas came and went. The festive season was the great success that my parents had wished for. I hated the decorations having to be taken down in the New Year. I felt as though my happy life would disappear with them into the box in the loft.

My feelings of security didn't fade away but life for me hit a plateau. I stayed at home and was my mother's companion. Why this was so was never explained to me. I was coming up to thirteen and there was no sign of me attending school. I asked my father once again about my schooling. "Well," he replied, "You were so ill and you're not strong enough to cope with other children." I thought this strange because I was allowed to clean the house and do masses of ironing, even cut the lawn with hand shears. In fairness to my parents, they were chores that I liked doing.

I used to always go to the town with Mum, I would even accompany her to the hairdressers. I used to watch the hairdresser do Mum's hair and occasionally I would hand the hairgrips to the girl working on her hair. Before long I was asked if I would like to go to the shop to help on a Saturday. The owners would give me a little pocket money. It was made clear to me that because I was only thirteen, I could not legally be employed. Theoretically, I was only at the hairdressing salon to observe. Within a short space of time, it was apparent that I was a natural. Legalities went out of the window. My mother's hair started being styled at home then I was asked to wash and set all her friends' hair and sometimes even the neighbours.

Life sauntered along. The war was still on, and rationing was in full swing but at least everyone was in the same boat. This made many housewives inventive in the culinary field. It really was remarkable how the women of that period kept their households going. My mother's favourite ingredient was dried egg. She conjured up all sorts of dishes made from it. Although my father worked in a food depot it gave us no advantage. In fact, it made us very aware that the country was prepared should the food convoys be sunk by German submarines or for an invasion. We really tried not to think about that too much.

It was around this period that my father formed a support group whose sole purpose was to keep an eye on the families who had loved ones serving in the forces. The support group grew, and it became remarkably successful.

Apsley Village Hall was the venue used for the dances and concerts. It really brought everyone together who lived on the Corolite Estate. Corolite was the name of the company who owned the Lime Works. The estate was built on their former land. There seemed to be endless parties of some sort. Every month in between the dances there was a party to celebrate the children's birthdays that fell within that month. All the young children were thought of, and it certainly made the estate a happy place to live.

What about the child who lived amongst this hive of activity? There was still no talk of me attending school. I was told that I was happy as I was and a big help to my mother but if I wanted to, I would be able to work as soon as I was fourteen. That was the final discussion about my education. I have never been able to fathom out the reasoning behind my parents' decisions. How did kind, caring parents become so indifferent about my education? How did they not foresee the consequences of the choices they made on my behalf? These significant decisions meant that my formal education finished at eleven and half years of age when in fact it should have been at the age of sixteen. No one will ever know what I may have achieved had my education continued. I would have liked to have pursued a career as a psychologist. Perhaps I would have failed the exams to gain entrance to the profession but then again, I could have attained passes. I will never know. One thing I do know for sure. I have often felt like an unqualified psychologist with so many goings-on in my life.

The following summer my parents decided that they would like to take a holiday in Leigh on Sea, a seaside resort that was immensely popular with East Londoners. They decided that I was very capable and therefore able to look after the household, which now had the addition of my two brothers, Alan and Sandy. Alan had returned home from Pixies Hill to attend the senior school in Crabtree Lane. He had made the decision not to sit for the scholarship. I thought his decision was a stupid one, as he was quite bright but like a lot of boys of that age, he dreamt of being a famous footballer. Every spare moment he had, he was kicking a ball around.

I adhered to the weekly household routines, and everything went well during my parents' absence. In fact, a little too well as this gave my mother and father a sense of assurance and made them feel comfortable about leaving me with the job on a more permanent basis. I was only thirteen years old. When my parents returned to Hemel Hempstead, they announced that they both loved the area around Southend and Leigh on Sea and planned to go back to the south coast with the sole purpose of looking for permanent accommodation. They hoped to rent a property from the local authority. Within a week they travelled back to Leigh on Sea and tried to fulfil their ambition. It all seemed incredible to me, even at that tender age. I carried on as housekeeper for around six months. I maintained the house for them as efficiently as an adult would have done. I worked out our food requirements and bought the groceries, cleaned the house and did the washing and ironing. I had no help other than from Sandy who used to give me a hand with the garden.

I was pleased and mightily relieved when I eventually found out that my parents were unable to secure a tenancy which was one of the deciding factors in their return home. The privately rented flat they were living in, was also proving too expensive. Life returned to what was normal for us. Dad retired and became interested in local politics. Mum returned to her role of housewife with me back to the role of companion.

The family was reforming gradually. Eileen had obtained a job as a secretary in a small company in St Albans and due to our shortage of bedrooms had rented a room in the next avenue. However, she came home to meals and was always accompanied by her laundry. I had now got used to calling my brother Horace by his nick name of Sandy. He too was working in St Albans at an electrical business. Brother Bob was expected home from India, but we realised his life would now revolve around his new family in Ipswich. Bette was still in Newquay and seemed to be incredibly happy. We were almost complete as a family.

My father carried on with his social activities and was constantly organising theatre trips to Golders Green Empire. These outings raised the spirits of many people. It was still an unstable time and the theatre trips helped many of our neighbours who were in a state of great anxiety. Some had lost loved ones; others had been told that relatives had gone missing in action, and a few had husbands in prisoner of war camps. Stories filtered through about the terrible atrocities happening in the camps to not only soldiers but civilians.

On occasions I used to babysit for our neighbours. They always treated me kindly and frequently used to leave out a little plate of supper for me. Reflecting on those times now, I realise how caring our local community was.

Stan Searles, Eileen's fiancé, joined the Royal Airforce. He was based at RAF Grantham which was eventually renamed RAF Spitalgate in 1944. Stan already held a pilot's licence so immediately became a

Pilot Officer. He used to visit us whenever he was able to get a forty-eight-hour pass. On one of these occasions Eileen and Stan decided they would use their time together to plan their wedding. They wanted to get married in St Albans and if possible, to have the ceremony in the Abbey. We were all excited about this forthcoming celebration. I was to be a bridesmaid and was overjoyed at the prospect.

Stan was constantly attentive to me. One day he whispered in my ear, "When you hear a plane coming over Jeannie, look up to see if it's a Mosquito and if it is me, I will loop the loop for you." I believed him and for the next few days I dashed outside whenever I heard planes overhead. One cloudy day I looked skywards and there in the distance was a de Havilland Mosquito. It circled a couple of times then as it approached the plane suddenly looped the loop overhead. It was Stan. He had kept his promise. It was the most exhilarating sensation and felt totally unreal. I had never observed such an exciting spectacle. How could something so magical happen before my very own eyes? The whole family were extremely fond of Stan and like many families we prayed for him and the safe return of all the serving men and women.

In March 1945 Stan's father contacted Eileen to inform her that Stan was missing. He had survived several sorties over Europe only to go missing, probably over the English Channel. Stan served with the elite Path Finder Force who, from 1942, led almost every raid over occupied Europe. These experienced airmen made a vast difference to the effectiveness of Bomber Command. However, the crew's odds of surviving were radically reduced with the more sorties they did. Stan's last radio communication relayed that he had dropped his flares and was turning and heading for home.

We were all devastated by this news. Regrettably, the many search aircraft that used to span the channel looking for ditched planes never found a trace of him or his crew. We will never forget him.

The Air Force's Runneymede Memorial is dedicated to some 20,456 men and women who were lost in air and other operations during World War II. Those recorded have no known grave anywhere in the world and many were lost without trace. The names of each of these airmen and airwomen are engraved into the stone walls of the memorial and Stan and his fellow pilots and crew are amongst them. After all these years the sadness of his loss remains with me.

Eileen was distraught. We both recalled a conversation we had had with Stan when he told us how difficult it was to exit from a Mosquito because the crew gained access via the belly of the aircraft;

not the side or top. That piece of information took away any hope Eileen had of his return. Stanley Oliver Searles was awarded the Distinguished Flying Cross posthumously.

I had now reached the age of fourteen and could legally leave school. I felt a sense of freedom. The prospect of further education had finally slipped away from me forever. This is something I have always regretted. Both my parents thought I was an achiever right up until their deaths, but they failed to realise what life may have held in store for me.

I was now able to work in the hairdressers as a trainee. Many apprenticeships had been suspended during the war, so it really was just a training period of three years without any legal contract or obligation. I worked there for over a year and didn't receive proper training. My job was menial, merely waiting on the hairdressers, washing the towels and capes and making tea. In short, I was a skivvy. Out of the blue a friend of my father's got me a placement in Watford to continue my training. I would receive an apprentice's payment of ten shillings a week, but I would be trained properly. I was delighted at the prospect.

This was my first grown up job. My previous employment was connected to my mother. No longer would I have to observe the private exchanges she had with the owner, wondering what was being said. This gave me the sense of being liberated. It proved hard for me financially. Ten shillings a week didn't go very far. My bus fare was six shillings which left me with practically nothing. I always said a silent prayer of thanks when a customer paid their bill and gave me a threepenny bit as a tip. The tips made such a difference to my life. I ticked over quite well and really enjoyed my job. Both the head stylists were French refugees who were very skilled and way in advance of British hairdressers.

We hoped the war was coming to an end in 1944 but the blackout was in full force and our town had its share of forces stationed here. British soldiers were stationed in Cupid Green, on the outskirts of the town and American soldiers were based at Bovingdon.

I started to enjoy my life so much more and was now allowed to go to dances which were held in the canteens of John Dickenson, the greatest and largest stationery manufacturer in the world. Often at the dances, on a Saturday night, there would be confrontations between the different forces. The M.P.s, military police, had to frequently sort out skirmishes. The resentment of the British soldiers for the Americans was palpable. The fact, or so they thought, that they were much better paid and could throw money around annoyed many. I heard them winding each other up but always felt it was friendly banter. The dances did enable some relationships to flourish and a few local girls became G.I. brides and ended up living in America. At the time I was so sorry that I had been forbidden by my parents to even dance with an American. My siblings were always just a stone's throw away, so I didn't get the opportunity to even try.

I was at the age to be impressed by the opposite sex, believing every word they said. At this time, I had no shortage of offers to dance. There were always lots of male family friends which gave me a steady supply of partners. Ballroom dancing became my passion. I liked its elegance. It was the era when all the women wore long dresses and got spruced up to go out. I was fortunate enough to own two long dresses. One was my bridesmaid's dress, the other, my mother had acquired from somebody second-hand. I used to spend an inordinate amount of time getting ready but not as long as my sister Bette, who by now had returned from Newquay. We only had the one tiny bathroom and there used to be constant shouting from one member of the family or the other about the length of time spent in the there. "You've been in there for far too long," was the common cry as the door was thumped. I always caught the end of it all as I worked. Saturdays were always very tiring days. After work I found it difficult to get on the buses as they were full of Saturday shoppers returning home. After getting off the bus I had an awfully long walk up a hill to the top of Belmont Road. When I eventually reached home my mother would be waiting to greet me with a lovely smile but with wet hair. The curlers and hairdryer were already to hand. After setting Mum's hair I could finally eat then get ready for my favourite evening of the week.

I did enjoy this time of my life. I was growing up. At fourteen I looked like a seventeen-year-old. I was very slender and fairly tall. This gave me quite a selection of dancing partners. Yes, boys were coming into my life thick and fast. I was allowed to go to the pictures with dates so long as I was home by nine o'clock.

Amongst this throng of boys was one called Dennis. He had brown hair, was slim and about three inches taller than me and lived quite close to my house in Pamela Avenue. I was soon invited to meet his parents. I really enjoyed their company and their household always seemed so much saner than mine. Dennis was more special than the other boys that I danced with. I was made to feel special by his family and I really cared for his little sister Iris. Dennis felt the need to join up. The navy was his choice, the Merchant fleet. He signed on and was soon allocated a ship. We corresponded weekly. I still went to dances and enjoyed dates to either the pictures or cycle rides to Ashridge or Dunstable Downs. Looking back now I suppose I basked in the attention. My inferiority complex rapidly diminished. It was only then that I realised what a burden I had carried from my childhood.

People were preoccupied with the prospect that the end of the war was imminent, and they were longing for the return of their loved ones. However, the aftermath of the war brought a different reality for some. Couples with newly formed relationships discovered that they really didn't know each other; many found their homes became overcrowded, partners had gone astray, and forgiveness was not always forthcoming. Tension was paramount in so many families. We knew all about this as my father was involved in local politics.

My father who was a strong Labour supporter was persuaded to stand for the forthcoming local election. Our house became a hive of activity. Like minded supporters were in and out of the house for months and there was no privacy for our family. My father had become a staunch Labour supporter during the pre-war time of the great depression. Although at that time he was employed he felt compassion for all the thousands that were not. The industrial and mining areas of the north of England, Scotland and Northern Ireland were the hardest hit by the economic problems. Unemployment reached 70% in some areas at the start of the 1930s (with more than 3 million out of work nationally). Many families depended entirely on payments from local government known as the dole. Even so families were cold and hungry. As children we always included them in our nightly prayers. My father now felt the same emotional attachment for the returning troops.

Election Day came and the months of hard canvassing paid off. Father was elected by a large majority and was Hemel Hempstead's first Labour councillor. The town had always previously been a Conservative stronghold. Life in the Bailey household changed considerably. Father was voted chairman of the housing committee. He was elated but didn't realise what an impact this would have on our household.

Our house was small with only the one sitting room. When people visited Dad, we all had to retire to our various bedrooms, even our mother. This situation had many draw backs. Our only toilet was on the ground floor. To use it we had to go downstairs then walk outside and go around to the back door. On receiving complaints from us all, including my mother, my father admonished us. "You should be ashamed to complain. Plenty of people have nothing and through no fault of their own." He was right and we did feel the shame of complaining. This intrusion into our household was unrelenting and lasted for a couple of years.

My father continued with his social work and good causes for many years. He formed Darby and Joan clubs. The first was in Apsley but in due course they spread out across the town. His ambition was to have a centre for the elderly and lonely. He wanted a place where people could call in and have a cup of tea or coffee but mainly some place where they could talk to people who were in the same position as themselves. Dad's dream was realised, a recreation centre for senior citizens in Half Moon Yard. It is still there today and now called The Centre in the Park.

I do not know if my father had a conscience about the dreadful things he had done in his past. He was his own judge and jury. What I do know is that he spent his last forty years doing good things to promote a better world. My family found so many letters of appreciation and thank you cards amongst his keepsakes when he died. They were a tribute to his kindness and caring for the underprivileged. He achieved a lot in his lifetime. I forgave him for his past transgressions. I valued and loved him for his courage and tenacity.

I had experienced very sore hands and had had a rash for a few weeks. I was dealing with the problem and trying not to draw attention to my dilemma. I didn't feel too worried about it as no one I had been in contact with seemed to be affected. Nevertheless, the problem didn't go away, and I had to consult a doctor. I underwent various tests and was diagnosed with dermatitis undoubtedly brought on by hairdressing. It was a bitter blow for me as I loved my job and had reached examination level. I had no choice and had to leave the salon with immediate effect. The soreness and rash took a couple of weeks to clear before I could go job hunting.

The time off work coincided with my brother Bob's wife, needing some assistance to travel to Hemel Hempstead to await her husband's return from India. As I was the only member of the family available, I was delegated and more than happy to do so. This was the first trip I had made on my own as an adult. It was a good journey and when I arrived, I was greeted warmly by my sister-in-law Jean. I knew that I was staying in Ipswich for a week, and that I would have a little time to take in the sights.

During my first day we were swamped with visits from neighbours and friends. Most of the calls were to do with preparations of some sort, for the summer fete the following Saturday. Apparently, things were well under way. This fete was in honour of a young soldier who had been a prisoner of war. He was released on an exchange with the Italians. This young man was one of over 170,000 British POWs, prisoners of war, who were taken by German and Italian forces.

Saturday duly arrived. Jean and her mother were doing their good deeds and helping the organising team. I didn't fancy going to the fete as I thought this wouldn't be my cup of tea, so I offered to take the baby for a walk into the town. I thought that I'd like to mooch around the shops. My sister-in-law was delighted that I had volunteered to take baby Robert as it freed her to help in a more constructive way.

It was such a beautiful day and the glorious weather helped make the fete a success. Jean was busy helping when the guest of honour, Leslie Hunter, spoke to her. "Hello Jean. I hear you are now married to an airman and have a baby." He then cast an eye around, "Where is the baby?"

"My sister-in-law has taken him for a walk. Would you believe it, she's just arrived back." Just at that moment I walked onto the field not knowing where to start looking for Jean. Quickly I became aware of this handsome young man with blonde hair running towards me. He then blurted out in one breath, "Hello. I'm Leslie Hunter. I'm the one this shindig is in aid of." I just laughed and then let him do the hard work of pushing the pram over to Jean. Leslie was called upon to present various prizes and told me not to move until he came back. Jean and I giggled at his eagerness and intensity. I didn't move from the spot and my first date with Leslie was organised for that same evening.

Leslie was so pleasant and very courteous. We went for a drive to Felixstowe. This was extremely exhilarating for me. The only people I knew who had cars were in jobs of national importance. I later discovered the car belonged to Leslie's father. We both enjoyed the evening, and a second date was arranged. I only hoped that Jean's parents, who were my hosts, didn't object. Our second date was a bit strained at the end of the evening because he wanted me to stay in Ipswich for longer. Silence enveloped the car on the return journey. Suddenly all in a rush Leslie said, "When you walked onto the field I expected an old-fashioned sister-in-law, not this wonder on long legs with a beautiful smile. My heart jumped out of my body, and I don't think it has come back again. Now I'm in a terrible quandary. I am twenty-eight years old and in love with a sixteen-year-old girl. What am I to do?" I was very shocked by his strength of feelings for me, and I could see that he was in such turmoil. A mature man had fallen in love with me. He went on to say, "I know from Jean that you have a young boyfriend in your hometown. I neither have the wish or the time to play the games of the young. I will write to you every day and telephone when I am able."

Wow! I found it all so remarkable but because I was mature beyond my years, I took every word he said to heart. Our next two days together were so tender and without pressure. During our last evening he turned towards me and uttered, "I want to marry you and look after you. I can provide a home and you will always be cherished." How do we ever know in life what is going to happen from day to day? Leslie made sure that when he dropped me back at the Allard's house, he had time to chat with Jean. After he had driven off Jean said to me, "Leslie has really fallen for you."

On my return home to Hemel the excitement, with regard to my family, was all for the new baby. He and Jean had joined our over-crowded household. It was chaotic with people everywhere.

I spoke to my mother about Leslie, and she wasn't a bit interested. "A mature man of that age couldn't seriously be so enamoured with such a young girl." She then went on to ask if he had taken advantage of me. She wouldn't have made those remarks had she met Leslie.

Letters came from Leslie daily and telephone calls once a week. I now had to sort out what I was going to do about my two younger boyfriends. I found it hard to come to terms with the fact that I had several young men who were obviously extremely interested in my future. I went from feeling not special to anybody to having people who were very fond of me and caring. I could feel the difference in my self-worth. I didn't think I was pretty so it had to be something else, but I was too inexperienced at that time to define it.

Now the dermatitis on my hands had cleared I could seek employment at John Dickinson's. The paper mill employed thousands of workers. They even had their own school. I was advised to go to see their recruiting officer, who was based in the school.

I turned up at my appointed time and more or less told the truth about my lack of education and how that had come about. Mr Newton, the head of the school, talked to me for around an hour and finished by saying, "I don't need any paperwork. In the past hour I have gained an insight into your potential and your future capabilities. I am offering you a job as a junior in the Book Office." I glided home on winged feet. I was employed and it was on merit and not my background. That day I came to terms with the realisation of how one's education can steer you through life. In my case, the appraisal of a very astute gentleman helped me to realise that it was not the looking back into the past but looking forward that would help me to achieve my ambition. Mr Newton's interest and faith in me changed the course of my future. He had in such a short time instilled in me a sense of self-esteem. I left the interview feeling that I was able to take on anything the future threw at me.

The following Monday morning I was collected from the Time Office by a pleasant mature woman who informed me that I was to be a junior on the secretarial division. At the time I didn't appreciate that it was a fantastic opportunity and an excellent position. All the ladies in that section were secretaries to the managers and they were very discerning in picking their juniors. I really had been given a head start. Bless Mr Newman he had done more than his best for me. I was enrolled in the school to learn shorthand. I received lessons twice a week which were paid for by the company. I hated learning Pitman shorthand but liked the general office training. I was now meeting other young girls like me. During our breaks we talked about clothes, dances and boys.

Dickinson's held weekly dances. The tickets were 'must have' for most of the younger generation of Hemel Hempstead but they were so hard to obtain. The company devised a fair system of distribution. Each department in turn, had the first pick. Any tickets that remained were sold to the other departments, also in strict rotation. We tried to secure tickets from the older people in our department who had no wish to take part. Each week I, along with members of my family, was lucky enough to be at these wonderful dances. They were held in the Guild house which belonged to the company. Often the top bands of the day played there. It was the most glamourous setting and I thought ladies in long frocks brought elegance to any dance. Every weekend all the local young men assembled at the ends of the dance floor to eye up all the girls. The girls too had the same intent. These are blissful, happy memories for me.

It was at this time that I acquired the name of Jane. Jane was a cartoon strip drawn by Norman Pett that ran in The Daily Mirror from 1932 to 1959. The young boys in the Book Department decided that I looked like her and started to call me Jane. This caught on and whenever I walked through any of the departments 'Jane' echoed around. This was a daily occurrence as part of my job involved going from department to department. Eventually everyone was calling me Jane. It used to embarrass me whenever I was asked how the name came about as Jane was considered a little risqué at the time. Now after so many years I can confess how it all began.

I was still attending my classes but found my daily work uninteresting. As a junior I seemed to spend the entire day delivering papers or filing notes. I was young and failed to realise the opportunities that were there. All I could see was what was happening in the here and now.

Whilst on my various excursions through the departments, of which there were dozens, I observed that all the other workers appeared so happy. I used to stop and talk to some of the young girls I knew and concluded that I would be much happier working with them. My parents were told that I was going to apply for a transfer. They were furious and were quite right to be so. In hindsight I realise they were, at long last, thinking of my future.

I applied for a transfer into the Stationery Department where I already had several friends. I stayed there until I married and was incredibly happy and content. The extra wages enabled my wardrobe of clothes to expand. This didn't impress my mother and one day she told me that she was going to visit all the shoe shops in Hemel Hempstead and Watford to tell them that I was banned from buying more shoes. How my life had turned around in such a short time.

I enjoyed every moment of day in the new department. I worked very closely with my friends and learned how to create beautiful presentation boxes of stationery which were padded and bedecked with ribbons and bows. It was a skilled job and rewarding. Joan, one of those friends from over seventy years ago, remains a much-loved friend to this day. The years have passed but the loving strength that we gained from each other has endured. We often talk of the past and wonder about our future.

The new job with extra money and freedom had distracted me but I was all too aware that I had to deal with the boyfriend situation. The prospect of what I had to do didn't come easily to me as I didn't want to hurt anyone. However, with regard to Dennis, his lovely mother Cis had anticipated my plight and invited me to supper for a talk. She began by saying, "You are much too young to settle down. I have explained this to Dennis and told him that I have cancelled the money order which he used to send off for an engagement ring." I was astounded by this news but also appreciated that he had such a lovely caring mother who only wanted the best for her son and his young girlfriend. I continued to write to Den for some time. Our courtship gradually tapered off without any issues.

I started going to other dances which were held at the Town Hall. I loved the atmosphere of the old Victorian building. It was steeped in history and the long dresses didn't seem out of place. One night I was taken there by a young man called Ken Humphries. Whilst he was at the bar getting our drinks, a huge fellow came and stood next to me. He asked if I went to dances at The Town Hall regularly. He also asked me where I lived. Ken soon returned from the bar. He resented me being chatted up, so he told this chap to shove off. I thought this was a brave thing to do. He was such a huge guy I thought something untoward might happen, but it didn't.

At the end of the night the usual crowds walked en masse in the same direction, talking and laughing. Suddenly the big guy loomed up from nowhere. He walked alongside me and started talking. We continued our discussion until we reached The Plough which was where people dispersed in various directions. The big guy walked off. He didn't get far before he turned around and called out to me, "By the way my name is Bill. You won't forget it because it goes with your surname," He was of course referring to the song Bill Bailey Won't You Please Come Home. I laughed. Ken was livid and said, "I'm not being made a fool of." He walked me as far as Belswains Lane, where he lived, and left me there. I laughed and caught up with some people walking my way home. I had no further dates with Ken for some time. We did have the odd dance afterwards but with no reference to the big guy. It was on one of these rare occasions that Ken asked me out to the pictures. I cannot recall now what the film was, but it was showing at the Rex in Berkhamsted.

It was a very balmy night, so Ken suggested that we walked home via the canal towpath. All was well until we reached the bridge at the Roses Lime juice wharf. This quiet boy turned into a very amorous man who was hard to handle. Gone was my assurance that I was able to handle any man. I just about managed to control the situation. Ken was now an incredibly angry young man. He stormed off and yelled out, "Oh you … the calm, cold and immaculate Miss Bailey." He left me on the tow path to walk the rest of the way home on my own. Thankfully, I arrived home safe and sound. A lesson had been learned. I now knew that my young boyfriends had turned into men.

During this period, I was still writing to Leslie who now thought that there was no boyfriend in my life. He knew that the Dennis situation had been resolved. Leslie wanted me to decide. I was only sixteen and my parents had not even met him. I certainly was not sure of what falling in love really meant. I thought I knew it all but of course I didn't. Leslie was aware of how I felt but thought with his maturity and experience he could handle the situation for both of us. Bless him, he had such a lovely strong character. I am sure that had he lived nearer; things would have been different. The letters and the telephone calls kept coming. I had to stop him showering me with gifts. Eventually things calmed down. I kept going to dances but Leslie did not move on. I felt so guilty but when I was older, I realised that is how life is. We all must learn to move on until we feel the time is right.

CHAPTER SIX

My sister Bette had not arrived home from Newquay and my parents couldn't fathom out why. Evacuees from all regions of England had been returned to their original homes. Weeks went by and still my sister hadn't returned. My parents wrote to her and asked if she had any information on the repatriation, but Bette's answer was always no. After a while, my concerned father contacted the War Office to ask for information and an explanation for the delay. He was stunned when he was told that all the Newquay evacuees had returned to their parents other than those who had elected to remain with their foster parents. Birth parents or legal guardians had been sent forms to sign about their final decision on repatriation. My parents had not received or signed any documents. My mischievous sister Bette had decided she wanted to stay and live at Mrs Arthur's forever. She had forged papers and even found herself a job. My exasperated parents arranged for her immediate repatriation. She had to return home under her own steam. I now had to share my bedroom with her as we were so overcrowded. This meant losing my own precious space. However, we managed. Bette sought employment and found a position at John Dickinson's in the Plastics Office. Over the years I tried to find out from my sister where she worked in Newquay, but she wouldn't reveal anything. It remained her secret.

We now had another member of the family competing for the bathroom on a Saturday night. Bette joined the family's forays to the local dances. We were all good ballroom dancers, but my sister Bette outshone everybody in the foxtrot. She always had serious dancers waiting in the wings to dance with her. It was on one of these occasions that Bill, the big guy I'd met previously, sought me out. We only had the one dance before it was time to bid goodnight to each other.

During the week it was the norm for me and Bette to meet up at lunchtime and walk to the village shops. Dozens of cyclists used to stream through the village at the same time, some going for lunch, others returning to work. Bette drew my attention to a cyclist riding a very attention seeking bike. It was made from stainless steel and was very shiny with dropped handlebars. It was ridden by the big guy. Every day we used to watch out for him. He would smile and I would try to be a split second faster and turn my head away. It was all a game to me. The poor man had to cycle so fast to reach the entrance gate, deposit his bike in the bike sheds and then run, depleted and out of breath, just to pass in front of me to say hello. On one occasion, completely breathless he approached me and asked, "Will you come to the Charter's Ball with me?" I replied by telling him that I would think about it. I knew I had to get my parents' permission to go and the fact that they didn't know him might influence their decision. My parents agreed with the proviso that I took Bette with me. At our next lunchtime encounter I told Bill that I would go if he asked his friend Dud Stratton to invite my sister. This he did and the stage was set.

The Charter's Ball was an incredibly special dance, held annually in the Town Hall. As the name suggests it was an annual event held in honour of the town being granted a charter by Henry VIII. Not only were the tickets expensive they were exceedingly difficult to obtain. The tickets were first offered to the local bigwigs then the remaining tickets were sold to the hoi palloi. Years afterwards Bill told me that when I agreed to go with him the panic set in. He had no idea how or from whom he could obtain four of these precious tickets but obtain them he did.

It was a very relieved pair that knocked on the door for that special date. Bette already knew Dud as he worked in her department. My parents thought Bill and Dud looked and sounded fine, so we set off. The bus stop was only a little way from the house. Bette and I both teetered on our high heels, holding up our long dresses. We all sat at the entrance to the bus and could see our glamorous selves reflected in the windows. I could hear Dud speaking to Bette and they kept laughing. Bill and I didn't say a word for the whole journey. He just stared at my reflection which made me feel uncomfortable. *'This is going to be a very strange evening. I wish I hadn't said yes.'*

I was so wrong. The evening proved to be one of the loveliest evenings one could wish for. We all sauntered home and when we saw the familiar sight of The Plough, Dud said his goodnights. Bill walked both Bette and me home to Pamela Avenue. As soon as my parents saw Bette shut the door, leaving me outside with Bill, they flew outside and

74

announced, "Goodnight. Thank you for bringing them home safely." Bill was crestfallen. He thought he would at least get one goodnight kiss, his first, from me.

More dates followed the dance. We had several trips to the Luxor and Princess cinemas. The Princess picture house had a small box for patrons. I never wanted to see a film from the side view plus I knew all about the naughty goings on. It was mostly the American soldiers who liked its privacy. We all used to discuss the shenanigans that went on and concluded that you only went into that box if you were a certain type of girl. How we typecast people and I reflect now on how judgemental we were. I hope I've been forgiven but that is how it was in those days. Cinema goers had to pay a lot more money for tickets in the box and yet you shared it with the brooms and vacuum cleaner. Bill imparted this piece of information to me. I thought he was being serious, not joking. He went on to say that the saying, 'sweeping the dirt under the carpet,' came from using that box and I believed him.

Bill became a regular visitor to our house. Each visit to the cinema or to a dance he collected me from the house, and he always walked me home. I still was in contact with Leslie and spoke to him by telephone. He confessed to me later that he made the mistake of thinking he would stand back whilst I was finding my way. My parents now accepted Bill, but my mother had done her best to put me off at the start of our relationship. She used to relate stories about his mature life and compared it with mine. Her ultimate put down was to say, "Don't you know that he plays darts in a pub and goes around with a gang of men." This so-called gang proved to be his school mates who were gradually getting demobbed. They used to all meet in the Kings Arms in the town on the first Friday of their demob. I thought it all rather glamourous and took no heed.

It was the winter of 1947, a winter to remember. Britain experienced several severe cold spells that brought large falls of snow. The snow drifts blocked roads and railways, which caused problems with transporting coal to the power stations. Factories had to close to conserve fuel and household electricity supplies were restricted. Even radio broadcasts were limited, and television services were suspended. However, all the young were making sledges and having fun. We had beautiful hills surrounding us and we used to climb to the top of the highest hill, sit on the sledge and descend at a terrific speed. It was tremendous fun and all the young people, me included, were totally unaware of any danger. Giant snowmen sprang up all over the place.

The boys were extremely competitive and tried to outdo each other and were persistently trying to impress us. Three sisters from one household gave them a challenge. As well as having fun we used to gather firewood from Hob Jo Wood to help with the lack of fuel. Oh, such cheerful memories that I can recall with a smile because I was young. In reality, it was a very hard time for so many people. From late January until mid-March, snow fell every day somewhere in the country. The temperatures rarely rose more than a degree or two above zero. People shivered in overcoats both indoors and outdoors. Pipes froze. There was a scarcity of food and unemployment was high.

It was that same year that my life altered course. I was on a bus returning from the pictures with Bill. We sat on the top in the front seats and as usual Bill looked at me through the reflection on the window which still made me feel ill at ease. Unexpectedly I heard him say, "Will you get engaged to me on your eighteenth birthday?"

I was stunned. "I will need to think about it and in any case, I am not eighteen this birthday, only seventeen. When you originally asked me my age, I thought that I wouldn't be going out with you again, so I told a fib."

It was now Bill's turn to be shocked. "I don't believe you." He thought about what I had said and then went on to say, "In fact, when we first met, I thought that you were around twenty. If you don't want to get engaged just say so, don't make up such stories." It wasn't long before we arrived at home and when my mother opened the door I said, "Will you tell Bill how old I am next week."

Mum looked puzzled then replied, "Seventeen."

Bill just uttered two words, "Good God."

However, he still went ahead and asked my father if we could get engaged. My father said, "As long as you look after her and you know what I mean."

Then my mother joined in. "I have something to say. You can get engaged but she is not going to get married until she is twenty-one."

We got engaged on my father's birthday 2nd May 1947. Bill's parents were introduced to mine and after meeting me they too got over their reservations about my age. They once described me as bursting into their lives like a firework. I was spoilt and immediately showered with love by them both. We had an extremely close bond which was maintained for the rest of their lives.

Now we were an engaged couple we felt we could go ahead and plan a holiday for the coming July. It was customary for the whole of

Dickinson's factory to shut down for two weeks. We thought we would go ahead and book. My mother found out about this and was horrified at the prospect and quickly restrictions were soon put in place. I could go away with Bill providing my young brother Alan shared Bill's chalet and I was with some other female, yet unknown. All my protesting was to no avail. The conditions were not negotiable. We booked our holiday with Butlin's. As soon as the written confirmation plus other documents arrived in the post they were perused by my parents. How strange it seems now in today's society. Saving began in earnest for both the wedding and holiday. At last, my life seemed 'normal' with a happy future ahead.

When I first saw Bill, I always described him as, 'the big guy,' because he was six feet three in height and had a forty-eight-inch chest. I was five foot eight but as slender as a reed. I always knew that he would watch over me in a protecting way. Due to his size various people said, "I wouldn't like to upset him." Conversely, Bill was a gentle giant. When I said that to him, he said, "Don't tell anybody that I am a kitten really. My size protects us both."

Preparations were made and the evening before the holiday we decided to go for a drink at Ye Old Fighting Cocks in St Albans. The pub was built in the eleventh century and is in such a delightful setting, adjacent to both the Abbey and lakes. Bill had arranged to pick me up in time to catch the eight o'clock bus. He always biked to our house and then we used to get local transport to wherever we were going. I was almost ready to leave when a car drove into our crescent. This was an unusual event.

I looked out of the bedroom window and saw it was a small Ford and wondered which house it was bound for. As the driver got out of the car I nearly passed out with shock. It was Leslie. I rushed downstairs to tell my mother and nearly fell down the entire flight as a result. "Mum, Mum. It's Leslie," I called out. My heart was pounding, and I started to shake. He rang the doorbell. I opened the door breathless, a bright pink with all the emotion. Leslie was an absolute darling and said immediately, "It's all right. I know you are engaged to somebody called Bill." He came into our house and told us an utterly amazing story about how he'd found us. He knew that I had dealt with the Dennis situation but didn't know about Bill. How I let that happen is to my shame. I still cannot believe that I handled it so badly.

Leslie had been to Lord's Cricket Ground to watch a match and thought he would travel to Hemel Hempstead afterwards and sort things out in person. When he arrived, he realised he hadn't a clue to the whereabouts of Pamela Avenue. He drove down Marlowes, which was the main street in those days and stopped his car to allow a woman pushing a pram to cross. The woman looked up to thank him when they both stared in amazement at each other. The pram pushing lady was my sister-in-law Jean, the very person who had introduced us. Jean felt she had to tell him that I was engaged. Leslie decided he still wanted to see me, and Jean directed him to the house.

Bill was about to arrive any second. My mother in her wisdom told us to sit in the garden and she would bring us some tea and biscuits. We had only just sat down when Bill approached us with an outstretched hand to Leslie. Initially the situation was very strained. We sat drinking tea and making polite conversation. Bill ended up inviting Leslie to come for a drink with us. Leslie accepted and offered to take us in his car. The journey was completed in silence apart from directions being given.

We found three empty seats in the pub. Bill went up to the bar to get the first round and whilst ordering the drinks Leslie pleaded hurriedly, "Please break off the engagement." When I looked up Bill was watching us from the bar, his face set and angry looking. On his return he set down our glasses and we talked about cricket and the test results. Both men were knowledgeable about sport, but I don't think either of them had that at the forefront of their minds. In the following hour or so I felt I advanced a few years in age. Leslie went outside for a breather. Bill turned to me and said, "I can see you are finding this hard to handle. Well, I can tell you now, I am not letting you go. I've waited a long time for the right girl to come along. I am deeply sorry that he was a prisoner of war in an Italian camp, but I've survived being torpedoed so that makes us even."

Leslie returned and spoke directly to me. "I am going now. I will return to Ipswich tonight instead of staying over. Enjoy your holiday and I will speak to you when you return." I walked to the car with him without any words being spoken but when I saw the tears running down his face, I was jolted into being the adult that I thought I was already.

Bill and I walked to the bus stop in silence and hardly spoke to each other on the journey. On our arrival home he collected his bike and said goodnight without even kissing me goodbye. Both men had experienced life and seen things to make them more mature. I was so young. This was my very first truly emotional experience of what loving someone really meant. Bill told me a long time afterwards that he had intended to break off the engagement and do what Leslie had done - wait for me to grow up. He went on to say that he couldn't find the strength and was afraid that I would find someone else in my maturity.

Getting up the next morning to be in the right frame of mind for Butlin's Holiday Camp was nothing short of an ordeal. My young brother was so excited and broke the silence because he didn't know what was going on. Unfortunately, his excitement only lasted for twenty-four hours because he became sick and was confined to bed in the chalet until our return home. We called the camp doctor, but he couldn't make a diagnosis, so my brother returned home a very sick teenager. All his plans for chatting up girls didn't come to fruition. We knew that he had to feel terribly ill for him not to take advantage of a dream holiday. Each day he told us that he thought he felt a little better, but we knew he only said this to delay any thought of him being admitted to hospital.

We had longed for this holiday and now all three of us wished for every day to pass quickly to accelerate our return home. It was a peculiar feeling wishing away the holiday. Bill and I were very anxious about Alan. We knew that something was seriously wrong.

The journey home seemed to never end with every jolt of the coach causing great discomfort to Alan. How pleased and relieved we were to see my parents. Within hours of our arrival home my brother was seen by a doctor. The doctor ascertained that the week prior to our holiday something had happened to Alan which he hadn't discussed with anybody. Alan was now an apprentice plumber at Dickinson's. He was on a job and following the plumber, carrying a large pipe on his shoulder. As they turned a corner, they came across two boys playing with a paper football. One of boys went to kick the ball but misaimed and his foot flew into Alan's groin. Unable to bend with the pipe on his shoulder, the full impact of the kick did considerable damage. His crotch had swollen to such a degree that it was now impossible for him to walk. He hadn't told anybody what had happened because of the holiday. The injury altered the course of his life in many ways.

None of us could have foreseen what the next ten years would mean for him and the family. His condition deteriorated and he was placed on the hospital's critical list. My parents were asked if they could afford to pay for a private consultant.

Whist in hospital Alan confided to my father that during a procedure to aspirate fluid, the tip of the hypodermic needle had broken off. My father made enquiries to the ward sister who denied everything.

She said it was utter nonsense and that Alan must have overheard the staff talking about another Alan Bailey. My father wasn't convinced. He left the hospital, drove home and telephoned the hospital reception. He enquired that he needed to establish the wards of both Alan Baileys. He was informed that there was only one patient with that name, and he was in the Windsor Ward. Nothing was ever done about this incident, there wasn't even an apology.

Alan was seen by a consultant from Charring Cross Hospital called Mr Warner. He was with Alan for less than five minutes before he informed my parents that Alan's body could float off the bed with all the fluid it contained. "Alan is dying. Are you prepared to take the risk of him being transported to London?" Obviously, my parents wanted the best care that they could possibly get for my little brother. He was transported immediately and that was the start of many years in various hospitals.

In hindsight I wondered if I should have either sent for my parents or taken Alan home sooner. I was reassured that he was now in the right place to be cared for and that he would hopefully recover.

I grew up rather quickly during that period of my life, trying to come to terms with the facts of what had happened. I wrote to Leslie and told him of the turmoil within the Bailey family and that I was sorry for any pain that I had caused him. He answered with his usual caring spirit saying, "Just look after yourself and be a support for your family. Please keep me up to date with news of Alan. Be happy. Please write again unless it proves difficult."

I asked Bill if he minded if I wrote to Leslie. "Yes, I bloody well do mind, but I guess you will take no notice. Never sign the letter with love." I smile as I write these words because if Bill were alive today, he would utter the same comments. I did continue to write to Leslie, and he used to telephone me occasionally. The letters became less frequent as my wedding day drew nearer.

Life at this time was not only hectic but full of concern for Alan. He was transferred to Mount Vernon Hospital, the fluid had now been diagnosed as TB, tuberculosis. His few weeks of hospitalisation had now turned into an unknown length of stay. We rallied the troops and made sure that somebody visited the hospital every day. Bill's mother undertook to see him once a week with other friends visiting whenever they could. Very few friends had cars in those days and the buses to the hospital were infrequent and expensive. Bill and I were frantically saving for our wedding.

Contrary to my poor mother's wishes we booked our wedding for June 1948. The lead up to the special day was frenzied. We fitted in appointments, jobs and shopping around Alan's hospital visits. My wedding dress was bought during a day's visit to London when Alan was in Charing Cross Hospital. My bridesmaids' outfits were made by a dress maker in St Albans. She had been recommended to me by a friend of my mother's, but she turned out to be useless. What a disappointment. The dresses had to be altered twice to even look acceptable. Had I been in a better financial position I would have bought replacements.

Alan was depressed because he wasn't able to attend the wedding. His ward sister was very compassionate and asked the consultant if Alan could leave the hospital for the day. She promised the doctors that if Alan was allowed to attend, she would accompany him in the ambulance. The outing was agreed to, and the family were over the moon for him.

I left work the week before the wedding. No one could understand because I had chosen to do so, as everybody was saving hard for the future. I was given a very pleasant send off by my friends in the department. Bill had already said to me, "You don't have to work as I can keep you." However, I had something in mind. I really yearned to be a seamstress, but I kept these thoughts to myself. I didn't even share them with Bill.

The week before the wedding, I worked hard in the house helping my mother prepare for the many guests that would be camping out at our house, even though most of them would be sleeping on the floor.

On the Friday afternoon I informed my mother that I had finished all the tasks, enough was enough. I wanted to give myself a facial and a manicure. As I climbed the stairs, I glimpsed through the window two women approaching the front gate.

"I think we have a couple of Mormons" I called out to my mother. "I'll speak to them." I rushed down the stairs, opened the door and smiled. "Good afternoon."

"Can I speak to Mr & Mrs Bailey?" I called my mother to the door. The same woman spoke again. "Can I come in? I have a private matter I wish to discuss with you."

Mother invited them in. "Please sit down. How can I help you?"

"I am Mrs Lees, Colin's wife."

Colin Lees was my sister Eileen's boyfriend and they had been courting for a couple of years. We were stunned. My mother and I looked at each other dumbfounded. Mum telephoned both my father and sister and told them to return home from St Albans immediately, without telling them why. Time seemed endless waiting for them to arrive home. During that time Colin's wife related the sad saga. She and Colin had three children. One was incredibly young and still in nappies when he started his affair with Eileen.

When my sister and father arrived home and were confronted with the news, they too were shocked. My father especially so because he had asked both Colin and Eileen, months prior, if Colin was married and they had denied it. It was all horrendous and very disturbing. Colin then arrived having been summoned by Eileen. He had been warned by her that he would have to face a distraught wife and her sister plus our family. After much talking over cups of tea Mrs Lees and her sister were told that it was the day before my wedding. Colin's wife came across to me and took both my hands. "I am so sorry. I would never have come today had I known you were getting married. Don't be put off. There are so many happy marriages. They don't all end up like mine."

I burst into tears and ran upstairs to my bedroom which was festooned with wedding paraphernalia - bride's and bridesmaids' dresses, shoes everywhere, plus my suit for my honeymoon in its tissue cover. I couldn't stop crying. I curled up on my bed in utter misery. Everything had been spoilt. I stayed there for a couple of hours, all thoughts of my facial, nails and hair had vanished. Lying on my bed was an ugly swollen, red eyed person. The happy bubbly girl had disappeared. *'What will people say when I cancel the wedding? What will my parents tell them, certainly not the truth?'*

Both my parents came to talk to me, but I just told them to go away and start to cancel the wedding. They did the only thing they could do and sent for Bill. My father had only told Bill that I wanted to cancel the wedding. He omitted to relate what had happened that afternoon.

Bill was ashen when he arrived. "What have I done?" were his first words to me. The poor man. He climbed onto the bed and cuddled me which made me sob uncontrollably. Eventually he heard the full story behind the afternoon's events. He was so relieved that it was not our wedding causing my distress.

Bill spent the next couple of hours bathing my eyes, creaming my feet and cuddling me. He told me what a wonderful husband he was going to be and that he would never do anything to hurt or jeopardise our relationship. After he left, I felt a lot better. Up until Bill's arrival I felt all the joy had left me and that I would look a mess on my wedding day. My parents spent the time that Bill was with me, discussing how they would handle the problem on the wedding day. "We will just forget it happened for now. Only the immediate family will know."

'How about the bride?' I really don't think, to this day, that my parents thought it was an ordeal for me, but it most certainly was.

CHAPTER SEVEN

My wedding day, 5th June 1948, started off in quite an unusual way. My father brought a cup of tea to my bedroom. He had never done that before, as I never drank tea in bed.

I went downstairs and discovered a hive of activity with people laughing, neighbours had also arrived with greenery and flowers for the hall table. Everybody was in high spirits. My mother gave me a kiss. "You don't do a thing. It's your wedding day and you must enjoy and make the most of every minute."

I was euphoric but things felt very strange. I decided to go and see the rabbits in their hutches, at the end of the garden. I took one out and cuddled it close to me. They were magnificent creatures, Angoras with beautiful white fur. I fantasied about them coming to the wedding. I pictured myself holding them instead of trailing red roses. My thoughts made me smile.

I returned to the hubbub of the house to find that my relations from London had arrived. It was all kisses, presents and hugs topped with glasses of sherry.

The wedding was at 3.15 p.m. at St John's Church in Boxmoor. I was eighteen years of age and William Leonard Durrant was twenty-four. It started to drizzle with rain when we arrived at the church.

All our guests were seated as my father and I advanced down the aisle. I made a conscious effort to look and smile at the congregation but then I couldn't believe my eyes. Colin was sitting next to Eileen with the rest of my family. It threw me completely. The service progressed and just as we were making our vows thunder and lightning lit up the stained-glass window behind the altar. I remember thinking quite clearly, *I hope this isn't a sign.* Bill looked at me, smiled and squeezed my hand.

The rest of the ceremony went off smoothly. The rain had stopped by the time we came out of the church. Our wedding was distinctive in that we had church bells ringing even though St John's Church has no bells. My brother Sandy had recorded pealing bells from various well-known churches then rigged up speakers in the big tree by the front entrance.

I was surprised by our guard of honour. Bill and I left the church under an arch of axes formed by the John Dickinson's fire brigade. Bill was a part-time fireman. An open backed fire engine was waiting to take us to the reception. It was certainly impressive. The firemen rang the bell continuously drawing attention to members of the public who called out their good wishes.

Everything that was planned and executed on that day was done to make our wedding day the best day possible. Bill and I felt that everybody had succeeded in accomplishing that goal.

We left the reception to change into our going away clothes and then had to catch the Greenline to London. We had booked a taxi to take us home and then on to Bury Road bus station.

We cut it fine for our train to Margate and just managed to board, as it was pulling out of the station. There was a couple already sitting in the carriage. He was in a sailor's uniform. They told us that they had just got married and were on their honeymoon. We did not confess to them that we were in the same boat.

We had almost arrived at Margate when the train was shunted into a siding. We were there for two hours without any explanation. As it was the last train to Margate, we concluded that it was shunted into a siding for the night. Somebody eventually walked along the line and informed the station. The train started to move but as soon as it got a full head of steam up, we were in Margate.

We caught a cab to Cliftonville, our honeymoon destination, only to find that the guest house was locked up. It was 1.30 a.m. Bill banged the door several times and we wondered what we would do if no one answered. Finally, the owner unlocked the door. We could hear the person on the other side struggling to undo the bolts. The door was opened eventually, and we discovered the poor woman only had one arm. We were shown our room which was up in the attic and we both fell into bed exhausted. No honeymoon that night, just a welcome bed.

We arrived in the dining room the next morning and the entire room of guests gave us knowing smiles. We were both mortified and shrunk into our seats as quickly as possible. We ate little breakfast and made a quick retreat.

The sun was shining as we walked the length of the esplanade, feeling better by the second. All the recent turmoil faded away. Bill stopped to light his pipe then uttered, "Are you feeling better Mrs Durrant?"

I certainly was. We were only away for four days as that was the only leave permissible, other than the annual factory closure of two weeks. It was a different pair of honeymooners that returned to Hemel Hempstead to start their life.

We were so fortunate to secure two rooms above the ironmonger's shop in Apsley village. Although the house was built behind the shop it was big, but it was without electricity. Our two rooms were on different floors. The living room was on the first floor. It had a big black, coal burning range which I soon got used to cooking on. A solitary gas ring stood by its side on the floor, just in case you didn't or couldn't light the range. The bedroom was in the eaves. It was gigantic and we both loved the space. A massive bed stood alongside the wall. We almost had to take a run and jump to get on it. Beside the bed stood an antique wash hand stand complete with china bowl and jug. We both loved our accommodation.

Mr and Mrs Court, the owners, were deeply religious and adhered to the teachings of the bible. We grew very fond of them and respected their beliefs. After we were interviewed by them and accepted as future tenants, we walked around the back of the building to see if there was a place to keep our bicycles. I noticed a factory built immediately behind the row of shops and took note of what they manufactured. I still longed to be a seamstress. Even then I made no mention of this to Bill or my family.

The first Monday that Bill returned to work I walked around the back of the shops to the factory and entered through the swing doors. The hall was empty with not a soul in sight. I could hear a whirling sound and the murmur of voices. After standing there for a minute or two I noticed a bell set into the wall with 'Attention' above it. My heart was racing, and my mouth completely dry. I pushed the bell. It was so loud, it sounded like a fire alarm. Within a minute a slender gentleman aged about fifty came towards me smiling.

"Hello and what can I do for you?"

He introduced himself as Mr Finney, the office manager. At great speed I told him my name and in the same breath asked him if there were any vacancies.

"What experience have you got?"

"I haven't any. I am hoping you can teach me."

"Well, you have taken me by surprise. Please sit down and wait whilst I go and talk to Mr Green who is the chairman and owner of the business."

I learned later from Mr Finney, who became not only a mentor but a dear friend what had transpired.

Mr Green had replied, "Well this is a first. Is she a cheeky girl?"

"No. I would say more ambitious. She is only a kid, but she has a wedding ring on. Let's give her a try."

This was the beginning of my life in the rag trade. When Bill came home from work, I was eager to announce that his new wife had found herself a job. We both couldn't stop smiling. We visited both sets of parents to share our good news. All the family were delighted that I would be working again. I think I was only without a job for two weeks.

I had kept my ambition to work in the rag trade to myself. I had even consciously planned on us having children and had concluded that I would be able to make all their clothes, as well as mine. It did not occur to me that I wouldn't get a job without any experience. That was my immaturity.

I started the following Monday. When I was introduced to my fellow workers all the machines were switched off as a sea of faces gazed at me. They were informed that I was going to be trained. There were lots of murmurs and raised eyebrows. The machining quickly resumed as the girls had targets to meet.

My training started the moment my bottom hit the seat of the stool in front of the empty sewing machine. There were no preliminaries, it was straight in at the deep end. The first coats that machinists were taught to make were the regular school coats of that time, known as Melton coats. The cloth was rather like the bouclé of today. The pieces of fabric came to the machinist after being cut by the cutters. Each layer presented to us was a complete coat ready to assemble, along with its lining. My skills improved and progressed, and I was soon able to join in with the other girls and their friendly banter. Many of the seamstresses were wonderful women from the East End with delightful humour and truly kind hearts. I learned so much from them and it wasn't all about sewing.

Towards the end of my first year, I was able to make women's suits with complicated velvet insets in both the collar and pockets. The skills I was taught have stayed with me to this day. After just one year with these lovely ladies, I became pregnant. I was so excited and told everybody my news, which turned out to be far too soon. All the other machinists were thrilled for me. However, the following month my bosses sent for me, and I was informed that I would have to leave. The company were anxious for my safety and were regretful but terminating my employment. In 1949 there was no such thing as employment protection.

I left with a joyful send off and an arm full of baby clothes. Mr Green and Mr Finney gave me money towards a pram.

It was only a short time afterwards that my mother heard that a house, quite near to them, was going to be vacated. Somebody that was already subletting. We were informed that we could move in the following month.

I became remarkably close to Mrs Court. Bill and I had been told that she had terminal cancer. I was very distressed on hearing this. Apparently, the Courts knew this when we moved in but were determined not to overshadow the newlyweds. As soon as Mrs Court became unable to leave her bed, I would take her washing bowl to her room and wash her then braid her beautiful hair before I went to work. It became a ritual. Mr and Mrs Court always called me young Mrs Durrant. If they ever needed me for anything they would the call out, "Young Mrs Durrant can you come down and help please."

It was an incredibly sad day for me when she died. Both Bill and I felt genuinely concerned at leaving Mr Court on his own. He told us it was his intension to sell the shop as soon as possible, and this he did.

We moved into the house in Sunrise Crescent the next month as planned. It was very poorly furnished, but we quite quickly stamped our mark on it. Money was short as I no longer earned. However, we were fortunate that I got asked by several ladies to do their hair. It proved to be a great help financially. The fact that we were subletting didn't seem to bother either of us. I went to the agents every month and handed over the rent book to be stamped. We took that as a sign that they did not mind the situation as long as we paid the rent.

My pregnancy seemed to go on forever. I so desperately wanted this baby that each day seemed like a week. However, eventually the inevitable happened on 26th May 1950 at 4.20 p.m. My beautiful baby was delivered by an American doctor. Just he and I were in the ward, and he talked to me constantly whilst we awaited her arrival. He told me that he had always wanted to be a doctor but couldn't afford the tuition fees. He became a successful businessman, made a fortune then retired so he could study to be a doctor. His only remaining qualification was obstetrics.

On my daughter's delivery he asked, "What are you going to call your child?"

"Jennifer Susan."

"Why don't you call her Rose Marie as she looks like a little rosebud?"

Melanie Jayne was our final decision. I liked being told our daughter looked like a rosebud. My mother's description of me at birth was somewhat of a contrast. "You looked like a cheap, scrawny rabbit, just like the ones I used to see hanging up in the butcher's shop." Every time she said the same thing and she always put the emphasis on the word cheap.

Melanie was given a wonderful welcome on both sides of the family. She was the Durrant's first grandchild and the second grandchild on my side of the family. I couldn't wait to show her off.

My first walk out with my little treasure resulted in me leaving her outside the grocer's shop. I purchased a few items, then left the shop without thinking. It was only when I got home and went to push the side gate open that I realised I had left my precious cargo outside the shop. I was mortified and ran like the wind with tears streaming down my face, fearing the worse. I continually said sorry to her all the way home.

That evening Bill hurried home from work to see his precious new baby. I cried again as I related what had happened to her. Over the years I have heard of new mothers doing the same thing.

Both grandmothers vied for her attention. I found going out with my lovely mother-in-law challenging. What should have been a lovely walk to the local shops was an awfully slow process because everyone had to see the new baby. Should some acquaintance miss us, nanny would steer the pram in their direction. I got so cheesed off with it that I used to take a book and sit on a bench on the moor and read. My mum-in-law was delighted with that arrangement and so was I.

Life was good for us with our little daughter who was growing so fast. After several years had passed, we discussed that it was perhaps time to give her a brother or sister.

We had one great concern that continually lived with us all. Alan was still in hospital and his T.B. was spreading in his body. Whilst he was at Mount Vernon Hospital, we were able to take Melanie with us on visits. We found a good vantage point where we were able to hold her up for her uncle to see her through the window. His face used to light up, especially when she became old enough to wave to him. Sadly, he spent so many years in one hospital or another.

I eventually became pregnant again, but it was a difficult time for me. I had experienced such a good pregnancy previously. It came as a shock to find that I wasn't able to walk far without pain or lift my little daughter up in my arms for a cuddle. The nurses at the clinic told me constantly that all was well. I assumed that they knew what they were doing but it became apparent that this was not the case.

At eight months I was cutting and setting the hair of one of my midwives. Whilst I was attending to her that morning, I remarked, "I think I'm in labour."

She palpated my belly. "You could be in premature labour. I'll inform the midwife on duty." I continued with her hair.

By 9 o'clock that night I was in serious labour. Bill called for a midwife who realised as soon as she examined me that things were far from normal. Unbeknownst to me, she could not hear the baby's heartbeat. After a while, there was thumping on the front door from another midwife.

"You're needed elsewhere in Cotterells."

"I am not leaving my patient. You'll have to find someone else." The delivery was catastrophic. The midwife realised the baby was not responding. "I can't do any more to help you. I need to call a doctor."

At this point she spoke to Bill and told him the baby was not alive. "The doctor will want Mrs Durrant to go to hospital. Whatever you do, don't allow this to happen. Your wife won't survive being moved downstairs, let alone the journey to Watford Hospital."

A traumatic time followed, but our little daughter was growing fast, and we centred our life around her. Melanie attended Lawn Lane Nursery and loved her nursery nurse Mrs Rose. My visits to the nursery reaffirmed that I still wanted another baby. When we announced our decision to the immediate family, they were aghast. They were concerned and fearful that I may have to endure another horrendous experience.

Once again, I became pregnant and was in good health throughout the nine months.

At 11.40 p.m. on 26th October 1954 Andrea was born, weighing in at 8lbs15oz. There was tremendous joy as the delivery had gone well. We had already discussed names prior to her birth. We both felt that our family was now complete. Our two little daughters were the pride and joy of the family.

As soon as our new arrival had got into a routine, I was able to resume some hairdressing. I scheduled my appointments around the baby's needs and that of the family. It helped us financially to have the little luxuries of life, like the purchase of a car. It wasn't too long before Bill found a car of his choice. This car was our very own. The previous vehicle had been purchased and shared with Bill's father.

My poor mother-in-law's health deteriorated rapidly. She eventually became wheelchair bound with chronic rheumatoid arthritis. My last walk out with her was a trip to Churchill's swimming pool when Andrea was in her pram.

Alice became completely dependent upon our help as Bill was an only child. My father-in-law changed his job so he could work close by, allowing him to pop home frequently during the day. I took care of the washing and ironing. Unlike now, there was no help from the local authority and certainly no financial assistance. It was a constant pressure caring for them and continued for sixteen years. It was only made possible by my lovely mother-in-law's patience and perseverance. She was in constant severe pain and endured it all without complaint. When she saw that my face showed concern she would always say, "Don't worry about me. I will be all right. I look worse than I am." She would then give me such a big smile that I would have to turn away so that she didn't see my tears. My father-in-law also did all he could not to ask us for extra help at weekends or when the children were off school.

One day I asked Bill if he would teach me to drive. My first lesson started well. I followed Bill's instructions and we progressed to the end of the road. I stopped at the junction to take a left turn but found the task of putting out the indicator and releasing the clutch all a bit too much. I kangarooed into the next turning and Bill yelled at me. "Any bloody fool can take one foot off the peddle and press down on the other." I was so upset that I left the car crying and walked back home. That was the first and last lesson from Bill.

During the next few weeks, I took the car off the drive myself and kept driving around the block. My parents lived on the corner of our road, and my father used to stand outside his house shouting encouragement and waving a tea towel as a flag. This was illegal but I took the risk as the roads were deserted in the late 1950's. After several weeks of jaunts around the block I booked lessons from a driving school. On my first lesson the instructor said, "Don't worry, you cannot do anything wrong, you are quite safe, as the car has dual controls." I drove away and almost immediately the instructor stopped the car. "You can already drive, why didn't you tell me?"

I ended up having the same number of lessons as anyone else.

Bill used to quiz me when I returned as to where we had been. He concluded that I was always going on long runs because the driving school wanted to get their money's worth. Thank goodness I passed my test and life for the family was made so much easier.

CHAPTER EIGHT

I had spotted for weeks, notices in shop windows and other odd places inviting women who would like to meet other likeminded women to a meeting. This intrigued me and every time that I shopped and read the posters it made me more determined to go and see what it was all about. I took note of the date.

On the evening of the meeting, I walked to Warners End Hall which was situated behind the shops. I was amazed at how many women were making their way in the same direction. We were complete strangers but many of us started chatting. We all had the same aim, to find out what this meeting was about. To our amazement, the hall was packed, and we sat wherever there was a space. I managed to get a seat at the end of a row which pleased me. Being tall it meant I didn't block anyone else's view of the stage and I could also make a quick getaway should I wish to.

The stage was a temporary rostrum set with four chairs and a table with glasses of water on. A woman walked onto the platform followed by three others. Everyone clapped, not knowing why, just polite acceptance. The first woman stood up and thanked the audience for their attendance and interest. The meeting then got underway. There was complete silence, and everyone paid close attention.

"I represent the Townswomen's Guild. How many ladies here have heard of us?" I couldn't see any hands go up. "We are a body like the W.I. except we are located in towns. We know many of you are finding it difficult to settle down into your new homes and feel isolated from your friends and families."

Murmurs of agreement came from many parts of the hall. During the next hour or so the speaker extolled the features and aims that the guild aspired to. Its creed being, "To encourage the education of women to enable them as citizens to make their best contribution towards the Common Good; and to serve as a common meeting ground for women irrespective of creed and party, for their wider education including social activities."

We were enthralled to hear about Townswomen's Guild branches that had been set up in other new towns. We were informed that we could have drama groups, arts and crafts and so on. In fact, we could decide what activities were best suited for our forthcoming members. The speaker declared that it was now time to make some decisions. "Would the audience like to form their own branch?"

There was resounding chorus of, "Yes."

"If this is the case, you now have to form a committee. In the first instance you must elect the officers, starting with the Chairman, Treasurer, Secretary and Membership Secretary."
Silence reigned. Just muffled murmurs rumbled around.

"Remember you will all be new and have to learn along the way. We will give you support for the first few months."

The deathly hush in the hall was broken by the speaker's next announcement. "We will vote for your first chairman. She will take on the role which I am playing now." The sound of voices filled the hall, but no one came forward. "Don't worry, this always happens at the inauguration. Someone here has the ability. Amongst all you interested ladies there will be someone interested in the role otherwise there would not have been such a good attendance."

Her gaze swept the audience. "The lady sitting to the back, at the end of the row, will you please stand up."

We all looked at each other. The ladies surrounding me called out, "She means you."

I was horrified and shook my head. The speaker then addressed the two ladies sitting beside me and the two sitting behind. "Do you think she could do the job?"

"Yes," echoed all around me from complete strangers. They knew nothing about my capabilities.

"You see, they don't know you, yet they have observed how you have asked questions this evening and fully support your nomination. We now have our first officer, the Chairman."

I sat down in astonishment. I recognised the skills of the speaker as she unearthed the rest of the committee.

As newly appointed officers we were told to remain in our seats until the meeting was adjourned but not before a date was set for the next meeting. We were relieved to know that we had support from the hierarchy for the first two meetings or longer if they felt we needed it.

Our next meeting was an informal one, for just the committee. It was held in a small room in Warners End Hall. Limited training was given to us. I thought I wasn't up to the job but everybody else was floundering too. We felt we had to support each other.

I couldn't sleep the night before our first meeting. Our supportive, experienced colleagues stayed in the wings out of site. I was petrified as I walked on to the stage and the auditorium fell silent.

"Good evening, ladies."

I received a standing ovation. I was overwhelmed that the membership showed their support and appreciated what an ordeal it was for this novice. The meeting progressed well with the various officers playing their part.

The skills of committee procedure had to be learned over time. We were all young and needed a challenge and a distraction from the everyday life of babies and household chores. The Townswomen's Guild creed was certainly imparted to each one of us. Our membership grew to 103 which was a remarkable achievement and the talent that we discovered over the years was a revelation. We had expert crafts women and a wonderful drama group capable of putting on amazing productions. It wasn't too long before we realised that we needed to appoint a social secretary. Outings were organised to theatres, museums, stately homes and the coast. The branch grew from strength to strength. Friendships blossomed and still remain to this day.

Alan was still very ill; a decision was made to transfer him to Stanmore Orthopaedic hospital. He underwent an operation to remove some bone from his leg which was used in the affected bone in his spine. He spent a year suspended above his bed in a plaster case only able to look at a small square of the ceiling. It was a terrible time for him and for those of us who loved him. He was so tolerant in such dire circumstances.

I continued with my hairdressing, fitting my appointments around our busy schedule. Bill helped in any way he could, being on shift work helped us manage our routine. Considering the strain, we were living under, our lives remained as calm as they had always been. It didn't matter which side of the family needed our support. If one of us could be there we would. Our loving relationship kept us going. However, there were times when we sat and cried about the things we couldn't manage, that were out of our control.

Our children were told that when your family are ill you must do your best to help them. Sometimes we had to alter our plans when we had organised to take them out. We were always honest with the children and told them the reason why.

After a year at Stanmore, Alan, was transferred back to Harefield Hospital. He was admitted to a two bedded room. If the weather permitted, the staff used to push his bed outside in the fresh air. No one was given any information about his length of stay. In hindsight, I realise that it was a good thing. I'm not sure Alan or my parents could have handled it, had they known.

After several visits we started to talk to the young man sharing the room. We had noticed that he didn't have any visitors. Furtive whispers from Alan told us that he had no family at all and had been admitted from Leavesden Hospital. We took Francis under our wing and before long Francis became an additional member of the Bailey family.

Alan and Francis were side by side in that little room for six years. Today this seems an unacceptable length of time for tuberculosis. Both were consumed by this dreadful disease and endured horrendous treatments which wouldn't occur today.

Alan realised that Francis only looked briefly at books and magazines. It dawned on him that Francis couldn't read. Francis never went to school and was placed in care until he was fourteen. The local authority didn't know or care that he had special needs. At fourteen he was placed in Leavesden Mental Hospital and just left there. Contracting TB was his good fortune, in a way, as he needed to be hospitalised.

Alan taught him to read and write and educated him about life, some of which he could have done without knowing. My little brother was particularly good looking and had an eye for the ladies.

Over the years Francis was accepted by my children as an extra uncle. When the time came for his discharge, my father learned that he was to return to Leavesden hospital. We were horrified and anxious for him because his life was so different now.

A meeting was arranged with staff from both Harefield and Leavesden hospitals. My father spoke on behalf of Francis. He explained that Francis had learned to read and write and that with backing he could look after himself. Dad went on to propose that our family would support Francis.

Leavesden hospital released Francis and Harefield hospital turned up trumps. They found him a job as an orderly. All the years in hospital had made him aware of what was required of an orderly. He was entitled to live in staff accommodation which was in converted Nissen huts in the hospital grounds. Everyone knew Francis, both patients and staff. It proved to be a perfect solution. Bill and I took him on as a member of our own family.

Alan was also discharged and quickly found himself a job with Addressograph Multigraph in Hemel Hempstead. He had gone into hospital a boy and had come out a man. He found living with my parents difficult and they found it hard to come to terms with him being a mature adult. I know he had flings with the nurses when he was in rehab and Francis was posted as the lookout.

"Good thing the laundry room couldn't talk." Francis once said.

Alan being at home released me from the extra burden of supporting my parents. He was a caring, loving uncle to my little daughters. He used to play with them and spoil them. He had been in hospital for ten years. His final discharge was a big relief to all of us, but it also gave us back much time and freedom.

CHAPTER NINE

Life was still so terribly busy, and I now wonder how I managed to fit everything in. My evenings were taken up with hairdressing, but my days were committed to anything I could do for the family.

Alice, my mother-in-law, was deteriorating by the day. Her rheumatoid arthritis was devouring her body rapidly. Her face was permanently etched with pain. Her limbs were now so deformed that she couldn't stand up even with help. My in-law's home overlooked the moor and Alice spent her days looking out of the front window of the cottage. Before Andrea started school, I always took her with me to Boxmoor and she used to sit by her grandmother looking at the wildlife on the moor. They shared a pair of binoculars and Nanny used to point out the nesting birds in the trees. My mum-in-law's powers of observation were amazing. Horse chestnut trees lined the moor and any changes in their leaves or unusual movement of branches she noted and memorised. Even the cows that grazed were noted for their shapes, spots, anything that distinguished them from each other.

I remember when it became a legal requirement for all new cars to be fitted with seat belts. My lovely mother-in-law counted all the vehicles passing her cottage and noted how many drivers were using the new belts. That was how she managed the constraints in her life.

Often my father-in-law would find an envelope on the doorstep. It would be addressed to 'The lady who sits in the window.' Sometimes it was a child's drawing, or an Easter or Christmas card. On other occasions a bunch of flowers would be left without any message. I feel close to tears as I remember an incredibly special lady.

Bill announced one day, "I have something special to talk to you about when you have a spare moment."

I laughed. "Well, it had better be now because I would never recognise a spare moment if I had one."

Bill had been contemplating and had come to a big decision. He

98

had altered his mind about adding to our family. To say I was surprised is an understatement.

"Why have you changed your mind?" He replied that he realised he would soon be forty and that this milestone would make him an old dad. It was quite a shock because I had decided to further my education. However, I thought I could put that on hold and accepted his change of heart.

Not long before Bill died, he confessed his real reason for wanting another baby and it was nothing to do with his age. It was because I kept talking about wanting to go to college. He didn't think it would be good for the family. Wow, what a revelation that was!

I became pregnant in 1960 but during my pregnancy I suddenly became extremely ill. I had double pneumonia and spent about six weeks in bed. This coincided with Andrea starting school. My anxious little five-year-old girl was taken to school by Nona, our kind next door neighbour.

I eventually recovered. Routine visits were made to the anti-natal clinic, and I steadily began to look the size of an elephant. I continued my hairdressing, except every week I had to stand further back from my customers. I was overwhelmed by the gifts of baby clothes I received. One dear lady arrived with her husband who carried a large parcel to the house. When I unwrapped it, the contents took my breath away. It was a complete layette for the baby. It had been made from a pattern in the Reveille magazine. It was a copy of the outfit Grace Kelly had had made for her new baby. Anything to do with royalty was certainly fit for the new member of the Durrant clan.

I was overwhelmed by the kindness of so many ladies who had become not just customers but my friends.

CHAPTER TEN

All too soon the baby's birth date arrived. Everything was prepared and ready, except the baby. My bump got bigger and heavier by the day. I was told at my ante natal appointments that all was well, and my date must be wrong. I got to three weeks overdue and then in my frantic fear I informed the clinic that I had been extremely ill at the start of my pregnancy, therefore believed my date to be more accurate than theirs. I was relieved to be told that I was to be admitted to hospital the following day.

The next day was a Saturday and instead of concentrating on my impending delivery I told Bill that we had to buy the girls new winter shoes. It didn't occur to me that their father was well able to buy them shoes whilst I was in hospital. We went, as we always did, to White's shoe shop in the old high street.

The tantrums started in earnest. Andrea screamed out, "I don't want new shoes." She wouldn't sit on the seat to be measured. The assistant tried to calm her down. "Everyone likes to have new shoes."

"I don't."

What a performance we had for the next half an hour. "I want Mummy to put them on." My large tummy prevented any assistance. Bill held her in a vice like grip with the little darling curling her toes to prevent them being fitted. This resulted in the baby inside me doing acrobatics in protest. Melanie had been watching this display and walked up to her little sister.

"Andrea why can't you be a good little girl and behave for Mummy? You are going to be a big sister soon when Mummy has the baby."

It worked and the shoes were put on to Andrea's feet by Melanie without another word. It proved to be the last paddy that Andrea ever displayed. My ten-year-old daughter had demonstrated to her little sister the correct way to behave. We left the shop all smiles.

The journey to the hospital was just five minutes away. When I kissed the girls goodbye Melanie asked, "Mummy does this visit mean that you won't come home until you have the baby?" I quickly realised how anxious she was for me.

On that Saturday after various tests, I was pushed into a delivery room to wait. I was left there all of Sunday and was in a very anxious frame of mind. My unfortunate experience of the past haunted me. By early Monday morning I was feeling at death's door, and I couldn't reach the bell to ring for attention. It had been tied to a trolley and pushed away. I called out so many times, but nobody came. I realised the baby wasn't going to wait any longer and I ended up delivering my baby without help. I looked down to my feet. Lying there was a huge baby boy who weighed 9lbs 2 oz.

A nurse's face appeared at the porthole window in the door. "Oh my god!" Everybody rushed in.

Nigel was so jaundiced. All his skin was wrinkled like an old person. He had to be isolated for the rest of his stay. He would have died had he been left inside me for another couple of days.

An informal enquiry was held and concluded that I was just unfortunate that the night staff had gone off duty and the day staff were being given their instructions.

Andrea was delighted with the new addition and Melanie was second in command. Within a couple of weeks, I could have gone away, and Melanie would have been capable of caring for her little brother. What a delightfully happy household.

Both sets of grandparents were enamoured with Nigel. It gave my mum-in-law such pleasure to have this new baby. It helped take her mind off her increasing debility. My goodness this new arrival to our family brought with him so much love. We were truly blessed.

My father gave up every spare moment to come and watch him being fed and bathed and he would rock the pram if the baby cried. He and Nigel formed a close bond. At the age of three Dad used to take Nigel to work at the steel works where he was the gatekeeper. Fortunately, the owner Mr Christopher was a good friend of Dad's and Nigel became well known by everyone at the factory. My father gave him a wage packet every Friday when all the workers collected their wages. He even used to 'clock in' with Dad.

Dad used to do another task for Nigel. It was a daily occurrence. He was continually replacing the tyres on his Dinky cars.

In later years I asked Nigel if he remembered going to work with his grandfather or the time, he spent playing with him but unfortunately, he didn't.

I eventually resumed my hairdressing and was still helping my father-in-law with Mum. It was a busy life. I coped but didn't know any different. I still had the enjoyment of the Townswomen's Guild and all the activities that came with it. When you have a new addition to the family you think you won't be able to do this or that, but you do. Life always has a way of adjusting itself and priorities change. If I hadn't been surrounded by a loving and caring family, I wouldn't have managed. My ability to drive was a great asset and made a vast difference, especially getting to Boxmoor, my in-law's home, and getting back home in time for the girls after school. I was always tired but blessed by my support.

One of my hairdressing clients owned a caravan in East Runton on the north Norfolk coast. Although she didn't let it out to non-family, we were fortunate that she agreed to let it to us. We had a wonderful time, and the children loved the beach. Fortuitously, the site was on the cliff top above the beach. It was safe enough to allow the girls to run to the beach ahead of us. Our friends had advised us to book a beach hut in the January. It was such a joy and worth every penny of the rental fee. It was a place of security and warmth if the weather was colder. The girls being shy at changing on the beach could change in the hut and hang their costumes up to dry. Chairs, windbreaks buckets and spades were stored in there too. We purchased a Calor Gaz camping stove and soon became very efficient at heating soups and making beans on toast.

Our first year of renting a static caravan proved so successful that on our return we booked for the next year. Sometimes when you repeat something you enjoyed, it doesn't always work out. However, in this case it did. The following year the same enjoyment was shared by us all. Nigel was growing up fast and able to walk, nappies a thing of the past. Bill used to take the girls rock pooling which they loved. They would spend hours searching in nooks and crannies and very often disappeared from my view. Eventually Nigel wanted to join them. He had many a grazed knee but soon realised that you had to tread carefully. When they all returned, I was like a mother hen. I was the dryer of wet bodies and had the horrible job of getting sand off their feet before they replaced their shoes. I enjoyed every moment. Whilst the family were busily occupied, I read books or knitted. My favourite occupation was to people watch. I am the same today. It doesn't matter where I am, a bus or train station, an airport, a seaside promenade, I always watch. I like observing people and their interactions, picking up on idiosyncrasies to try to guess their stories. I often look at couples and think they don't seem to belong to each other. I am probably wrong on all counts. At least it is harmless pleasure.

My brother Bob and his wife Jean joined us for a couple of days during one of our stays in Norfolk. They observed what a relaxed family we were and said they could see how much we loved East Runton. Shortly after our return from that holiday, I received a telephone call from Bob. He informed me that the builders were moving off site after completing the runway at the new Stanstead Airport. The site manager wanted to sell his caravan. My brother described the caravan as very solid with an individual bedroom behind its kitchen. There was a fire for heating and its chimney passed through a water tank to supply hot water. It was a six berth. Its only drawback, as far as Bob could see, was the fact, that it was bright yellow. The gentleman wanted one hundred pounds for it. That was the problem for us as we didn't have that sort of money spare. £100 in 1965 was a fair bit of money. We resigned ourselves to the fact that it would have been wonderful but wasn't to be.

My Mother came for a cuppa the very next morning and pressed one hundred pounds in my hand. "Buy your caravan and I don't want the money back. However, there is one condition. You mustn't tell anybody where the money came from. If your father thought I could save that amount from my housekeeping he would be horrified." That gift of a caravan set the pattern of our lives for the next twenty years or so.

It was with great anticipation that a visit to Stanstead Airport was arranged. We gave no thought about a site plot being available. We adored the caravan and handed over the cash. Our little family was over the moon. The site manager arranged to have the caravan towed from the runway onto a piece of adjacent land which was undeveloped. Stanstead Airport was still in construction and not open to the public. Now the reality set in. What to do first? We had to organise it being towed to Norfolk. We also had to acquire a site. It was all in the laps of the gods. We were filled with optimism.

The following Saturday we were up at the crack of dawn to leave for Norfolk. My parents looked after the children. It was dark, raining hard and very cold. It made us question whether we were doing the right thing.

We stopped for breakfast in the first cafe that we found open and arrived in East Runton around eight o'clock. We knew where the Abbs brothers lived who were the caravan site owners. Fortunately, we had spoken to them many times on our holidays. We were shocked to hear their answer to our enquiry. "We have a list of people waiting for a vacant plot on our site."

We were crestfallen and related the saga of how the caravan purchase came about. The Abbs were so contrite that they couldn't help us. "They are in such a position." One brother said to the other. "Can't we come up with something?"

Never once did those lovely gentlemen say, "You shouldn't have gone ahead with its purchase." They offered us a cup of tea then both went into their kitchen, shutting the door behind them. We could only hear murmurs. In due course Mr Abbs the younger, came out of the kitchen carrying a tray of tea.

"We cannot accommodate your caravan right now but get it down here and we will store it on the site somewhere until we have a vacancy. The trouble is, it is such a large caravan to accommodate. The larger plots rarely become available. Did you realise that the length prohibits it being towed? This means you must use a transporter."

We went home genuinely concerned but relieved that we were able to store the caravan should a site not be available. Within a week a transporter had been arranged and the caravan was delivered to the site without any hiccups.

The following Easter when the site opened, we received a telephone call from one of the Abbs brothers to say they had re-arranged some vans and made a space for us at the back of the site. We were thrilled, when we made our first visit, to find we were situated in the last row, right on the site's boundary. We had lovely grass areas at the sides, and no one had a reason to pass our caravan. How fortunate we were. It was the start of so many years of wonderful memories for us and the children. Whenever possible we would make our way to Norfolk.

After the euphoria of the acquisition and the caravan being sited, came the issues that we hadn't considered in the excitement of the purchase. Bill had made it clear to me that he didn't want to take any financial responsibility for the caravan. If I wanted it, I would have to organise the business side of things with respect to funding, budgeting, maintenance etc. He took sole responsibility for our family finances and made a first-class job. We never had debts of any sort due to his diligence. This was fine by me. I had worked out that my hairdressing would fund it. We decided that the caravan would not be let. It was for us and the extended family only. We kept to those rules for years.

I realised that if we were to get the full use of the summer months, I would have to re-adjust my hairdressing schedule. I discussed it with my clientele and with their support I was able to re-arrange all appointments that came within the half term holidays. I offered all my ladies the chance to go elsewhere but their loyalty was such that they stuck with me.

Our three children spent all the school holidays with me in Norfolk. Bill used to take us down and return some weekends. He was still doing the Sunday paper run and didn't want to lose that source of income. I too managed on my usual housekeeping. We were fortunate in so many ways. My mum-in-law was cared for by my father-in-law with Bill going to check every day after work. My parents were retired and when they wanted to, they would come down to see us in Norfolk for a couple of days.

There were times when the extended family would visit us in Norfolk. We had exhilarating hours on the beach and often picnicked outside the 'van on the grass.

My brother Bob visited us on several occasions. It was lovely to think that he knew just how much the caravan meant to us, as it was all down to him. On one occasion he and Jean booked into a B&B in the village. Bob and Jean were in their bedroom at the cottage and had settled down for the night when their bedroom door opened, and the owners walked through to access their bedroom in the boxroom. "Goodnight to you both. I hope you sleep well."

How we all laughed. That story has been told so many times. It was the time of simplicity and honesty. These days this wouldn't be accepted or tolerated.

CHAPTER ELEVEN

We always returned home feeling that our time in Norfolk had recharged our batteries. This went for the children too, but they were always eager to see their grandparents and their friends. We had very lovely neighbours. The Batchelors lived next door. Nona and Peter had four children, three boys and a girl. Living next to them were the Nocks. Gert and Harry had two girls. Marilyn and Pauline. Andrew, from next door, was Andrea's special buddy. Andrew, Andrea and Marilyn were an enterprising group of children. Their friendships have endured over the years. They are now in their sixties. I remain a courtesy auntie. Both sets of their parents have passed away but my connection to their children is steadfast. I value their caring, treasures from times past.

It was time to register Nigel for school. Both Bill and I were incredibly happy with the way things had gone for Andrea and we considered Mr Burgess a great Headmaster and highly rated the rest of the staff, so Nigel was registered at Martindale J.M.I. School.

Sometimes I walked Nigel to meet Andrea from school and on one of these occasions the headmaster, Mr Burgess, asked me if I could spare a minute for him, in his office. He asked if I could help him out by doing a few days playground duty. Of course, I said yes and planned my commitments for the next two weeks around the times he requested. After the two weeks he asked me to stay on as a permanent member of the kitchen staff. It would mean that I would be able to take the school holidays off with the children. It was an offer that I felt I could not refuse. I did lose a couple of my customers who came for their hair appointments during the mornings, but the evening ones remained loyal. The women that left understood what having school holidays off would mean to me. Once again, having the school holidays free enabled the Norfolk holidays to continue.

Owning our own caravan made such a difference. The onerous big pack up became a thing of the past. Linen, towels, costumes and all the essentials to make the stay enjoyable were only taken at the start of the season. We were now experienced caravaners.

My life was structured and more secure. Life had new possibilities enriched by a different kind of freedom. My salary was guaranteed although halved during school holidays.

Bill was a wonderful support. He never once questioned us wanting to spend all our free time by the sea. In those days we only had the one car. Bill drove us to and fro for many years, until the children were grown up.

We never knew from day to day what the schedule would be. Sometimes we walked, very often to the nearest town, which was Cromer. Going to Cromer meant a walk to the end of the pier and whilst there a look at the lifeboat station. I always found the crew willing to talk to little children and show them around explaining the boat's function and how important it was to the community. On other occasions we walked in the opposite direction towards West Runton which wasn't so popular. It didn't have a pier and the walk was longer. Andrea was always envious of her baby brother being in the pushchair. Sometimes on the way back I would let her stand on the back axle under the handle. As she grew, her weight made it hard for me to push so that little perk had to be abandoned. Other days, the best for me, we went straight down to the beach. I'd open the beach hut, and the children would hunt for their costumes then gather up their belongings for whatever they had in mind. Although rock pools remained a favourite pastime, they were never the same without their daddy. When lunchtime came, we would have one of our 'beach hut meals.' When Bill was with us, I was able to walk to the local chippy. That was always the most popular choice and top of the favourites list.

Those times spent in north Norfolk still live in our minds and hearts as the happiest of days.

CHAPTER TWELVE

On my first day at work in the school kitchen I felt like a child attending school for the first time. Our day started at eight thirty. I was fortunate to know the Head Cook, Bessie Kerwood. The rest of the staff were unaware that Bessie was one of my hairdressing clients. Bessie and I both decided that the connection remain private to enable the job interview to be without prejudice. Formalities had to be adhered to although I had already been offered the job by Mr Burgess.

I was given my uniform which included a little hat, rather like those worn by nurses. Lily Webb and Pat Humphries were assistants like me. I knew both ladies by sight. I was soon into the routine tasks required of me. As the new girl I got the grotty jobs. What I had not expected was the bonus of having a very kind-hearted boss. Bessie was not only efficient, but she also organised and delegated with a marvellous sense of humour, which uplifted our spirits. Throughout my life I have worked with countless people in many places, but the Martindale School canteen colleagues proved to be the best friends one could ever encounter. From the moment we arrived until the close of the day there was laughter and sometimes shared sadness, but we were all in it together. Mr Burgess, the headmaster once said, "I love to walk through the kitchen because it always uplifts me." That was a great compliment to a group of dinner ladies.

There was a standing joke between us. I once told my colleagues that if I concentrated hard enough, I could always make anybody standing with their back to me, turn around. It became a daily request from one or the other.

The dining room was often used as a classroom. Lessons concluded when the canteen hatches were wound up in readiness for serving lunch. It was a sign to any class that lunch was ready. There was always a teacher on dinnertime duty or sometimes the headmaster would supervise the children. The four of us used to stand in a line at the servery and then the smiles from us would start. We were always laughing with the children. One of my colleagues would suddenly call to me, "Now!" That was my cue and meant that the member of staff on duty had their back to the servery. I used to stare at their back and could always make them turn round. It must have been a coincidence, but it always worked. Mr Burgess was my favourite target. He was always on the move and constantly turning around. I always managed to time it perfectly. On one occasion he turned around and looked at me. "It is very strange, but I always know when Mrs Durrant's eyes are on my back. I can feel them."

I never found out, but I suspected that someone had told him about my magic powers, knowing that he had a good sense of humour. He was playing us at our own game. Bessie herself had a great sense of fun and could have turned the tables. If so, she kept her little secret.

Nigel had settled down in the reception class. His teacher was called Mrs Morgan. I greatly respected her. Her gift to every child was to make them feel special. She spent time listening and comforting them. Every child in her class loved her and thought that she cared for them individually. This is such an achievement for any teacher. Nigel was to call upon all her skills a little later in his school life.

My father had retired. Both he and my mother were in their early seventies. Dad was still involved in his good works. He started the Warners End Darby and Joan club in the newly built community centre. It gave the elderly somewhere to go and before long a lunch club was affiliated to it. The membership grew to one hundred members, which proved there was a need. Outings were arranged, and parties were held for any occasion that merited celebration. The building was well used by all age groups from preschool groups, Cubs, Girlguides through to wedding receptions and all our Townswomen's Guild meetings were held there. The centre was a great success and an asset to the community. Warners End no longer felt like a place tacked onto Hemel Hempstead.

The guild was becoming immensely popular, the membership now had a waiting list. I enrolled for a mental health course at Dacorum College and found it informative. It gave me a greater insight and understanding of the mental health charity the Guild supported. My friends were also pursuing various avenues open to them. Flower arranging was a favourite choice, but there was a surprising array of subjects for members to choose from. It took us far away from the continual commitment to housekeeping and childcare. As soon as we

109

entered the hall for our meeting, we became ourselves, not someone's daughter, wife, or mother. We were enriching our lives and passing on our new skills. I greatly enjoyed this time of my life.

My childhood had taught me to value the here and now. My family were and are everything to me. I constantly told my children that I loved them, and my aim was to not let life hurt them in anyway. I know this was a tall order, but I think I was making up for the emotional security that was lacking in my childhood. The path I chose was the right one for me. I follow that same path with my grandchildren and their little ones. The love just gets richer, and I feel truly fortunate.

My mother-in-law's health was deteriorating. She was being seen by consultants, but her condition was far too advanced to be considered for any surgery to help her with her ongoing pain. Our visits became more vital and sometimes we would get a call in the night. My father-in-law, Will, had never lifted so much as a tea towel to help in the past. In fact, my mum-ln-law wouldn't allow him or Bill to do any domestic chores. However, all that had changed. Will ended up doing all the chores and could turn his hand to anything. My brother Sandy also lived in Hemel, and he would help when he could. He was accomplished at DIY, and he placed castors on the legs of a dining chair so that Mum could propel herself, on a good day, to the window. It was a struggle for her, but it gave her a sense of freedom to go from one room to the other.

Mum would come alive whenever she saw her grandchildren run up the garden path towards her. Her family meant everything to her. Many times, I have seen the children lay against her for a cuddle and the pain would be etched on her face, but she would never tell them or ask them to move. Her love for the children was so overwhelming it helped her conquer the pain.

I enjoyed each day in the school kitchen, but my working life was to change yet again and in the most unexpected way. It was during a half term break that my father came to see me. He was very agitated because the cook had left the Warmers End Centre and there was nobody to cook the lunch for the old people's club. My father asked if I would go and see if I could help them in any way.

"You only need to cook them egg and chips or something like that. We can't let them down. There are about thirty people involved. It will be nothing to you."

I took myself along to the hall with Nigel. Andrea stayed with Andrew at the Batchelor's house. Melanie was off somewhere with her friends. How right my father was. All went well. I provided an acceptable meal for everyone that was appreciated by all.

I could see my father huddled in a corner with the Chairman discussing something in hushed tones. Both men had very grave faces. I watched my father approach me and heard the tail end of his conversation. "I will ask my daughter and see if she can help." He then asked his question. "The hall is booked for a dinner on Saturday. The mayor is the guest of honour. It is to celebrate the opening of the Community Centre. Can you do the catering?"

"What is expected?"

"Oh, it's a four-course meal, but we do have the menu."

"How many guests?"

"Two Hundred."

I was aghast. "How on earth can anyone cook for that amount of people on a domestic sized cooker?"

No one said a word. Other equipment was there but not a commercial cooker. It was a formidable task. The food hadn't even been ordered, which showed the irresponsibility of the cook who had scarpered. I think they had taken on more than they could chew. Now my father was asking me to get them out of this dreadful dilemma. It was true that I had catered for weddings and celebrations for the Guild and various friends, but these were done from friendship and were not commercial ventures.

I had no sleep that night wondering if I would be able to achieve some sort of acceptable meal, but there was still the logistics of how. This was more than a challenge. I needed better kitchen facilities. Bartletts, the kitchen manufacturers, were based in the industrial area of Maylands Avenue. The owners were practising Christians and knew my father through various charities. They had sat together on various committees. They agreed to come to my aid should I take on the task. I informed the Community Centre that I would try and help them out, but I could only do my best.

I enlisted six of the younger pensioners to help with the mundane kitchen chores and four neighbours to act as waitresses. I enrolled some men to put up the tables and to dismantle them after the meal in readiness for the dancing during the evening. Bessie, the cook from school, volunteered to be my right-hand woman. I was confident that I had surrounded myself with the right supportive staff. Now I had the meal itself to consider. The menu was already planned and set-in stone. I told myself I had no time for negative thoughts.

My lovely neighbours willingly helped me with this daring endeavour. I delegated my next-door neighbour Nona and her neighbour Gert, plus my mother and me to roast the turkeys slowly in our ovens overnight. With the cooking of the meat resolved I was able to deal with the vegetables. Stuffing and the wrapped sausages were cooked in the Centre's kitchen then placed in the heated trolleys leaving space for masses of roast potatoes. The first course was much easier. I purchased gigantic commercial drums of soup which only had to be heated. I made trifles, for the dessert, until they were coming out of my ears. The final course was a cheese board, therefore I only needed to buy the biscuits and various cheeses. That may all sound so easy, but it was a nightmare even though a remarkably successful one.

Just before the guests arrived, I slipped into my black jersey dress and became the manageress. All the guests were greeted on arrival with a sherry; at the end of the meal speeches were made. The mayor said his thanks and then introduced a lady called Mrs Reynolds, who was the head of the Schools Kitchen Service for Hertfordshire. In her speech she said, "I have just learned from Mr Bailey that the lady responsible for our splendid meal only had five days to prepare. Well, done to her and I would very much like to meet her."

Mrs Reynolds sought me out. "If ever you want to work for Herts County Council. I will give you a job." Little did she realise that I already worked for them.

At the end of the night, the whole team enjoyed the leftover food accompanied by a glass of sherry and concluded that we all deserved a pat on the back for our achievements. When I arrived home, I was exhausted but on a high. My lovely husband had been such an asset. His carving of the turkeys was the key to making all the other tasks possible. Earlier in the evening when we were plating up the meat, I realised we were around twenty portions short. We could have taken meat from some of the plates where maybe we had been too generous, but I remembered a new take away had opened in town. Bill was dispatched and returned triumphant, waving a bag in the air. It saved the day.

As a result of the success, I was asked if I would consider taking on the job of restaurant manageress. I was in a dilemma. I had enjoyed the stimulus and achievement of that one occasion but was unsure whether the daily grind of running the whole restaurant was what I wanted. This wasn't going to be just supervisory. I would be head cook and bottlewasher. I had to consider the school holidays and our trips to Norfolk. I didn't worry about letting the school down as there were plenty of ladies on the headmaster's waiting list should a post become available.

I started my new job almost straight away and had my own list of ladies that I wanted to work for me. My hours were the same. The restaurant opened at nine o'clock and I started work at 8.30. What I didn't know, was that there were many very hungry Irish builders who were constructing new houses in the Chaulden neighbourhood. I cooked full English breakfasts nonstop from the moment we opened. I was warned to be careful as they could possibly be rough and ready, but I didn't find this so. They always addressed me as Mam and behaved in a very respectful way with the waitresses. My food must have been reasonable because they never bought slices of the pies, tarts and cakes but preferred to purchase the whole thing.

As the Community Centre was new, the special carpeting in the entrance had only recently been laid. It was of the best quality and that beautiful red, you find in cinemas. The committee were horrified that these labourers were going to damage it, so a canvas tarp was laid over the carpet. The workmen always conformed to my request to use it. They always made my day with their sunny disposition and courtesy to the other customers and staff. I was sorry to see them go when their contracts finished.

The restaurant became established and was a regular meeting place for the electric and gas boards workers, mums coming in from the school runs as well as passers-by. The Darby and Joan club had dinners there twice a week. I think many people came in because they were lonely. Warners End hadn't been completed beyond Boxted Road. There were still many lonely people trying to start afresh.

I had to organise how I was going to have time off during the school holidays, so I started training one of my ladies to take over in my absence. Ella was diligent and she made the promise that as her two children were grown up and working, she would never let me down. She kept her word, and I knew she would manage well.

I was always tired. The title manageress sounded so grand but, I was the cook. My managerial dress of black jersey hung on its hanger until all the work was done. When I stood beside the waitresses at the entrance hall little did the guests know they were smiling at the cook. I was often given a tip as the manageress plus one for the chef. As all our tips were pooled it never was a problem. Sharing the tips equally gave validation to the behind-the-scenes workers. We became a close-knit group. Whatever the function, as soon as the clearing up began, I would

113

lay a table with a damask cloth and set the table with cutlery and wine glasses as if it was an official booking. We all sat down together and had the same meal. It was such a success and gave the staff a close bond. It was a thank you from me for their hard work and loyalty. I remember on one occasion one of them said to me, "Jane you ought to write a book. It would be a best seller if you repeated these conversations."

Fridays were my busiest days. As well as dealing with the usual Friday trade I had to start the preparation for the next day's function. Tables were laid, anybody who was free helped. Every task that could be done in advance, was. We had become very slick and professional, each person knowing their role and responsibilities.

One Friday we were preparing for the next day's wedding. I was placing the flowers on the tables when my mother's neighbour rushed in to inform me that my father had had a heart attack. He was on his way to Watford Hospital as the cardiac unit was unavailable in Hemel. I froze. It took me a minute to assess what I was going to do. My staff were wonderful and reassured me that everything was in place for the following day. I left for home to sort out the children and to put Bill in the picture.

I spoke to Alan in South Africa who said he would travel home on the first available flight. My mother, brothers and sisters and I all stayed at my father's bedside until he died on the Sunday. We were all devastated. My mother went to pieces. Alan unfortunately arrived home too late. He came home in time for the funeral.

The family were amazed at the tributes to Dad. We could now see the good work he had accomplished. Letters came from ex-service men, fellow councillors, Darby and Joan clubs, welfare committees. Many spoke of his great kindness.

The week after the funeral I just floated around in a daze. The staff had managed the wedding with the support of Ella. I felt I couldn't leave my mother as she just couldn't pull herself together. My father's death also had an impact on my in-laws. We were all so close as a family. This was the first death of that generation.

Life changed in many ways. I never returned to work in the restaurant. My mother's needs came first. Within weeks she wanted to move and was making all sorts of decisions that were not sensible. It was exceedingly difficult for me. My mother thought I had all the answers, which of course I didn't. She didn't take into consideration, for a long time, that I had a young family and in-laws that needed me too. It was very tough at times.

I was pushed from pillar to post into situations I couldn't resolve. I was trying to placate my mother, sharing the load of my mum in-law with my father-in-law, being mum and a good wife. I had also returned to hairdressing. I was very thankful that I had very well-behaved children. Sometimes I went to bed with such bad migraines. I would often look into the mirror when applying my make-up and think, '*Why doesn't my stress show? I look as though I haven't got a care in the world.*' I repeatedly told myself, '*Keep going until the next school holiday.*'

My children had had a wonderful relationship with my father, especially Nigel. All three found it hard to accept that their granddad had died. Andrea asked, "Does that mean that granddad is in heaven?"

Nigel was listening to this conversation. Whilst I was clearing the table from our meal, I noticed that he was scribbling on an old raffle ticket book. He had drawn a picture of a head. In the mouth was a smoking a pipe. My father always had a pipe in his mouth even if it wasn't lit. I felt distraught and it triggered off my own grief.

"I am not going to be a fireman. I'm going to be a pilot so that I can go up in the sky to find grandad." This wasn't the last sign of Nigel's anguish.

I was requested to see Mrs Morgan, Nigel's teacher, without him being present. I had such a shock when she told me that he had changed his name as he didn't want to be called Nigel any longer. This lovely lady changed the name on his clothes peg plus all his books. She went on to show me pictures that he had drawn. It was hard to believe they were drawn by a five-year-old. The pictures depicted horrifying scenes of raging fires with black figures and skulls. Mrs Morgan's opinion, which I valued, was that he didn't want to be the same little boy whose grandad had died. She thought that Nigel believed that by changing his name it would all go away. After a period, without any discussion, Mrs Morgan renamed his clothes peg and books.

It took quite a while for him to revert to the happy little boy that he had been previously. When I heard him arguing with his little mate Jonathan about which Dinky cars belonged to him, I knew he was getting back on track.

CHAPTER THIRTEEN

Melanie was growing into a young woman fast. I used to observe her getting ready for school. Her skirt length had to be exactly right and styling her hair took ages. I noticed a slight use of make-up, which was against school rules. She was still the same quiet helpful girl. She was approaching the school leaving age and decisions had to be made about her future and what she wanted to do. Her German teacher Mrs Helmich wanted her to take up German as she was particularly good at it. She even visited the house to ask me to persuade Melanie. However, Melanie knew her own mind, she wanted to be a nursery nurse.

Applications to train for an NNEB were completed, submitted and successful. She was allocated a place at St Albans College. That was the start of her adulthood. I tried so hard to get her to accept a place at the Norland College of Nannies. The course cost £2,000 which was a fortune, but I wanted her to have the best, as I saw it then. No amount of persuasion could budge her.

Bill and I had saved for some time towards the deposit on a house. We approached our local housing department but without success. The Labour government had a policy of not selling council houses. However, we did gain information from our enquiry. We were informed that houses were being built at Grove Hill and would be for sale by the New Towns Commission. Encouraged, we visited the estate and decided to buy one of the completed three storey houses.

We bought 181 Washington Avenue. Ironically, the house stood on a piece of land that had belonged to Bill's great uncles. Their land covered an extensive area and was a compulsory purchase by the New Towns Commission for £5,000. We were paying the same amount of money for one terraced house that was leasehold. They were Will's uncles and my in-laws felt hard done by. It was a disgusting price even in the early 1960s. We had to put that all behind us. We looked forward to starting to pay a mortgage and not rent. A new way of life for us.

My mother had now moved into a bungalow in Gravel Path, in Warners End. I was delighted as it was a quick easy move. The local authority was anxious to obtain a three-bedroom house for a needy family. My mother seemed to be a little less demanding, enabling me to concentrate on our move. I was still not working but I had a breathing space for a while. Nevertheless, if we wanted to maintain our standard of living, I really needed to get a job. I didn't want to restart hairdressing, but I knew that extra money paid for our times in Norfolk. Soon a decision was made for me.

I had a frantic call from a neighbour stating that my father-in law had fallen off his bike after leaving his allotment. He had disappeared but the bicycle was still propped against the kerb outside the Whip and Collar pub. Another neighbour had gone to look for him. Will was found wandering in the Marlowes and was confused so the neighbour took him straight to Casualty. He had a considerable gash on his head where he had hit the kerb. He was so confused that we couldn't ascertain whether he had hit the kerb with his bike and fallen off or had fallen off for another reason. I drove straight to the hospital. After he was patched up, I was told I could take him home and should return in five days to have the stitches removed.

Will obviously needed looking after as well as my mum in-law. Bill and I were in a quandary as to how. We had the children to think about and Bill had to work. We decided to do the caring between us and work in shifts at their cottage until the stitches were removed. His condition accelerated at such a pace that it was obvious that my gentle father-in-law had far bigger problems. My mum in-law was worried sick. She had observed him putting his clothes on back to front, he ate food with his fingers from only one half of his plate, he missed doorways and tried to walk through walls.

I was convinced that there was something seriously wrong with Will. I took him back to Casualty. Eventually I spoke with a very brusque, loud voiced doctor in his office. He bellowed at me, "Why do you think I should I admit him?" I raised my voice to compete with him.

"Why don't you read the notes in your hand? I've listed all our observations and concerns."

"If everybody wrote me notes, I wouldn't have time to see my patients."

I became so angry that he had written off my lovely father-in-law that I shouted at the top of my voice. "How dare you treat him in this way. He is a gentleman, and you are not God." Dr Sadiqi shrank back in his seat and shouted something to his right-hand man. "All right, I'll admit him."

I was told later by a friend of mine, who was a sister in the Casualty department, that the conversation was overheard in the corridor. Apparently, I had made the staff's day. The doctor had worked for years at West Herts Hospital, and everybody was intimidated by him.

That was the first time in my life that I had behaved in that way, and I haven't had the need to do so since.

Will was transferred the next day to St Bartholomew's Hospital in London. He was diagnosed with a brain tumour and was operated on within days. Unfortunately, nothing more could be done for him. He didn't surface from the operation with masses of tubes like his fellow patients therefore he reasoned that he was one of the lucky ones that didn't need treatment. Nevertheless, according to Will, the doctors thought he should have a good rest before going home to his wife.

It was a dreadful day. Both Bill and I let the tears flow down our cheeks on the journey home. We were then faced with the task of having to tell my mother-in-law. Bless her she greeted us with, "I know what you are going to tell me."

We now had to care full time for Bill's mum, travel up to London every day and look after the children. It was an exceedingly challenging time. We didn't know where to turn for help. Everybody we approached felt sorry for us but couldn't help. Eventually the surgery managed to cajole Highfield Residential Home into taking Mum for an interim period and they made sure we knew it was only until Will was discharged. She was there for three weeks.

On one of those Sundays, we invited Mum home to dinner. It was bitterly cold, too cold to be pushed in a wheelchair, but Alice was eager to see her grandchildren. Bill went to London to visit Will and I cooked a special roast dinner. Andrea had a remarkably close relationship with her grandmother and announced, "I will fetch Nanny to help out. I am capable of pushing her home." She was fourteen at the time. It was a good one-and-a-half-mile walk so with great trepidation I agreed. I knew that whatever difficulties she would encounter with kerbs and rough ground, Andrea would surmount them. They both arrived home for dinner in one piece. That day has remained special to all of us. Within two days my mum in-law was admitted to St Pauls Hospital with chronic health problems.

For reasons unknown to us, the hospital withdrew all her drugs. She was taking twenty-seven a day and within hours she was hallucinating. When the staff checked on her at four a.m. the following morning, they discovered she had died in her sleep. She was sixty-seven. We were so shocked and distressed. We concluded that she had just let go of life. Our children were heartbroken.

Our next journey back to Barts Hospital was to tell Will that his beloved wife had died. He took it well, considering how remarkably close they were, but we had to remind ourselves that Will's brain tumour had given him a different perspective. We returned home to the children knowing that they needed some of our time and compassion. Melanie had assumed the mantle of being mum. Although at college she returned home each day to give support. She washed the clothes and kept up with the ironing. Andrea kept a watchful eye on her young brother and made sure that the dog was fed and walked. We were so proud of them. Often children's grief goes unnoticed, but we observed that they were suffering too. Our close family unit gave us strength.

Organising the funeral was hard. Both Bill and I felt we were floating through all the arrangements. The funeral was on a bitterly cold day in March. So many people attended. We had issued invitations, but the word spread that anybody who wanted to pay their respects could do so and would be welcome at the house afterwards.

Will was too ill to leave the hospital, so we decided not to tell him when the funeral was.

When we visited him after the funeral, we were astounded by what he said. We walked into his private room, and he announced, "I know Alice was buried today. She came and said goodbye to me at 3.15 this afternoon. She was in a rush because she said she couldn't be late and had to catch 'them' up. On her rush out of the window she knocked the vase of flowers off the bedside trolley."

Will's room was several storeys high above the ground and the vase of flowers on the bedside trolley was at the foot of the bed, away from the window. I just had to go to the ward Sister to ask her what she thought about the story.

"I know, it is very strange. He told me what had happened, and I could see he was pleased to have said goodbye to her. Yes, the flowers were knocked over and he certainly couldn't have done it."

The story really affected us. Bill who was a sceptic on most occasions was utterly puzzled by his father's story with accurate timings. He said, "There is much that we don't know about this world."

Within days Will talked about coming home to live with us on his discharge. This was fine because we had already assumed that.

On one of our visits Will looked at Bill and said, "I am going to give Jane the cottage. I hope you don't mind."

Bill replied, "Will, you do what you like with it. If you give it to Jane, you give it to me too or vice versa." The subject wasn't mentioned again.

We collected Will from the hospital by car as he wasn't well enough to travel by train. As soon as the car pulled away into the heavy traffic Will panicked. He was petrified. Thankfully, I had sat in the back and was able to lean forward to reassure him. It was a typical London traffic jam with vehicles all around us. He was terrified of being enclosed. Will was like a child seeing it all for the first time.

I suddenly became anxious. *'How will his final days be if everything around him scares him after the peace of the hospital?'* This didn't prove to be the case. As soon as we left the hubbub of London, he became relaxed and more like his old self.

CHAPTER FOURTEEN

We were surprised that Will never mentioned Alice or talked of his home in Boxmoor. He kept to the same routine every morning. Will and I were by ourselves for breakfast. Bill often worked an early shift, and the girls and Nigel would be on their way to school and college. I set the table in the kitchen, and he always requested a full English breakfast. Afterwards we used to sit and talk about what was going on in the world. His daily ritual continued with his perusal of the racing pages in the newspaper. This was something he had never done before, and it was a joy to see his face. He behaved as though he was a member of the racing gentry making his selection. I used to telephone my sister-in-law's father who was a bookie then Will would place his bet. He never queried the cost, or any money lost. He was like a child in a toy shop. I loved it. He had worked hard for little money all his life. Most days he accompanied me shopping or I took him for drives to Ashridge or St Albans Park.

Before long, many people were introduced to him. I joked and said, "You think you are Lord Halsey." (Halsey is the Lord of the Manor for Hemel Hempstead.) He had no conception that his life would be cut short at any time. It made it much easier for us as we could laugh, joke, and involve him in plans for the future. Only one thing bothered him. He felt Grove Hill was too far away from his beloved Boxmoor, where he had lived his entire life. I used to take him to the cottage in St Johns Road at least once or twice a week. We would walk along to the shops where everyone would be delighted to see him looking so well. Locals often chatted to him about the old days, before the new town was built.

We had a family discussion about selling the cottage and the Grove Hill house. With the combined money we would be able to look for a house in Boxmoor. Will was involved in these discussions and was delighted with the idea. Our house was put on the market and sold straight away. We had only been in residence for just over one year. We were overjoyed when we found a delightful house in Ashtree Way, even though it needed a lot of work to bring it up to standard. We went ahead with the sale.

Will seemed a little off colour and I assumed he had the flu, as much of the town was infected. I kept him in bed and sent for his doctor. He was of the same opinion. Will gently slipped into a coma. I declined the offer of him being taken into hospital as I wanted to watch over him myself. Sister Rosemary McDonald, a district nurse, was allocated to him and visited daily. He stayed in his 'gentle sleep' for around ten days then passed away without any suffering. It was exactly five months from his diagnosis at St Bartholomew's. We had just started to recover from the loss of my father. Now we had the death of Bill's mother followed shortly after by his father. It was such a lot to process. Grief comes in many guises, as we had found from Nigel's behaviour. Both Bill and I were struggling. It was all too close and the grieving heavy to bear and believe. Later in life I trained to be a bereavement counsellor for an organisation called Cruse. I learned that our emotions at that time were the usual ones experienced by the bereaved. The pain and anger we felt were all part of the grieving process.

Rosemary popped in once or twice after Will had died to see how we were doing. On one of these occasions, she said, "You would have made a good nurse. I have seen you at work; you are a natural. The Dacorum Health Authority are setting up a new scheme to train auxiliary nurses. I think you should apply. I will be more than happy to recommend you."

I applied and was given a placement there and then at the interview. The panel offered me a position based on my interview and Sister McDonald's reference. I was the first auxiliary nurse for the Dacorum district, closely followed by Pat Record. I started my new job the week after we moved to Ashtree Way.

Three auxiliary nurses were appointed. We were assigned to different nursing sisters and spent a week with each one learning the ropes. We also attended courses in a couple of the local hospitals. We were then considered ready to work with patients but were still on trial. I was assigned to two district nursing sisters and was answerable to them both.

I was so nervous on my first day because I was going to be assessed by a senior Nursing Officer. The officer came from St Albans. We met outside a small cottage in Leverstock Green. As she got out of her car, I couldn't believe that she was old enough to be in such a senior post. She was so tiny compared with my five feet eight inches. She shook my hand and said, "We are making history today. Remember that the patient doesn't know you are new or that this is a new service."

We were invited in by the patient's husband. Hot water was boiling on an open fire. We progressed to the bedroom and the N.O. said to me, "I will just stand and observe." I was shaking whilst trying to remember to fold my coat inside out and place it on a chair alongside my nurse's bag. I then proceeded to fold back the bedclothes and asked my patient if she was comfortable. I am sure she could see I was incredibly nervous. She said, "I do like the colour of your new uniforms." As I folded back the sheet, I saw she was a double amputee. I nearly fainted with shock. I hadn't been prepared for this and had never seen a double amputee in my life. It had certainly not been included in our training programme. After washing the patient, I dressed her and all too quickly became aware that her two artificial legs, complete with stockings and shoes, were propped up against the wall. I realised I hadn't a clue how to attach prosthetics. My back was to the N.O. but the patient could see concern etched across my face. She kindly said, "Nurse, do you mind if my husband straps on my legs? He somehow seems to place them in the right position for them not to rub my stumps." The couple left the room and I cleared up and remade the bed. When we finally left the cottage, I looked at this young girl, who was my examiner, and awaited her comments. "Have you ever seen an amputee before?"

"Never."

'Well done! You didn't show any sign of shock. I think you will do very well in the Dacorum nursing division."

I was now thirty-nine and fit but amazed to find out how tiring bathing and dressing patients was. Every day for me was an education. My biggest fault was that I became too attached to most of my patients. Little did I dream that I would write about it in my eighties. My visits to one particular patient inspired my book, The Pain of Silence.

I worked until two o'clock each day which gave me time to look after my mother. Time away at the caravan became possible once more.

CHAPTER FIFTEEN

My sister Eileen and Colin resided in Kinloss in Scotland. They lived there for several years. Colin worked on the aircraft at RAF Kinloss. We all thought that everything was hunky-dory. Their huge mobile home was sited on the base, and they were able to use the officers' mess and the NAFFI facilities. Some years down the line, I had a tearful Eileen on the telephone informing me that things were wrong between them and that she wanted to leave Colin. I felt saddened by the news but apart from comforting her over telephone I was unable to help. I discussed the situation with my other sister, Bette, and we concluded that our mother had no need to know.

Things got out of hand and Eileen and Colin were requested to leave the base. Word got back to Rolls Royce, Colin's employer, and the company suggested he take early retirement. The retirement deal gave them enough money for a deposit on a pub. It wasn't too far from the family, right in the centre of Tring. The Victoria was an old building. I cannot remember whether it had three or four floors, only that it enabled them to take in bed and breakfast guests to supplement their bar takings.

Their first year went well. We used to visit them and often enjoyed a meal together. My sister was an excellent cook, and her presentation of food was exceptional for the time. Soon word got around, and their business boomed. We were delighted that they had put the past behind them. The Vic, as it was affectionately called, was hired out for parties with Eileen doing the catering and Colin playing host.

Slowly the situation changed. I used to receive telephone calls from Eileen telling me that Colin was being abusive. She inevitably asked me to go over to sort them out. It was evident that they had both returned to their bad habits. I knew it would only be a matter of time before the business suffered. Customers don't appreciate publicans arguing in front of them. Those who didn't mind, helped to drink the profits. They were on a slippery slope again. They sort counselling and for a while it worked. The counsellor ultimately suggested that they should move on again to help eradicate the past. They moved to St Albans. I found the whole situation incredibly demanding.

My mother also decided that she wished to move. She wanted to go into sheltered accommodation. She relinquished her bungalow in Warners End and was given a flat in Florence Longman, in Apsley, an area that she knew well. Another upheaval that Bill and I had to deal with. We hoped this would be my mother's last abode.

We seemed to be going from one crisis to another for years. I was showing great signs of stress from all the pressure. My mother's warden, who wasn't the most accommodating of women, told me that if my mother awoke in the night and pulled the alarm, and she deemed it nonessential, she would telephone me. I was habitually called to my mother in the middle of the night. I used to still be half asleep when it was time for me to get up. On seeing my mother, the following morning, she did not allude to the call out in the middle of the night. To her this was normal behaviour.

Dead on my feet, one morning, I reflected on her selfishness and decided to confront her. I told her how her frequent calls were affecting me. We talked for quite a while, and I thought I had got through to her. As I left, she called after me.

"I should come first, and be before anybody, even your family because I am your mother." I despaired hearing this, as I knew nothing was going to change. And it didn't. I still had call outs plus twice daily visits.

My mother thought things through and came up with a solution. "If I came to live with you, all this stress would stop, and you wouldn't have to visit me. It would make your life easier."

My mother couldn't fathom out that she had created all the pressure. Her flat was in the latest purpose-built block with all the facilities imaginable. It was close to the village centre which had all the usual amenities. Everything was on her doorstep, what else was my mother looking for?

Bill wasn't impressed. "Jane that cannot happen. Our lives as we know it would be destroyed. We have your mum every Sunday, every bank holiday and you devote many more hours every week to her. That is enough. We have to have something left for ourselves."

I told my mother that I had discussed her proposition with Bill.

"It won't be Bill who has made that decision, it will be you. I know why you think that. You think things like your weekly fund-raising stall on the market will have to stop or that you won't be able to attend your women's meetings. You put other people before me." I left the building in tears. In the end, all the caring counted for nothing. The very next morning my mother behaved as though nothing had happened or been said. The subject matter was never raised by her again.

Eileen and Colin's final move was from the Harrow in St Albans to the Boar's Head at Piccotts End. It was yet another period in their lives when they thought they would make another fresh start.

It was a delightful olde-worlde building with a great history. It had the most delightful views with pretty gardens, all in all the perfect setting. The pair of them kept to their promises of reducing their alcohol consumption and they kept on the straight and narrow for a couple of years. Eileen's reputation for excellent pub grub soon had the Boar's Head packed with customers.

Whilst at their previous pub, The Harrow, my brother Bob had managed to get Colin a job as an engineer at Heathrow airport. He continued to commute to the airport. This supplemented their income from the pub. It should have helped them financially, but it didn't. It enabled them to wine and dine out, leaving staff to cover for them. They assured the family that their relationship was now in a much better place.

Colin started to go to a gym and sauna on his way home which was the start of things sliding backwards. Eileen being by herself, helped herself from the bar optics every time she walked the length of the bar. It was so sad. I visited her daily in the hope that I could steer her from this downward spiral. I couldn't. All she gave me was empty promises or falsehoods.

I was back to being called out in the night to bring her home when things got out of hand. Colin had met up with an old girlfriend and she visited the pub, as a customer, every night. It was so blatant that the customers were aware of the situation.

I contacted Bob and asked him to go to the pub unannounced to see for himself. Our sister was threatening to commit suicide and I needed some guidance and support. Something had to be done. I investigated private housing associations for Eileen. I eventually contacted Hightown who owned various premises in Hemel. Although expensive, residents from Dacorum could apply when there was a vacancy. Within a couple of weeks, a flat became available.

Bob and I devised a plan to help Eileen leave the pub. We didn't want a confrontation during licencing hours. We hired a van and arrived at the pub in the afternoon when it was closed. Bob, Bill, and I gathered up all of Eileen's essential belongings and packed them into the van. We had some items of furniture, gifts from friends and family, already on board. Eileen couldn't believe the move had gone ahead as planned. We settled her into her flat in Cornfields. I stayed until the evening. I knew it would be extremely tough for her with no customers or alcohol to help herself to.

A frantic Colin telephoned. It was a massive shock to him that evening. I was informed later that within hours of Eileen leaving, the girlfriend and her husband were helping in the bar. It was as Bob, and I envisioned. We had in fact done Colin a favour, but as far as we were concerned, we had given our sister her respect and dignity back.

We hoped that in time her pub life would be a distant memory. Initially it was hard for her to adjust. She didn't want to go out. However, she persevered and in due course saw an advertisement for a cashier at Halfords. She applied and was successful. My sister was on the road to recovery. Although the wages were low it supplemented her pension which she had just become entitled to at sixty. I was fortunate enough to be able to help by paying her rent for six months. During that period, we hoped the council would find her a cheaper flat which would enable her to live within her means. One did become available after a year. It was sheltered accommodation, a first floor flat in Chapel Street. It was ideal for her as it was just off the High Street. Eileen could walk to work. We were all delighted to see her so much happier. Each Sunday she came to lunch which gave her contact with the family. She liked her accommodation and was finally in a good place emotionally. She still liked the odd drink but kept it under control for the rest of her days.

CHAPTER SIXTEEN

Another remarkably busy time in our lives was the lead up to Melanie and Ken's wedding in the summer of 1971. The church and reception venue had to be chosen and a date confirmed. Melanie chose her sister, and her cousins Carole-Anne and Sarah to be the bridesmaids. She wanted to make their long dresses which was quite an undertaking. Melanie, always the perfectionist, had to have the best of materials and the design entailed the making of minute lace flowers with tiny buttonholes all the way down the back. The hard work paid off because the dresses were beautiful. Her own wedding dress, although bought, fitted her like a glove. She looked breath-taking when she walked down the aisle.

Our own Silver Wedding anniversary followed over a year later. We celebrated with a party in a local hall, not far from our home. We invited as many guests as we could trace from our wedding day. By now most of them had families of their own which swelled the numbers. Melanie, once more, used her sewing skills to make me an incredibly special dress. The black material had silver threads running through it, making the ankle length dress glimmer as I moved. I was thrilled to have a one-off designer dress made by my own daughter.

The party continued into the next day. We provided lunch for thirty or so people, some of whom hadn't gone home from the party. They just slept where they could. I know Bill and around ten male guests played cards all through the night. It was certainly a party that we wouldn't forget.

Bill and I were not surprised when Andrea told us that when she left The Cavendish School she wished to train as a teacher. It hit home that she was leaving the nest when we helped Andrea pack her bags and all her possessions to move into the student halls of residence at Wall Hall College. The car was packed to the gunwales. Andrea and I followed behind on her Vespa scooter. Bill and I had bought the second-hand scooter for her sixteenth birthday, and it was her faithful friend. It was my first time as a pillion, but I was reassured by Andrea that there was nothing to it. I soon learned to lean with the driver when negotiating bends. However, Andrea once called out in desperation, "Mum please stop crushing my ribs, you are really hurting me when you squeeze so tightly."

We arrived at Wall Hall in one piece. However, I cried on the way home at the realisation that I now had another child leave home. Bill was cross with me. "For goodness' sake Jane, Wall Hall is only up the road. You could visit on your bike!" I failed to see this as funny at the time. I laugh thinking of it now.

Alan used to telephone me regularly from South Africa. The calls were always from his office which meant they were lengthy as he didn't have to pay for them. During one of our conversations, he mentioned Bill's love of South Africa. "Why don't you save up and come out for a holiday? You will have to be here for a month if you consider that you'll be paying two hundred and fifty pounds for your fare. You will need a little spending money, that's all."

The idea was now in my head. I discussed Alan's proposition with Bill then started saving in earnest. Bill was such an easy-going man and had no qualms about me going. In fact, he said, "I love the country so much and will be interested to see what you make of it." Bill had stayed with a wealthy family during the second world war, but I would be going to stay with family. Bill thought this might make a difference and wondered if his judgement had been clouded by the opulence of his surroundings.

I soon arranged my leave from work and purchased my ticket for a whole month in South Africa. What a thrill. Unbelievably, at the time, not many married women would consider taking off for a month without their husbands. Bill was thrilled that I was willing to travel such a distance on my own.

It was a wonderful flight. I sat next to an elderly couple who were getting off in Salisbury, Rhodesia, as it was then called. All ongoing passengers alighted there also whist the plane refuelled. When we arrived at Johannesburg, I descended the steps and gasped at the heat. It was ten in the morning, and I remember thinking would it be as hot in Durban, where my brother and his family lived. It was! I had to connect with a local flight for the onward journey. It was a small aircraft and made me feel a little nervous. When the plane flew over the Drakensberg Mountains it lost height suddenly and I was petrified. I was sitting next to a thoughtful man who talked me out of my fear. It never ceases to amaze me how many friendly people you meet when travelling. Since that period of my life, I have flown many air miles and could write a book on the people I have encountered on my journeys.

I fell in love with South Africa and genuinely appreciated escaping from all the pressure at home. Alan and his family made me very welcome. I returned home a different person and with a determination to say 'no' to the demands of my extended family.

Bill asked me what I felt about apartheid, and did I think that I could live in South Africa. He had seen an advertisement in his company magazine for a printer in Durban. This was serendipity. "You will not have all the worry of your mother and other family problems. They have all managed whilst you were away." It was a lot to take in and consider but so tempting at the same time.

We now had our first grandchild, Lee. This baby boy was so welcome as Melanie and Ken had been trying for a baby for some time. Andrea was in her last year at Wall Hall College and might need support. Nigel was only fifteen and would have to come with us should we make the decision to go.

Bill had lived for two years on and off, in South Africa whilst in the navy. Many South African people entertained and showed tremendous benevolence to the serving forces. The Royal Navy, in the main, needed their hospitality. Bill was one of the survivors from a bombing raid on his ship. The Waters family in Pretoria took in Bill and two of his shipmates whilst they awaited their next ship. To a village boy like Bill, it was an unbelievably different lifestyle. The Waters could horse ride for two days and still be on the land that they owned. Their compassion was beyond measure. After the war I took over from Bill and corresponded with members of the family.

Bill survived another bombing and stayed with the Hollies. They were sheep farmers and like the Water family had extensive land. Bill said Mr Hollie was a sweet old gentleman who was always falling asleep. Standing on the piano was a beautiful, framed picture of Princess Elizabeth, the present Queen. Bill looked. at it. "This is a lovely picture of the princess Mrs Hollie and it's personally signed."

"Oh, yes," answered Mrs Hollie. "She is my cousin, and such a lovely person."

We were still deciding about emigrating to South Africa, but my visit had proved fruitful. My brother was already established in Durban. Alan's friends had already made me welcome. What a dilemma it was me. Bill found it much easier. Both his parents had died. My mother was still demanding but much to my surprise she thought it would be a good move for us. Hearing this did make it easier for me.

Andrea couldn't stay on the campus for another year. Fortunately, she already had her name on the housing waiting list and was allocated a small bedsit in the old town opposite the fire station. It was near the town centre. She was thrilled and so were we. By the time she moved in she had made it her own. She still had her faithful old scooter which meant she could transport herself to college. When she moved, she took Chippy, Bill's parents chihuahua, with her. The little dog adored her and was small enough to live in the flat without presenting any problems. Gadebridge Park was on her doorstep which proved a big asset. Our own springer spaniel was old and had been put to sleep sometime before. It appeared life was slotting into place.

My sister Eileen was devastated at the thought of our move. Bill applied for the advertised job. As it was with his own company, he didn't think that he had to be interviewed. Company policy dictated otherwise. He arrived home from the interview feeling confident as he was one of the company's top printers.

Bill wasn't selected. We couldn't believe it and Bill was furious. The printing machines in Durban were earlier versions of the machines Bill used in the UK. Dickenson's in Apsley Mill had the latest technology, and the old machines were shipped to Durban.

We found out from one of the senior managers that the company hadn't given Bill the job because they couldn't afford to lose him, as he was the most experienced of the Apsley printers. He could not be replaced before another printer was trained up. The company immediately offered him staff status. This would have made a big difference to his future pension plus many more benefits, but Bill resigned anyway. He was angry and hurt at Dickenson's treatment of him. Alan obtained a managerial position for him in Durban.

Nobody could believe that Bill had resigned. He had worked at John Dickenson since leaving school, apart from his war service. Even I found it incredulous. Bill loved an ordered life and change was rare. Eventually everybody started to take us seriously.

A 'For Sale' sign was being knocked into the ground in Ashtree Way when a gentleman pulled up in his car and asked me if he could talk with me. He informed me that he was extremely interested in buying our house. He went on to tell me that he was a solicitor and was obliged to do the things correctly. I asked him if he would like to look around the house, which he did. He returned later that night with his wife.

I knew the moment the gentleman looked around that there would be a sale. As he left, he said, "It's no good making you an offer, is it?"

"No, I'm afraid not."

That sale must have been completed in record time. Nobody objected to anything and the purchaser, Michael Green, did his own conveyancing. It all went like clockwork. With the money in the bank, we felt secure and that our future was ensured.

Now we had to wait. We had obtained all the documents that were required but the South African emigration department kept us waiting and waiting. After a month of no post or telephone calls from the embassy as well as our endless telephone calls to them, assuring the powers that be, that we had all the relevant papers, I went every day, except Sundays to the South African Embassy. There was always a long queue. Most enquiries were about passports, ours should have been straightforward. Not one person during that tense period could tell me why there was a delay.

Alan telephoned daily for news as he also couldn't understand the delay. It was eventually resolved. My brother was sitting outside his house in Durban as his neighbour arrived home. He called across to Alan. "Hi. How are you doing? When is your sister coming out with her family?"

Alan related the saga and apparently his neighbour Yanni was furious. He worked in a government department. Within one hour of that conversation, we had a telephone call from the embassy requesting us to pick up our immigration documents. It was certainly a question of knowing the right person in the right place.

We weren't sure when our flight would be. When you emigrate, your flights are organised by the embassy. You can't choose the date; they issue the tickets for new immigrants.

It was such an emotional time and awfully hard to deal with. Negative thoughts pervaded my mind, *'Have we made the right decisions?'*

My sister Eileen had offered to put Bill and I up for the last few weeks. Nigel stayed with Melanie and Ken.

We gave away a lot of our home to my sister, to help her furnish her flat and other possessions were offered to other members of the family or friends. All too soon much of our home was disposed of. It was only when I saw those pieces in other people's homes that I realised their loss was a form of sorrow.

The week before we were due to fly, both Bill and I were exhausted. The goodbyes had taken their toll. I was lying on the settee resting with eyes closed when Eileen said, "Aren't you supposed to be saying goodbye to somebody tonight?"

"I am so tired. I wish I could put it off until tomorrow. But I can't as we have no spare slots to fit them in. I'll wash the cups up while you wash your hair."

I was at the sink when my sister came up from behind and threw her arms around me. "I am so sorry for how I treated you in the past. I know I was always cutting you down to size in front of people. When you were born, I was fourteen and you were just another baby in the house. I couldn't believe that that baby blossomed into such a lovely girl. I was so jealous. I was thirty and my life was in such a mess and there you were, all laughter and boyfriends."

I cuddled her. "Eileen, it doesn't matter. I am fine and if it helps you, look at my life today. I have a husband that loves me and three beautiful children. All things in the past have gone. I love you very much and I know you love me too. That is all that matters."

With very red eyes and a very tired face we said goodbye to a couple of old neighbours. Nona and Peter Batchelor were taking us to the airport, so we didn't need to say farewell to them. Our last call was to Ken's parents. We clambered up the path towards the front door, but the house was in darkness. It looked as though they were either out or in bed. It was nine p.m. We banged hard on the door and Doris greeted us whilst switching on the lights. The house was full of our family and friends. We were speechless. The gathering had been organised in complete secrecy. My poor sister said she had been so anxious when I had mentioned to her earlier that we were too tired to go out. It was a wonderful gesture from Ken's parents. I have never forgotten that special night.

Our flight wasn't until six thirty in the evening, the next day. The last-minute messages and phone calls were difficult to cope with. Tears were constantly being shed. It was a relief when Nona and Peter collected us after lunch. Our check in was at 3.15 p.m. The car was strangely silent for the whole journey to Heathrow. We checked in and decided it would be better to go to the departure lounge straight away. We hugged our lovely kind friends. I was filling with tears when Nona said to me, "Don't forget we have an agreement. No tears." She then said something to me in her native Welsh, "God bless and keep you safe." It was years afterwards that I asked her what she had said.

We waved until Nona and Peter were out of sight. Bill said, "That is it, no more tears, from now on it's going to be smiles all the way." Nigel wandered off to buy a few goodies, his pockets were jangling with money that he'd been given. Bill said to me, "Let him do what he likes. It has also been extremely hard for him to leave the family and his friends."

CHAPTER SEVENTEEN

We knew it would be a lengthy flight and were prepared with newspapers, books, goodies to eat and all the paraphernalia that you take on long-haul. The refuelling-stop at Salisbury, now Harare, was a welcome respite. We didn't reveal to each other how we were feeling but I am sure that our thoughts were similar. *'Had we done the right thing? Would we like this new life?'*

Our reverie was broken by the sound of the stewardess announcing that the captain would like to say a few words. "Would Mr and Mrs Durrant and their son raise their hands." We were astounded and complied. "Welcome to South Africa. Folks, this British family has chosen to emigrate to our beautiful country. We wish them well and I think we should give them a good rousing welcome." Everyone in the plane clapped and cheered which made me cry. Alan who was a frequent flyer with the airways had spoken to one of the bosses and arranged the whole thing.

After a short internal flight of an hour, we arrived in Durban. Alan, Kath, and their son Wayne were there to greet us with big smiles and hugs. It was only a short journey to Pinetown from the airport. Alan drove home through the city so that we could see the contrasting architecture of modern Durban with the old colonial buildings. We were suitably impressed but extremely tired.

I had been to Alan and Kath's house on my holiday but both Nigel and Bill were seeing it for the first time. We were told to rest and to have a couple of drinks by the pool. The situation felt completely unreal. A pleasant buffet of food concluded the day and we all crashed into bed exceedingly tired and a little apprehensive.

Bill and I both awoke unrefreshed, with the enormity of our decision now a reality. The nervous tension was apparent to us both. Bill was expected at his new company at ten o'clock. He was to be introduced to his colleagues and the shop floor. The company had given him a week to settle in which was a godsend, as we had so much to arrange.

Registering Nigel for school was first on our 'To Do' list. At the interview, the headteacher stated, "We are a very disciplined school. See that basket of canes, (which was huge and tightly packed,) we use them for any infringement or breaking of rules." He then barked at Nigel, commanding him to stand up straight. Poor boy, he was white with fear. He knew things were going to be vastly different compared with his relaxed schooling at The Cavendish. We were all on tenterhooks and remained silent. When we left the school, we headed for the nearest restaurant in Pinetown. As we sat down Nigel blurted out, "I want to leave before I start. They run that school like a prison."

My heart sank but I did what any mother would do and tried to placate him. "That head made his school sound very disciplined to see what you were made of."

One positive outcome from the interview was that the head discovered Nigel had played basketball for the county. South Africa was introducing the game to all their schools. I hoped this would make life easier for him, but it didn't. It only excused him from learning Afrikaans which was compulsory in their curriculum. It was a battle that Nigel had to face on his own. At first, I drove him to school, but we soon found that the school bus stopped almost outside our house, so we took advantage of that. Bill also got a lift to work from one of his colleagues which freed me to house hunt.

It had been our intention to stay with my family until we bought our own house but within days, we realised that we were crowding their space. One of the estate agents found us a flat to rent, which was conveniently situated, near to both Nigel's school and Bill's place of work.

Estate agents in South Africa at that time, had a different approach to their English counterparts. I viewed houses every day with various agencies. The agents were completely unethical. If we passed a house with a 'For Sale' board outside with a different agent and I remarked, "That looks nice," they immediately responded.

"If you like it, I will go and knock to see if the seller is in." It really was an eyeopener.

Bill joined me at the weekends to view properties. On one occasion we were in an agent's office in Pinetown. We were both talking to the agent face to face but within ten minutes he had turned his chair away from me. I continued to answer some of his questions, and he completely ignored me and waited for Bill's answer or next question. Bill spoke up as soon as he realised what was happening.

"I think you should address my wife. It is she who will decide what type of home she wants. In fact, I don't think we can do business with you."

As we walked out, he called after us. "Perhaps we can do business on another occasion sir." He didn't realise the irony of this last statement.

After weeks of searching, we finally found a property in New Germany which borders Pinetown. It was a huge bungalow with a large overgrown garden. Bill and Nigel were overjoyed that I'd found a property to all our liking. We celebrated by dining out on Durban's seafront. Nigel couldn't believe that it was large enough for him to have his own annexe, complete with a private entrance onto the garden. The bedrooms in the main part of the house were large with adjacent bathrooms. I had a dressing room for the first time in my life. We were able to buy the house outright from the sale of our English home.

We anticipated that the completion date would be relatively quick and had already bought some furniture which had been delivered to the flat.

Week after week went by without completion papers. Everything had been signed for, all we needed was the keys. We got to worrying and I ended up visiting the solicitor's office every day. There was always a cock and bull story as to why I couldn't see the solicitor in charge. One day in desperation I told the office staff that I would not leave until I saw the head of the practice. When I finally saw him, I was fobbed off with a promise that a call would be made to Pretoria, the seat of government, to find out what was causing the delay. I left the office that Friday with a heavy heart.

All three of us felt despondent. Alan's friend invited us to a barbeque the next day which we readily accepted hoping it would cheer us up. After we had all eaten the dancing started. A young man who was a friend of the host's daughter asked me to dance. We chatted about this and that whilst we danced. Then he asked me how things were progressing with the house. I related the sorry saga and then he surprised me.

"I can tell you the date of when you will get your keys."

"How could you possibly know that?"

"I work in that office as a trainee and your money has been loaned out. They have lent it out for a month. On its return they will transfer it to the seller and then you will have your house. It is nothing to do with Pretoria holding on to the deeds. It's the greed of the solicitors. They invest your money."

Armed with that information I took myself to the solicitor's the next morning and waited for them to open. The boss walked by me to enter the office and said all in one breath, "Oh I am so sorry, but we are still awaiting news from Pretoria."

"I have got news for you. I want our house deeds and keys by this afternoon, or you will answer to the high court for fraudulent use of our money."

By 2 p.m. that day we had both the deeds and the keys. I didn't want to get the young boy into trouble, so I told the solicitor that I had a friend in high places in Pretoria and they had given me the information.

We had little packing to do in the flat. Most of our possession were in cardboard boxes and the new furniture was still wrapped in polythene. We went to bed that night in a state of euphoria. I undressed, took my jewellery off, and placed it on the dressing table and fell into bed only to lay awake until the morning.

It was pouring with rain and much to our horror an open back lorry turned up. I rushed out. "This must be a mistake."

"All our furniture is moved by these lorries," said the man in charge. Don't worry we have covers for everything." Bill joined me in protest but to no avail.

"It's only local, we only use the covered vans for the long hauls."

We gave up and followed the open van to our new home. As we got to the bungalow, I suddenly remembered that I hadn't picked up my gold bracelets from the dressing table. I asked the removal men about them, but no one had seen them. I was distraught. We were not insured at that time. Bill tried to console me by saying they were not important. In England each bracelet had been valued at five hundred pounds. What a start. We contacted the police after the removal company had left. Two detectives were sent to interview us the next morning. Their indifference was unbelievable. They left saying they would make enquiries but not to be too hopeful.

Bill's cousin Henry lived in Durban and was in the police force. Bill intended to telephone Henry and tell him of the loss but before he had time to do this there was a surprise knock on the door. It was the senior man from the removal team. He reported that they had looked everywhere on the lorry and in the flat, but the jewellery was nowhere to be seen. We knew that they couldn't have looked in the flat as we had the keys. As the gentleman was leaving, I said, "We have family in the police in Durban and they will take over the enquiry."

He left saying, "I am very sorry."

I thought well that's that. We had so much to unpack and that had to take priority.

We had heard about the rainy season in Durban, but I was totally unprepared for the volume and intensity. I was incredibly grateful that we had plenty of garage space to keep the packing boxes dry. The car would have to stay on the drive for the foreseeable.

The following day I watched the rain pour down the drive like a river. Now I knew why there were substantial drains in front of the house and garage. When it was time to collect Bill from work, I made a dash to the car, virtually throwing myself onto the driver's seat. When I went to buckle up my seat belt, I couldn't believe my eyes. There on the passenger seat were my gold bracelets. They had been returned. We were told by Henry that when the thieves knew that the police were involved and that one was a family member, they must have decided to return the lot. Thank goodness!

On my brother's advice we employed a team of young men to help us with the task of clearing the garden. It was a shock to discover that we had a secondary garden that had been hidden from view by overgrown hedges and trees. The garden was three acres in size. For a month I supervised the clearance. The team of garden boys came up trumps. They removed all the rubbish and consulted with me before they dug up plants and bushes. Bill had employed the team for one month, but we soon realised that we would need at least two workers full time every weekend on a permanent basis.

One of the young boys stood out from the rest. He had an abundance of common sense and a great feel for the needs of the plants. His name was Selby. He was a most handsome young man of fifteen. We asked him to choose who he wanted as a co-worker. Jerome was his choice. When I asked him why he had chosen Jerome he said, "Well mam he does as he is told and won't dig up anything unless I tell him to."

What a revelation those grounds proved to be. We unearthed beautifully shaped flower beds with the most delightful plants and shrubs. They certainly had been lovingly attended to until the property had been vacated over a year ago. Most days I worked outside which gave me great delight and helped me to adjust to my new life.

When we gained access to the side plot, I couldn't believe what

139

pleasures awaited me. We had fifty-six banana trees, red and white grape vines, lemon trees laden with masses of fruit. Pineapples laid like a golden rug under the lemon trees. I stood talking to myself saying repeatedly, "I don't believe it. This is all ours." I am sure that various people who would have looked around the property with a view to buying it, failed to realise that its biggest treasure was the overgrown garden.

The bungalow was built on a corner plot with rolling lawns. I wasn't surprised to learn from a neighbour that the previous owner was a builder and his wife a landscape gardener. The annexe had been built for his parents.

A barbecue with tiled areas for serving food was built into the bank. The area even included a tiled floor for dancing. The view extended to Signal Hill in Durban.

It wasn't too long before we gave the first of our parties. It was reassuring to know that we could plan weeks ahead of time and not have to worry about the weather. On this first occasion we invited all our English friends and Bill's work colleagues. Everyone was very complimentary about the beautiful grounds and seemed genuinely pleased for us. A few of our guests were not so fortunate and had emigrated without funds and were in rented accommodation with no opportunity in the foreseeable future to attain their own property. I remember looking up into the trees and watching the lanterns twinkling, thinking I am going to wake up anytime soon.

When we fell into bed that night, we both looked at each other and started to laugh.

"Is this for real Jane?"

"Too right it is. I can pinch you if you like."

CHAPER EIGHTEEN

Every morning I arose early before Bill and Nigel to prepare breakfast. I always included Gladys, our maid. I was told by many friends that I wasn't handling having a maid correctly, especially when I greeted her every morning with breakfast. They suggested that I stay in bed and await my breakfast. I didn't ever change my ways and we had happy staff working for us.

On Saturdays I started the morning by cooking breakfast for the garden boys. I had noticed that they always brought with them mealie meal, a milled white maize, not dissimilar to porridge. It didn't look very appetising. On one of the first Saturdays that the boys worked for us, they smelt me cooking breakfast. I overheard Selby's conversation with Jerome. "Isn't the boss lucky to have such good food." Every Saturday after that, they made sure they worked around the back, near the kitchen door. I started to make them a full English breakfast from then on. I was told that I was the greatest 'mam' in South Africa. They used to come to the kitchen when it was ready and take their breakfast to the front garden. Selby would often call out to the garden boys across the road. "Look what we have! You must get yourselves jobs with the English. Their ladies do their own cooking." The banter between the young boys always brought a smile to my face.

Selby was a decent young man and very caring, especially towards his mother. Most of the children that we got to know had absent fathers. Every week Selby used to bring items with him that needed to be repaired. It was generally something to help his mother. He always asked Bill if he could use his tools and bench during his lunch break. We were happy to encourage him. Different friends warned Bill that he would lose his tools etc. but we never did. However, we did wonder what was happening to our empties.

We used to buy bottles of beer and soft drinks by the crate, which were returnable. Slowly they vanished but never too many at one time.

Bill always watched the boys ride off on Selby's cycle after they had been given their wages so we knew it couldn't be them. On one of our walks around the garden Bill caught sight of a plastic carrier bag concealed within the hedgerow. It was full of empty bottles. Our young boys were so artful that they had worked out, that once they had said their farewells, they could cycle around the corner to retrieve the empties. My brother and our friends all advised us to sack them. We talked it over and decided to confront them and give them another chance. They were both regretful but only because they had been caught out. Bill took them to task. "If you take as much as a plant without permission you will be sacked." As far as I know it didn't happen again.

Gladys worked for us full-time and soon became part of our family. She was a very loyal person, and it was hard to remember that she wasn't a family member but paid staff. We gave her every weekend off from around lunchtime on a Friday to Monday morning. She should have returned to work by 7.30 a.m. but never did. She used to saunter in much later. I often saw her ambling up the road where she would stop and stand gossiping with anybody she encountered. On her arrival in the house, she would look at me and say, "I have been here for an hour already Mam." This was how she was, and nothing would change it. It didn't matter how kind you were. On one occasion I was looking through my bedroom shelves and couldn't find my tights. There was well over a dozen pairs of new ones, still in their packets, plus more that I had worn. When I enquired about the tights, Gladys said, "Oh, Mam I took them and sold them in the township. You don't wear them." I was speechless. A few strong words from Bill were uttered to Gladys. Afterwards she said, "Oh, Mam my daddy is so cross with me."

My friends had warned me about the stealing that went on. We had to live with it, and we got used to it. Apartheid was still in existence and employment for the majority of black South Africans was extremely limited. Stealing, for some, was a way of life and supplemented their income.

After breakfast I used to have a leisurely bath. This has been one of my luxuries for all my adult life. I used to put masses of lotion into the water, lie back and reminisce. When I was younger, I used to sing songs of the era. I think my pleasure of soaking in a bath came from the fact that there were always people surrounding me and the bath was the only place of solitude. My bathroom in Durban was huge. When I sang, I used to have a fit of the giggles because my voice would echo around the room.

I often decided to meet up for coffee or lunch with one friend or another. We often visited a new phenomenon called a shopping mall. On my first visit I was astounded at the luxury. Marble was in abundance with vast expanses of gleaming glass. All the global brands were there, as well as every type of restaurant that one could wish for. It was 1975. I was forty-five and still enjoyed window shopping. After a light lunch in the mall, I would return home to be there for Nigel and Bill's return.

After a time, I began the find this routine boring and only went to the shopping malls with Bill on a Saturday, when Nigel was at school playing basketball. A few visits were enough for Bill, he saw no attraction in the mall. He often said to me, "I would rather be on Hemel market any day."

The once exciting barbeques became very mundane with the same people attending. Conversation was constrained, enquiring about family or passing comment on the political changes happening in the country. Polite smiles or "Can I get you a drink?" weren't enough for me. Life was beginning to lose its sparkle.

We had the odd visitor, but I was particularly looking forward to having my two nurse friends staying with us. Janet and Maureen were coming for a month, and we had planned many things. Bill was excited to show off South Africa to them.

The moment they got off the plane they were greeted by heavy rains. They really teased us about our beautiful climate. We drove from the airport with heavy rain beating against the car windows. Their first view of the country was that of thousands of black bin bags covering the illegal shanty dwellings that lined the road. Not an impressive sight for any visitor. I have been told that they still exist today. This is not just a South African problem but a global one.

We soon arrived in New Germany. It gave us such pleasure to show them our home and garden. This was the start of a wonderful month for us all. We visited various places from the Sharks Board on the waterfront to the city's sugar factory, temples, and mosques. Gladys was pleased that Janet and Maureen were staying with us and asked me if they could stay forever. She liked that the house was filled with laughter every day.

All five of us were ecstatic about the forthcoming weekend trip we had planned, to the Drakensberg mountains.

It was a long journey. Our first impression of the hotel was that it was very grand and situated in beautiful grounds. We checked in and went straight to our rooms. I sat on the double bed, and it collapsed. I think the laughter must have filled the whole hotel.

It proved to be a wonderful weekend. We went on a horse trek. I had never ridden a horse before, so I was last in line with a member of staff following behind on foot. We traversed at a snail's pace until the horse was given a tap with the guide's riding crop. The horse swiftly began to trot under trees and over small streams. I was petrified. Suddenly, all the horses went into a walking pace. They were used to doing this trek with tourists and visitors and realised that they were halfway. Eventually, we trotted back to the hotel.

Whilst we were walking back up the drive a horseman rode across the path in front of us. He looked like a rider you would expect to see in an Australian setting. He had a huge leather coat down to his riding boots and his Stetson had corks dangling from its brim. He put his hand up in greeting then suddenly motioned us to stop. He struck the ground hard with his knobkerrie. There in front of us was a black mamba, a highly venomous snake. He smiled at us and said, "It's okay. It's dead." Maureen chuckled and spontaneously retorted, "If he isn't dead now, he will have a bloody big headache." All of us convulsed with laughter.

On our final day we went into a local village. It was like entering a wild west movie. There were splintering wooden sidewalks and the general store was incredible. It had various tins of food for sale, but all the cans were rusty. In the store were two African women in full tribal dress with red ochre over their faces. They wore bangles not only on their necks but on their legs too from their ankles to their knees. It was remarkable to see them and totally unexpected.

It was with great disappointment and with tears in our eyes that we said our goodbyes to Janet and Maureen. Their company had been uplifting and was what we all needed. They promised to return.

I formed a friendship with a German lady called Brunhilda, or Brun for short. She was the wife of a director at Alan's place of work. We really gelled. Our trips out and the conversation we had were an absolute delight. We had so much in common and were soulmates. Although we haven't seen each other for over forty years I know should we meet, we would be able to resume our friendship as if the intervening years didn't exist. As old as I am, I know my life would be further enriched.

Our anticipation of a visit from Andrea lit up our lives. She had finished her final year at college and could now relax and enjoy a holiday with us. We waited with bated breaths at the airport for her plane to arrive. Our excitement cannot be exaggerated. All three of us were on a high. She arrived to so much love, we couldn't stop hugging her. We didn't know what to do first on our arrival home, show her the house, the garden or eat our prepared meal. She chose to fuss the dogs then view the garden.

Gladys stayed on specifically, shook Andrea's hand and greeted her in Zulu, calling her 'daughter of the house.' Whenever Gladys referred to Andrea, she would always refer to her by that name. She never used her first name.

We enjoyed every moment that we shared with Andrea. Every day was filled with the excitement that you get when showing off your locality. Andrea and I spent our mornings exploring various places with the late afternoons reserved for Bill and Nigel. We often strolled along the sea front in Durban plus the docks where we watched the twinkling lights of the huge passenger liners that queued in line to get to their berths. The waterfront in Durban had been redeveloped. It was quite an exciting place to visit. All the old warehouses had been renovated and there was a profusion of trendy shops. On the edge of the jetties, there were dozens of seals basking on the pier supports or wherever they could find a perch. Their shrieks and cries could be deafening.

Andrea and I were often invited to Brun's for lunch or tea and Brun joined us on several day trips. The three months with Andrea flew by and we hated that she had to return to the UK.

Greta and Peter, an English couple from Lowestoft, lived behind us. Alan introduced them to us, and they became our staunchest friends. We would often enjoy meals at each other's house and attend may other social functions together. Greta walked her incredibly old dog Sparky, past our house daily, and our two dogs would frantically scramble to join them. Tara, a small terrier, was the right size for Greta but Ringo, our bull mastiff, was far too large to join them. I would have to placate him with a walk around the grounds.

We had acquired the dogs from a rescue centre before we moved. Alan had visited the centre with an enquiry and decided to walk around the kennels whilst waiting to be seen. He spoke to the various dogs through their cages and stroked their heads. One cage had the name Ringo above it. The bull mastiff crawled to the front. He was emaciated and tried to hold his paw up. The effort exhausted him and made Alan want to cry. Alan came to see me that night, at the flat, to ask if we would take the dog when we moved. Bill protested. "We don't want to start off with a sick dog." Alan had to return the next day for business reasons. Of course, he asked me to go and look at this dog. I was open minded and didn't make any promises. We arrived at the rescue centre and went straight to Ringo's kennel. I cried. Ringo's whole body was covered with scars, evidence of him having been beaten. Every rib projected from his body. Alan called out, "Ringo!" This skeleton of a dog got up, came over to us and tried to lift his paw. I knew we would have to save him.

I was worried what Bill would say about my decision. He knew I would be coming home with a dog but not poor Ringo. That evening Bill and Nigel came to the kennels with me. On reaching the kennel, Ringo heard my voice and made the effort to crawl to the front, lifting his tail just enough from the ground to wag it. Bill's first thought was that Ringo wouldn't live long enough to get home. Then he questioned how we would afford the vet bills. We hadn't sorted out our own finances; now we were adding to them. Bill soon capitulated and all the relevant paperwork was completed. On our way to the exit, we passed many cages. I caught sight of a little terrier type dog with enormous bat like ears. Her name was Tara. Her little paws were through the netting and her tail was wagging so ferociously, it looked as though it would fall off. She was an unwanted Christmas present. In two minutes flat I said, "Why don't we take her, she is so small compared to Ringo and is in a perfect condition." Tara was now part of the family.

Pets were not allowed in the apartments where we lived. I went to see the caretaker who was a very understanding Scotsman. I explained that we were paying board for Ringo and if we had to pay board for Tara, we would not be able to rescue her. He was so kind. "How can I deny a little dog a home?"

Tara lived at the flat with us and I visited Ringo every day for the following two weeks. I collected him the day after we moved in. Alan came with me as we were unsure as to how he would travel. I was so shocked when I put him on his lead as he was in a far worse state that I had assessed. He lay on the back seat of the car and instantly relieved himself from both ends.

After cleaning Ringo, he was put in the kitchen to lay on the cold tiles of the kitchen floor. We realised that he had never been in a house before. Tara looked at him and sniffed around. There was no confrontation.

As soon as Bill returned from work, he took Ringo to the vet. The vet was small in stature, so Bill lifted Ringo onto the surgery table.

"This poor dog will never make it. He has been starved and ill-treated for far too long." He lifted Ringo off the table and stood on the scales with him in his arms. "This is the first time in my career that I have ever been able to hold a bull mastiff in my arms. I think he is past saving but it's your decision."

Ringo stayed in the same position on the kitchen floor for one month, only leaving when nature deemed it necessary. I used to sit beside him and tempt him with morsels of food. When I felt that he was accepting a little more I hit on the idea of dipping bread into beaten eggs then frying it in olive oil. This started his recovery. Ringo stood up within a couple of days and I was able to take him for short walks in the garden. We were all overjoyed. Bill returned with him to the vet after one month. He too couldn't believe the improvement.

Our dogs proved to be such an asset. Not only were they a loving part of the family, but they were also an incredibly good deterrent to any prospective burglars. On one occasion Andrea and I were sitting on the stoop at the back of the house. I could hear Tara yapping. She was tied up at the front of the house. I went around to the front with my knitting still in my hands. A man advanced towards me and asked if I could give him a job or some money. He had a knobkerrie in his hand. He noticed that our small dog was tied up and no one else was around. He advanced towards me in a very threatening manner. I shrieked out, "Ringo" several times. He rapidly bounded out of the open door and jumped at the intruder who ran off with the dog pursuing him. Ringo chased him until he left our property boundary. It was very scary and made me much more cautious. It was a lesson to both Andrea and me.

With Andrea's holiday at an end, we suggested to Melanie that she and the baby travel to us in the new year. Both Bill and I already knew the value of family visits.

Preparations were made for Christmas. We dressed a tree and hung a few decorations around in the attempt to recreate the Christmases we had had at home. It was to no avail, all three of us went around with gloomy faces and heavy hearts. In England, our house had always been at the centre of all family celebrations with Christmas being the most special. A hard act to follow with very new friends replacing family.

On Christmas day Alan and Kath had organised a barbecue on the beach in Boulders Bay. Alan had booked a game of squash before leaving for the beach. Kath, Wayne, Nigel, and I collected Bill and Alan on the way to the beach. All I wanted to do was to sit down and cry. I felt bereaved. I think that was the day when Bill could see that we had an uphill battle before us. I know I did, but we kept the truth from each other for a considerable time.

Our next visitor was completely unexpected. A telephone call from Rhodesia came as a complete surprise. An acquaintance from the Townswomen's Guild had gone there for a month's holiday and decided that she would like to travel to South Africa and extend her vacation. We were put on the spot. What could I say other than yes, come? She wasn't a close friend and it proved to be an awfully long month. I found it hard going and both Bill and Nigel protested, "We told you so. It would have been easier if you had said it wasn't convenient from the start."

Nigel had settled into school but still hated it, but his social life had improved greatly. He had taken to South Africa his prized set of drums. As his apartment was so large and away from the main living rooms, he was able to practice whenever he wished. This uplifted his spirit. He and some friends formed a group with guitars, drums, and keyboard. He was counting down the days until he could leave school and get into the music scene. His improved spirit and attitude did alleviate our worries.

Bill always had a smile for me and yet I knew he was finding things a little hard at times. I would catch him looking into space with a sad expression on his face. When I enquired how he was he would always reply that all was well.

Bill was asked to attend a special meeting at work involving the management team and company directors. He confessed to me that he felt a little concerned as he had not been given any paperwork concerning the matter being discussed. He was also aware that colleagues had sometimes stopped conversations when he walked into the management rest room for his breaks.

"I really cannot think of a thing that I have done with respect to my job." All the machinery used in Durban had been sent from England. Bill knew it inside out. He was already experienced in the new computerised machines and was technically way ahead of anyone in the Durban management team.

Bill left home looking very strained. I was extremely anxious. I wished I could have attended the meeting instead of him. What a long agonising day it was, waiting for him to return home.

I watched the car come down the drive, my heart was beating so fast. Bill caught sight of me and gave the biggest smile possible. I couldn't wait for him to get out of the car to relate his news.

"Jane put the kettle on and make us some sandwiches because it's going to take me an hour to tell you what it was all about,"

"Bill, go and tell Nigel to join us." I had completely forgotten that he was at a basketball practice.

"I don't want him to know. It's not a good story and shows the immoral side of the business world."

Apparently, Bill was shown lots of paperwork, sheets and sheets, then asked to read enough to get the gist of what this enquiry was about. Bill suggested that if it was important enough to convene an upper management meeting then he should be given time to read it all. For over an hour he sat and read all the paperwork whilst the board talked, drank coffee, and smoked. It was difficult for him to absorb what he was reading. However, he finished, noted the signature at the bottom of the final page, then handed it back to the chairman.

"It looks a shamble. I really don't know why you want my opinion."

"Is that all you can say when the loss of that order has cost us hundreds of thousands of Rands, and that company has now cancelled all future business with us. Can you give us a reason why you allowed this catastrophe to get past you? You cannot deny that you signed for it."

"Yes, I saw somebody had written my name on the final page, however it was not me and that is not my signature."

Bill said the board huddled together and there was a lot of muttering. He felt very embarrassed but also concerned that somebody had signed his name. He wondered how it was all going to end.

"I felt sick Jane and just wanted to run away."

The papers were still in Bill's hand, and he kept staring at the signature waiting for divine intervention. Nerves made him play around with the papers. He rolled his wrist which made the first page uppermost. He stood up from the board table. The whole boardroom fell silent. They thought they were about to witness Bill walking out or resigning.

"Mr Chairman and members of the board please look at the first page of your brief and note the date. This transaction was instigated two days before I arrived in your country. Start your inquiries there."

After an in-depth investigation, two men were dismissed from the company. However, Bill never felt the same about working there. He sensed there had to be more than one department involved.

This experienced coupled with our homesickness prompted us

to make the decision to sell up and return to the UK. The whole South African experience enriched our lives. When I reflect on the time, it is always with a smile and great affection. Bill once said that he thought of it as an expensive holiday. At least we both felt the same. We didn't count the money that it had cost. The experience was beyond price.

CHAPTER NINETEEN

Our journey back home was completely different. Outward bound was exciting even though we were apprehensive. Everything was unknown but at the same time we were organised. Now it was a different kettle of fish. We had to live with Melanie and Ken whilst looking for a home and a job for Bill. Dickinson's had said that there would always be a job waiting for Bill should he return from South Africa. However, his senior position had been filled, making things vastly different. Me finding a job immediately wasn't important. The priority had to be the purchase of a house. Nigel was now of the age to leave school or go on to further education which he didn't want to do. He found himself a job in one of the Dickinson's offices. We were not happy that he had found an easy solution too swiftly. However, he was employed and for that we were grateful.

Bill went for an interview with Waterlow's at Dunstable. He came home very down in the dumps because the company's technology wasn't as advanced as he was used to. Bill felt his options were limited. He returned to Dickinson's for a further interview with his old bosses, who were delighted that he had reconsidered their offer. He was now back to where his career had started.

I house hunted daily. We realised that we couldn't afford a house similar in standard to our previous home. House prices had risen in the eighteen months that we had been away. It was another difficult time for us all. Ken and Melanie were sharing their home without complaint but having three extra adults was a bit formidable for a young couple with a toddler. Our intrusion was a daily concern for me. Bill's aunts had offered us a couple of rooms in their house, which was so kind of them, but we would have been in the same situation.

My search was restricted by the fact that the property had to be under £20,000. We wanted to pay cash and not have a mortgage. I became apprehensive. I always dropped Bill off at work before house hunting. As he kissed me goodbye, he said the same thing every time. "Don't worry Jane, today's the day. I know you will find something." After a few fruitless days of search those words of comfort failed to console me.

I finally found an older, reasonably sized house, in the older part of the Hemel. It was very solid, needed a bit of T.L.C. but I knew I could make it into a home. It was priced at eighteen thousand pounds, but I managed to get it for seventeen. The saving allowed us to spend a thousand pounds on alterations to make a larger sitting room. Eventually our furniture arrived from South Africa, and we were able to move in. That was such a relief and extremely heartening. We were able to settle back into a routine. It almost felt that we hadn't been away.

On one of my shopping trips to the town, I bumped into an old friend from the Townswomen's Guild. The Guild were having a committee meeting that night and she asked me to join them. I eagerly accepted as I realised, I would be able to see at least a dozen of my old friends. I arrived after they had completed the business side of the meeting and was given a lovely reception plus an informal welcome home supper. There were shrieks of laughter as we recalled all the fun we had had in the Guild's infancy. We were all novices at that time but now the ladies of the Stoneycroft Guild were mentors to newly formed guilds.

After we had finished eating the current chairman spoke to me. "Jane, you don't want a job, do you? I need to employ another receptionist at my surgery." I couldn't believe my good fortune. I was delighted and promptly replied, "Please set up an interview."

"You don't need one. The doctors already know you and I am the one that makes the final decision. Can you start on Monday?"

I drove home on cloud nine then celebrated with Bill and Nigel. I felt it was a gift from heaven. We would be able to live comfortably. How fortunate we were. Our South African adventure had been a costly one but now we would be able to build up Bill's pension fund after his break in service. The future would be of our own making.

The following Monday morning I got ready for work, with more than a few butterflies in my stomach. I had never worked as a doctors' receptionist before. The position entailed much more than making appointments in a diary. Something was going on every moment of the working day. There were clinics for every major illness known to humanity. My many years of working on the district gave me an advantage, in that, most of the surgeries I was dealing with knew me. It wasn't too long before I felt competent and experienced on the front desk.

Every day was different. Most patients were polite, others not so. One patient used to brandish his walking stick and hit the desk. One of Andrea's friends, who worked for the D.H.S.S. related a story to us of a man who regularly attended the office. She hated being on the other side of the counter when he came in because he aggressively waved a stick and always struck the counter. It was of course the same man.

Life at the surgery was busy and often demanding but I adored my job. Staff came and went. It was a teaching practice for G.P. training which meant that we had many new young doctors passing through. It made life at work so interesting. The doctors came from across the globe. Whenever we had a social gathering, family members were invited. Everyone used to bring special dishes from their home countries for us to enjoy. What a delicious variety of worldwide cuisine we got to taste.

The reception staff started to sense that something was going on within the surgery. We were excluded from conferences, and this went on for weeks. In the end, the senior partner invited us to the upstairs office where he revealed plans for the future. The surgery was going to relocate to a brand-new purpose-built surgery in the heart of Hemel Hempstead's town centre. We were astounded. It was going to be cutting edge. All the equipment would be new, and every doctor would have their own examination room. It was so luxurious we found it hard to imagine and hard to take in. It would take two years to complete. We were already updating patient files but now discovered they were for the future computing system.

In those days, the most senior member of the office staff was the head receptionist. Suddenly we were presented with a practice manager. She had her desk upstairs with the secretarial staff. We didn't understand her function at the time. She often popped down to look at how we organised the various clinics, and we willingly showed her. How gullible we were. It didn't take long for our head receptionist to resign.

To my surprise I received a letter giving me a raise in salary and thanking me for all the hard work I was doing for the practice. The very next day I received yet another letter offering me a further rise in salary and promotion to head receptionist. It was all overwhelming, but I accepted as I felt I had worked hard for the position. Life at work didn't really change for me. What did change was the surgery. It had been like a family but now it was like a commercial office. Even the junior partners seemed to take over from the senior partners. It was called progress and moving with the times.

My mother lived quite close to the surgery which proved an asset at times and was intrusive at others. In the time that I lived in South Africa my mother had become friendly with another tenant. She seemed a very considerate woman, without any family of her own. I had met Grace on several occasions before we emigrated and felt relieved that my mother would have a nice friend in her. On my return I couldn't believe what had happened to their relationship. My mother was doing nothing in the way of domestic work. Grace was doing everything, almost like a paid servant. My mother just sat and expressed her wishes. Grace had taken over and my mother had allowed it to happen. She liked having an unpaid housekeeper.

My mother was now eighty years of age. She could have easily completed most household chores with a home help. I couldn't believe what had happened to my mother's independence in eighteen months. Mum was in a dilemma. Grace had now taken over completely. My mother didn't like it but couldn't get out of the relationship. Now I was back in Hemel she thought I would take over and she could push Grace out. A crying Grace was often outside the surgery waiting to relate the latest saga. On other occasions she would enter my kitchen at eight fifteen, in the morning, to walk with me to the surgery and relate more tales of woe. It was becoming intolerable for me. I called my siblings to request a meeting to discuss the situation which had put an enormous strain on me.

The warden informed me that she had had enough of Grace complaining to her and my mother ringing her. When my mother called for the warden, the warden called me. It wasn't uncommon for me to walk down to Apsley over the dark and sinister canal bridge at 3 a.m. in the morning, only to find there was nothing wrong with my mother, she couldn't sleep, or Grace had walked along the corridor in the early hours to see if she was awake and wanted a cup of tea. It was becoming a nightmare for me. Bill supported me but felt powerless. He knew that I couldn't ignore her. Each time I thought, *'What if she really is ill?'*

The discussion with my siblings resulted in zilch happening. Eileen, my eldest sister lived close by, but she and my mother always fell out if they were in the same room for more than ten minutes. Bette, my second sister, travelled from Chepstow on the coach every two months. She used to spend a couple of hours with Mum then take herself off to Watford or St Albans to shop. She declared that one hour of Grace and Mum was enough. My eldest brother Bob called every couple of months before returning home to Crawley from his job at Heathrow airport. Sandy, my second brother, lived in Norfolk and only came once in six months. Alan lived in Durban and only visited when business required him to visit England. Life was proving tough for me, and I couldn't see a way to solve the problem. My headaches were proving to be permanent. Work was my only respite from the pressure of my mother.

I was at work and an incoming call asked for me personally. It was from the Casualty department, informing me that my sister Eileen had been admitted, suffering from a cardiac arrest. It was imperative that I made my way to the hospital. Of course, I left work instantly and arrived at the hospital within ten minutes.

My sister was still on the stretcher that she had been brought in on. It was placed on the floor. This was 1979 and I couldn't believe what I was looking at. I rushed to the first member of staff to complain. Apparently, my sister was waiting to be moved to the cardiac unit at St Paul's, which was at the other end of the town. Eileen was able to talk to me through her oxygen mask, but I asked her to be quiet and to save her strength.

I followed the ambulance to St Paul's and waited outside the unit only to be informed that she had arrested again and was now on a life support machine. It was all unbelievable. I contacted my siblings who all descended on Hemel from various parts of the country. I visited Eileen several times a day. After a week it was decided by the cardiac doctors to turn off the life support. It was an incredibly traumatic time. She had only just become independent and loved her little flat. At sixty-three, life still had a lot to offer. She was the happiest she had been for years. Earlier that year Eileen told me that she couldn't believe that she now had a normal life and had made friends with Betty, who lived in the flat below. *"We go shopping together on my days off from Halfords. I can do anything I like now."* Remembering those words comforted me.

My mother never asked about Eileen. I waited for her to complain about Eileen not visiting. I thought, as did my siblings, that when she mentioned Eileen, that would be a good time to tell her what had happened. It never arose because Mum never discussed her. The funeral came and went without her knowing.

Three years later my brother Sandy became extremely ill. He had severe headaches which required him to have sedation. Eventually the headaches became life threatening. He was admitted to hospital in

Yarmouth with a terminal brain tumour. Once again, we were devastated. Sandy was only fifty-seven.

On the day of the funeral, we experienced severe snow fall and people were advised not to travel. We travelled in a convoy but only got as far as the garage near the M1 motorway before Andrea had to abandon her sports car. By the time we reached the far side of the county the snow had disappeared, making the journey less hazardous. After the service at a crematorium near Yarmouth we came out to find the rear window of the car had been shattered into fragments. It made the journey home difficult for both driver and passengers on the back seat.

Although my mother knew Sandy had been unwell, she didn't enquire about him. For a couple of weeks, I kept repeating how ill Sandy was to prepare her for his death. Once again, she made no acknowledgement. My mother went on for the rest of her days never mentioning either of her two children. I always looked for signs of stress or for clues as to whether she was carrying the grief, but I never saw them. I had studied a course on bereavement and had qualified as a counsellor for the Cruse organisation. I was surrounded by professionals and heeded their advice. Life for Mum seemed to be the same.

Unbeknownst to me the warden arranged for a social worker to assess my mother. This was a total surprise. Mum only left her flat on Sundays when she came to our home for the day. She didn't socialise in the communal areas of the building, so all the information that the warden obtained had to be sourced from Grace, who was a very emotionally disturbed lady or from listening in through the intercom. However, I went along with this as I felt I might learn something from a professional.

The meeting was a complete whitewash. Some statements about my mother were true but others were skewed in Grace's favour. Yes, my mother did lock her front door to keep Grace out. The fact that Grace sometimes called at 6.30 a.m. didn't enter the equation. I listened very carefully to all that was said, although I felt the interview and its findings was a foregone conclusion. My main concern was to break Grace's hold over of my mother by getting professional advice. Mum was booked for a further assessment, but this time it would be residential, to determine if she needed extra care. It was a little hard to take on board when my mother saw me seven days a week. She didn't have the usual problems of the elderly. I dealt with her grocery shopping and clothes, plus her personal hygiene.

After the interview I was told I would be informed as to when and where the next assessment would be held. Only a couple of days passed before the letter dropped through my letterbox. I was horrified to read that the assessment was to be based at Hill End Hospital in St Albans. Hill End was a mental health hospital.

My frantic call to Social Services revealed that the assessment unit wasn't in the main part of the hospital but a facility in the grounds. I was then informed that Social Services would arrange transportation.

"You will not," was my stern reply. "She will be frightened. I need to take her myself, so that she knows I am there to support her."

It was so difficult to make this proposal sound as though it was an everyday occurrence to Mum. I packed a case, and a very reluctant mother was driven to St Albans. I spoke to her constantly as we drove there, but my sad, frightened mother was silent.

On entering the grounds, I found that the department was away from the main hospital and there was no suggestion of it being a mental health facility. We were greeted by very friendly staff and Mum was shown her bedroom. We were then introduced to the other elderly patients who were being assessed too. It was all very friendly. I left a very tearful mother but tried to reassure her by telling her that I would see her that evening.

I kept my promise. Mum was the only one with a visitor. She was tearful but I was delighted that she introduced me to one or two of the other guests. I left promising her that I would see her the next day.

My visits were productive. Mother's pleasure on seeing me was evident. I could see she was developing her social skills again. Her spirits had been raised by meeting new people. My visits were usually at the weekend which meant the staff on duty couldn't give me information about Mum's progress. I telephoned the social workers but was usually fobbed off with, "She is doing fine." After three weeks there was still no discussion about when Mum would be discharged. I sensed that something was going on, or decisions were being made and I was being kept completely in the dark. I questioned Mum about what she did during the day and concluded that the patients were only being watched regarding their ability to relate to each other. I made the decision to take her home back to her flat. I knew something didn't seem right.

I arrived on the Saturday and told Mum that I was taking her home. Of course, she was delighted. Apparently, the warden went crazy and tried to get hold of the emergency social worker. I questioned how empowered a warden was to have such an influence over a tenant's life. The warden's use of the intercom system in that building had a lot to answer for. Much was overheard, including private family discussions. I am pleased to say that now there are the means to prevent this intrusion.

Monday came and my battle with Social Services started. Evidently, my mother had been doing well and the end of the assessment was in sight. I persuaded my mother to complete the course and she went back to the unit with the assurance that she could come home if she wasn't happy. I dropped her off and promised to visit as before.

It was a week or just over when I visited the hospital and couldn't see Mum. I checked the toilet, couldn't find her, so asked a member of the night staff where she was. "I don't know but I know a lady has been transferred to another ward."

"That can't be her, because unless she is ill, she wouldn't be in a ward." A telephone call was made, and the same member of staff confirmed that it was Mum who had been transferred.

"Was she ill?"

"I don't know. You won't be able to visit her tonight. They don't allow visiting at night."

I was enraged but very frightened. I asked where the ward was and found my way into the heart of the mental institution. I knocked heavily on a door and heard a voice calling out. "I am coming. I am coming." The door was opened by a petite nurse who informed me that she was the Ward Sister. She said she would prefer me to return in the morning as they were getting people into bed and were short staffed, but I refused to leave without seeing my mother. I think the sister could see my determination and perhaps fear.

"Come in. You may have to wait. I will go and consult my colleague."

It transpired that my mother hadn't been put to bed. I waited for a while in the office before being taken to see my her.

Nothing in this world could have prepared me for the sight I was about to see. The double doors swung open; my heart plummeted. I felt I was entering hell. There must have been forty beds in the large space. There were beds down the centre of the ward with their iron headboards resting back-to-back and all the beds lining the sides of the ward were about a foot apart. Every conceivable space had a bed. The noise was alarming, literally bedlam. At the far end of this hellhole were some armchairs with patients sitting in them. Some had their hands fastened to their chairs. I found Mum there, wearing a nightdress that wasn't hers. She looked terrified. I found it all unreal. I cuddled her and she shouted out, "I told you that my Jeannie would come and find me." Mum wasn't confined in her chair, she had freedom of movement but was so petrified she didn't want to go anywhere. All the ladies seated in that row of chairs could move around wherever they wished, and the staff did chat to them. So why were they in such a mixed environment, one that was detrimental to their mental health? I recognised one of the women patients, a friend of Mum's.

I asked if I could talk to the sister. I wanted to know why my mother was in this ward. I also asked her if she knew of a Lily Humphries. This lady had been a good friend of my mother's. They had both belonged to the W.R.V.S and used to serve in the canteen at the local hospital. Sister recognised the name instantly.

"Do you know she sits in the chair next to your mother and neither has recognised the other." How sad that was. As soon as I reached them, I called both their names. It seemed to trigger something in their brains because they grabbed each other's hands and smiled. I will never know if they did recognise each other, but I would like to believe that. Sister told me that after that evening visit both Mum and Lily walked around hand in hand.

As I recall this black time, I wonder if there are still places out there that are unmerciful and frightening. Are people crying out for help, but we do not hear them?

I needed to know what infringement my mother had done to warrant her transfer. Evidently her assessment was complete, and the warden didn't want to take responsibility should Mum return. I was never given a detailed explanation. When I contacted the social workers' office, I was told that they were not involved with the case. It was up to the hospital to give me the answers. There wasn't a reason other than a request from an unfeeling warden. I knew I wouldn't get any further, so I decided it was time that my siblings visited and appraised the situation for themselves. When Bob and Bette arrived, they left the building within fifteen minutes. They told me that they could never visit again as it was so appalling, and they couldn't cope with the distress. I told them I had no choice. To keep our mother sane, I knew I had to visit every day.

A new purpose-built home for the elderly was being built in the town. It was called Gadebury. I went to look at the new building. The officer in charge informed me that the home would be organised into small house groups with a mother figure in charge. It was an attempt to recreate family groups. The bedrooms would have two beds with a small bathroom. It was perfect. I badgered Social Services until they agreed that Mum would be considered when she was discharged.

Mum would have to be released from Hill End Hospital but what did that mean when she hadn't been admitted in the first place? I had another battle on my hands. I found out which day Gadebury was taking its first residents. I went straight to Hill End and walked onto the ward to get my mother. I took her to her locker to collect her clothes and found there was only a few items left. All her nice clothes had been lost. I found her coat and one shoe and helped her dress. By now the staff were getting agitated waiting for a senior member of staff to block her discharge. I just marched her out of the door and drove straight to Gadebury. She was frightened once more at the unknown, however, I placated her and said that it was a special place for elderly people who needed to be cared for.

She settled down and spent the rest of her years in a place befitting older people who depend on extra support. There are not enough words to praise the care she received during her last few years in Gadebury.

It was around this period when Nigel was made redundant from John Dickinson's. Jobs were hard to find. Bill and I realised that being unemployed was not something we wanted Nigel to get used to. It was all too easy for him to lie in bed and listen to music instead of job hunting. He was twenty and had no idea of what he wanted to do. I was not happy in my own job. Things had changed at the surgery, and it had too quickly become a business centre. This of course was my opinion and not the term the doctors used. Their phrase was, more efficient. I handed in my notice and joined my son as unemployed. Bill was now carrying the household financially.

There was a glimmer of hope on the horizon for Nigel. Alan came home from Durban on a business trip. As usual he stayed with us. He suggested to Nigel that he went back to South Africa to try and gain employment there. If he decided that that was what he wanted to do he would be able to stay with the family until he found a job and accommodation. Nigel thought it was a good solution to his predicament. Alan returned to Durban to discuss it with Kath, his wife. The suggestion was acceptable to her, and plans were made for Nigel's departure. I was very apprehensive but did my best to keep a smile on my face.

Our next project was to organise a party for Nigel's twenty-first birthday. It would serve two purposes by being his farewell too. The party was a great success. All too soon it was time for his departure to the airport and our farewells. As he went through the final gate I was in floods of tears. Bill put his arm around me. "He will be back before long."

Bill's words were prophetic. Nigel was back in less than two weeks. I had given him money to deposit in the bank for his return flight, should he find living in South Africa again wasn't for him. He used the emergency fund to return home in less time that it took to take a holiday. To say we were angry is putting it mildly. I should have listened to Bill who told me not to give him the emergency money. He would have to have given his proposed new life a chance. How right Bill was.

I now gave some consideration as to what I was going to do with the rest of my working life. I needed to boost our income and replenish the money that we had spent on Nigel's departure and return. I always looked in the jobs vacant advertisements even when I was in full employment. On the following Friday of Nigel's return, I saw an advertisement in the Gazette, our local newspaper. It was for a Warden with Hanover, one of the local housing associations. After my experiences with my mother, I felt I knew only too well the demands of such an appointment and the responsibilities that went with the job. I applied in writing and received a telephone call from the Hanover Office in Cambridge. They asked if someone could visit my home to talk to me. I was delighted and an appointment was made.

I couldn't wait for the day to arrive. Fortunately, in my adult life, interviews have never bothered me. I always believe that if you have told the truth on your application, you have nothing to fear. I was very keen to get this job.

Mr Thomas introduced himself and settled into the armchair. He initially informed me that I did not have the qualifications that the company usually require but I had two that were above their requirements, my district nursing employment and my years of experience at the surgery.

"Surely there's plenty of employment for someone with your skills? Why are you applying for a warden's job?"

I gave him my reasons and explained the dire experiences I had witnessed and experienced with my mother's warden. I felt strongly that if I was appointed no one should be afraid to approach me and it was crucial that all the residents should trust me and know that anything discussed was confidential.

"Your story about your mother's housing association concerns me greatly. However, I think we will be extremely fortunate to have you join our team. I am pleased to say that I am offering you the job without any need to short list."

I was delighted. Bill had been on an early shift and had been given orders to stay out of sight. He sat in the car, hidden on the drive, smoking a cheroot.

After Mr Thomas left the house, I called out, "You can light up a King Edward. I've got the job." King Edward's were Bill's favourite cigars.

CHAPTER TWENTY

Nigel was actively looking for work, scanning the Situations Vacant columns and presenting himself at various recruitment offices.

I had a close friend staying with us for several weeks. I was helping her recover from a nervous breakdown. Peggy had been heading for a nervous breakdown for a couple of years. Her mental health had been on a downward spiral for some time. She always looked upon me as her sister, her elder sister, even though I was five years younger than her. I had known Peggy since the age of fifteen. My father had introduced her to me whilst we were having drinks in a pub at Bridens Camp. She and my father both worked at Brocks Firework Company in Cupid Green. She lived less than five minutes' walk away from our house in Lawn Lane so little effort was required to pop in to see each other.

During her stay with us, Peggy's doctors checked up on her regularly. Her GP was very caring and came most days to see her. Dealing with a nervous breakdown is difficult to the untrained. We could not see any obvious signs other than Peg's heavy smoking. When the doctor told her that she was ready to go home and that visits to the clinic in St Albans were in place, it was obvious that the news upset her. Peggy's doctor calmed her down and reassured her by saying that he would continue to visit her every day.

We sat down for our evening meal in near silence. It was hard to find something to talk about, that included her. After we'd finished our meal, I left the table informing everybody that I was going up to have my bath. As soon as I reached my bedroom, I discovered that Peggy had followed me. She asked if she could talk to me. We both sat on my bed and our conversation continued for about two hours. Bill came upstairs several times to ask me if I was okay.

My lovely friend begged me to let her live with us on a permanent basis. She said she would pay her way and help us with the housework and gardening. She suggested that we would be much better off financially. She told me that living with us had made her realise what life should be like, a home filled with lots of love and laughter. I tried to explain to Peggy that that would not be possible. My lovely Bill had to come first. He had already shared my stress for so long. I pointed out that her bungalow was only five minutes away, she could visit us whenever she wanted. Although she said that it would not be the same, she seemed to accept my reasoning.

I had my bath and then the telephone rang. It was Peggy's friends who were minding her dog whilst she was staying with us. They informed me that they could not have the little dog any longer and would not be able to in the future as they were both getting older, and it was too difficult for them to take it for walks. Peggy screamed into the telephone several times over, "You are betraying me." She completely overreacted. Peggy's friends had been kind to her for so many years, but this was all forgotten in the heat of the moment.

I took Peggy to her home the following day. We unpacked her groceries and checked things over in the bungalow then waited for the dog to be delivered by her friends. All seemed well. I walked around the block with her to exercise the dog then we returned to my house for the evening meal as planned. I felt I had done as much as I could to prepare her for her return home. Later that evening I walked her home and stayed for some time whilst she prepared for bed.

As I saw her into bed I said, "Peggy I've just realised you'll have to get out of bed and put the safety chain on the front door."

"Don't worry about that. You said you will come at nine o'clock in the morning and let yourself in with the key, then we will take the dog for its walk. That was our arrangement."

"Okay."

Next morning, I walked around to the complex, but stopped at the first bungalow to enquire after Peggy's neighbour's health, as she had been extremely ill. She asked me in, and I spent around ten minutes with her. As I came out, I saw another neighbour who called across and asked after Peggy's progress. "You will be able to ask her yourself as we will be coming by soon when we walk the dog."

I walked down the path and saw that Peggy's heavy curtains had not been opened. My heart lurched. I unlocked the door, and the little dog ran to greet me, wagging its tail. I called out to Peggy and walked into the bedroom. Nothing on earth could have prepared me for what I saw. Peggy was sitting up in bed, glass in hand, half filled with water with tablets scattered in the hollow of her lap. She was dead. She looked quite lovely. She had applied her makeup and looked as though she was on a stage set. My legs gave way and I hit the floor. I could not get up. I crawled into the lounge to the telephone. I contacted her doctor first. He was out so I gave his wife the information. Next, I rang the ambulance service. However hard I tried I could not rise from the floor; my legs would not support me. I was sobbing and shaking.

It didn't take too long for the police to arrive. When the police doctor came out from the bedroom he said, "This lady on the floor is the one who needs attention." I was in shock. Even though Peggy had said for years that she was going to take her own life, I didn't ever envisage her doing so. After Peggy's body was removed, the police interviewed me and then I was permitted to go home. Bill had been informed about what had happened and by the time I walked home Melanie had arrived to take care of me. I started to shake and could not stop for hours. My own doctor was summoned by Bill, and he gave me a sedative.

An inquest followed. I was the first witness on the stand. Although I shook with nerves, I managed to answer all the questions asked of me. The following week the local paper reported the story, stating Peggy was an alcoholic. The inquest had revealed that the drink in her hand was not water, as I had assumed, but was gin. I wrote to the newspaper protesting at the biased reporting, but they did not print an apology. I often think of my friend and understand, with maturity, more about her troubled life. To outsiders she seemed to have everything. No one knew that she was only nineteen, a new bride, when her husband Lesley was taken as a prisoner of war, in the infamous Japanese camp that built the railway. He returned home from the war, unable to live a normal life. He slept on the floor and kept his distance from Peggy. Both youngsters could not handle the consequences of that horrendous time. Post war, counselling was unheard of. Both faced the world as best they could. Lesley eventually died of cancer and Peggy just descended into this black place. I can still feel her pain.

The prospect of my new job gave me something to look forward to. I related the tragic event to Hanover, my new employer, and was given a couple of weeks to recover from the ordeal.

My brother who was now living in Cape Town telephoned to say that he had found a job for Nigel with a large company. He was happy to look for a flat for Nigel, should he wish to return. All of this happened within weeks of Peggy's death. Nigel felt that he would like to have a second crack of the whip. His ticket was bought but this time there was no return ticket money in his bank account. After all the emotional turmoil that I had been through, I still felt distraught that he was leaving us yet again. All the family and our friends tried to convince me that he would be back again. "You won't have time to miss him."

I was given a pleasant flat, which came with the job. My life within the Hanover Housing group had begun. I was to live in Great Palmers, the Grove Hill complex but had to oversee Hanover Green daily, which was in Boxmoor. This was very convenient for me as it enabled me to visit my mother daily, on my way to or from work. Mum was happy in her new home although she asked, almost daily, if she could come and live with me. Both the staff and the home were first class. I felt we were fortunate to have Mum reside there.

I enjoyed my new job. The residents were nice people and only called upon me when they really needed to. The flat was adequate for Bill and me and there was a guest room next door should we want to put up visitors. The previous warden had only moved to the flat below. When I discovered this, I was a little concerned, however I need not have worried. The ex-warden and her husband were always very pleasant and helpful to me.

On my days off we stayed at our house in Lawn Lane. We had left it furnished, as though we still lived there. We prevaricated about whether to let the house or sell it. We were in the fortunate position of being able to take our time before coming to a decision.

Nigel seemed to have settled down ln Cape Town. Alan took Nigel around the city flat hunting. Whilst they were in an agency a call came in about a property right in the city, in a prestigious position. Alan and Nigel went straight away with the agent to view it. As it was an old building the rent was within Nigel's budget. He was in seventh heaven. Alan promised to find him a few pieces of furniture and a bed but told Nigel he would have to manage everything else. I made the decision to fly over and stay with him in his almost bare apartment.

My son was delighted to see me and had borrowed a camp bed for himself. I could not believe Nigel's good fortune. The flat was next door to the Italian embassy with wonderful views over the park and government house. I spent my first week buying bits and pieces for the flat. Money was too short to buy ordinary armchairs, so I bought four garden chairs, but they looked good, and we started to fill the flat with similar cheaper furniture.

Nigel told me that he had met a girl that he liked. His aunt told me that she was too old for him and much more mature. Her name was

Maria. She was originally from Scotland but had lived in South Africa for some years.

Nigel took a day off work to take me on the cable car to the summit of Table Mountain. Maria was to join us, and Nigel had arranged to collect her. We arrived at her delightful little cottage. A very slender girl, with long hair down to her bottom, greeted me with such a delightful smile. She was so tanned that you could have questioned her country of origin. She looked lovely. I could see she was far more mature than Nigel, but I did not see it as a concern. We spent a lovely day together and I travelled home feeling much better about our son's future. He had been given the opportunity to make his own way in the world. I returned to the UK feeling much happier about him.

My Mum was settled or as much as she would ever be. Visiting her every day at Gadebury meant that she was so much easier to manage. My life was settling down.

Our house in Lawn Lane sold relatively quickly. At that period houses coming onto the market were scarce and selling instantly. We did not have a vast experience of selling houses. Had we been savvier we would not have sold the house at that time. However, it was done, and we started looking around for another in the Hemel district. Our investments were not keeping pace with the market.

Andrea had returned from teaching in Brunei. She had decided to take a term off before starting in a new school. She was often free to help me property hunt. One day we were so despondent with what we were viewing, we decided to call it a day. On our way home we cut through Horsecroft Road and saw a board being placed outside a three-storey house. We booked a viewing and made an offer the same day. It was never our intention to live in the house but to rent it out. We did this for a couple of years. We paid a fee to the agents for managing it, but our tenants were filthy. The first let was to three young men all of whom had doctorates. The agents wrongly thought that brains were the only requirement for good tenants. The second let was to a couple of young women who had come to work at Kodak. They were training the office staff how to use new equipment; something called a computer. They too rented the house for a year with the same dire results as the previous tenants. We decided to never rent out a property again. The cost of re-furbishing just wasn't worth the cost and worry.

When my friend Peggy died, she left me a legacy of money, even though it was not a fortune, I wanted to do something special with it. Although we no longer had the caravan, we still used to spend the odd weekend away in Norfolk. We were in Kings Lynn at the time and like always, spent time looking in estate agents' windows with retirement days in mind, even though they were a distance away. On one agent's board we spotted a section with older properties in need of restoration. One small cottage caught our eye, as it was only nine thousand pounds. We walked away after contemplating that it would require more than modernisation. The cottage was in the middle of a row and had been originally part of a farm. It was in the village of North Runcton. We stopped for a coffee and discussed the pros and cons. I convinced Bill that it would not hurt to look at it, as the sale price was within our budget.

We obtained the key and took ourselves off to find this little gem. North Runcton proved to be a small but really nice village. We could see the cottage from the road but had to reach it by walking across the two neighbouring cottages frontage. We saw instantly that it had a glass conservatory built on the front. Upon reaching the glass lean to, we could not believe our eyes. The conservatory was its bathroom, complete with a toilet. All in view of anyone who wished to look in. A tatty old piece of net curtain covered the bottom half of the panel to semi obscure the toilet. We both laughed so much that the lady next door came out to talk to us. She was a very friendly soul but wanted to know all about us within the first two minutes of meeting her. The ground floor room was a decent size but the whole place stank of dampness. The cottage had a lovely fireplace and behind that was a second incredibly small room which had a table and had obviously been used as a kitchen of some sort. By the fireplace was a door which hid the staircase, at the top of which was an open bedroom and to its left was a large front bedroom. We descended the stairs.

"No wonder it is so cheap," said Bill. "It would take a fortune to put it right, that's if you could."

I thought the same, but my mind's eye could see what could be done with it. As we locked up, the lady next door invited us in for a cuppa and a piece of her home-made cake. Her husband had been a county cricketer and enthralled Bill with his stories. We were there for a couple of hours. Before we left, they showed us the enormous garden that belonged the cottage. It was in a row just out of sight. You could have built a small house on it.

We drove back to the agents with the key. Bill said, "No way." I could see its potential. We told the agent that we were interested but had to work out the cost of restoration. During the journey home and for the rest of the following week, the cottage in North Runcton was the focus of most of our discussions. I made some enquiries from a friend of mine as to what grants might be available from the local authority. We were not sure if we could even apply, as our main home was not in Norfolk. Grants were available but Bill still needed convincing.

We eventually purchased the cottage. We were excited but knew there was a lot of hard work ahead. Plans were drawn up and builders engaged. On the odd weekend we went to Runcton to check on the progress. Our neighbours proved to be wonderfully understanding about the whole project. They put up with vans unloading outside plus there was an enormous sewer and drain gully for them to negotiate every time they left their properties. Our workmen told us that the neighbours also kept them in tea for the whole time they were there. They were so kind, and it made things much easier for us.

The weekend after the cottage renovations were completed, we set off early with our estate car loaded to the gunwales. We drove up to the front of the cottage expecting to clear away bits of rubble but everywhere was clean. We discovered that our next-door neighbour had cleaned both the outside and inside of the cottage and had left lovely toiletries in the bathroom.

We now had a delightful property which was quaint but true to its character. The front of the cottage now had a delightful kitchen with fitted units and pretty windows. The lounge retained its fireplace and the original door to the staircase. When we made a closer inspection of the cottage after we had purchased it, we lifted the front room carpet and uncovered an earth floor. It was not a problem for the builder, with his experience, he expected as much. He simply lowered the floor so that anyone over six foot could stand upright.

The cottage enhanced our lives. We spent many weekends and longer holidays there. Our friends and family stayed there too. Many said it gave them a sense of peace and an appreciation of days gone by.

Mum's health was failing in many ways and yet at nearly ninety she looked marvellous. Christmas was approaching and I was concerned that she would not be fit enough to come to us as usual, plus the winter of 1985 was very cold. I consoled her by saying that I would still visit for a couple of hours on both Christmas Day and Boxing Day. On Christmas Eve she was sitting in her wheelchair, and I took her into the communal rooms to talk to the other residents. She was a little hot and assured me. "I'm all right. I just feel a little iffy." I visited several times on Christmas Day and stayed with her until nearly midnight. I don't know why as she didn't seem stressed only a little hot. "See you in the morning Mum." On my way out I spoke to the duty officer and requested that she turn my mother over at one o'clock or so. My previous training kicked in and prompted the request.

At one o'clock I received a telephone call. Apparently, the duty officer had gone to turn my mother over and discovered she had died.

I returned at around 7 a.m. the next day to see Mum. I gazed down to see she was in the same position I had left her in, her hand with pink varnished nails resting over the white sheet. Her face with its beautiful complexion looked more like that of a woman of sixty. My last words to her were, "Oh Mum you look so beautiful."

I was still enjoying my job with Hanover, and I became quite attached to the tenants. The residents of both complexes were very friendly, and I found the housing association and my immediate bosses exceedingly kind but professional. On one of their visits, I was told that Hanover were completing a new build at Abbotts Langley and every warden within the company was invited to visit. I think most of the wardens in the locality took up the invitation and it was good to meet them over a cuppa. Hanover Gardens was built in the grounds of an old manor house and most of the large, mature trees had preservation orders. They were protected and left for future tenants to enjoy. It was a beautiful setting.

A week after that visit I was offered the job of warden. This was a great compliment. I was informed by someone in the company's higher echelon that the first warden of any complex was crucial, as they set the standards for the future. I was flattered and extremely interested as the accommodation was large, a flat with three bedrooms and the warden's office was adjacent, plus it came with a big salary increase. All very tempting but it would entail Bill having a longer journey to work and needing to use the car. However, the decision was taken out of our hands by circumstances we had not foreseen. Out of the blue, Dickinson's, Bill's employer, asked him if he would like to take early retirement. He was sixty-one. This was wonderful news and I said yes to Hanover.

We moved into Hanover Gardens a month before the tenants. It was a lovely building, built with a lot of thought and no expense spared. I loved it and got great pleasure from seeing the tenants move in one at a time. I made sure that I met all of them before they moved in.

I now had a pleasant office but had to learn about the paperwork. Everything necessitated forms, and in such detail. I had to employ various cleaners and gardeners. We also needed a handy man and my boss suggested that it would be a little income for Bill in his retirement. He was delighted and now had an interest in the running of the building.

I was concerned that one ground floor flat had not been let. Hanover informed me that it was for an assistant warden, should the company think there was a need. I did not think there was a need as everything seemed to be going well. However, it was explained that the problem arose when Bill and I took time off. Hanover advertised and soon had a short list to choose from. I was requested to attend the interviews. Amongst the applicants were a confident couple called Eileen and Ernie. He was a retired policeman and she had been a nurse. They had all the qualities that were required, as far as the company were concerned, but I felt a little misgiving. They were selected and soon moved in. My concerns faded as the months went by. They proved to be a wonderful support team for the next five years.

We had alternate weekends off, starting from Thursday evening until Monday morning. It allowed us to use the cottage on a regular basis. Eileen and Ernie would often stay at the cottage in Runcton on their free weekends. They would do any little jobs that needed attention, especially the garden. Ernie was like a professional. The arrangements worked out so well and we became close friends.

Hanover Gardens was a happy, lively complex. We arranged outings and parties were in abundance. We celebrated birthdays, and any anniversary. Each morning we all had coffee together. It was a time of much laughter. It gave the residents time with us, they got to know our families and we theirs. I started one morning by telling one resident that her glasses were very dirty. I took them from her and cleaned them. When I gave them back to her somebody else said, "Would you clean mine Jane?" That task became mine every morning until I retired.

We enjoyed our jobs but at the same time the complex was run efficiently. Both Bill and Ernie were a big asset, their skills covered most of the jobs that ever needed doing. Both men had easy going natures endearing them to the residents. We constantly had requests from people in the village who wanted to move in. I had proved to myself that old people can live in a sheltered complex and be happy in their remaining years.

CHAPTER TWENTY-ONE

Maria and Nigel had been married for several years when they dropped a bomb shell and announced their marriage was on the rocks. Bill and I knew they were going through a difficult time. We had been to their home in Hemel and had talked with them on several occasions, but it was to no avail. Our main concern was for the three little boys and the fact that Maria was pregnant again.

The separation culminated in Maria returning to Scotland with the four boys. We were desolated. Both Bill and I adored our grandsons and had so much contact with them. Our anxiety was for Maria too. It had been years since she had left her home in Scotland. Although her parents had long since died, her siblings still lived there and were incredibly supportive.

Bill and I drove to East Kilbride monthly to visit them. Maria had been re-housed, and we stayed with the family on our visits. It was always a joy to see them and heart-breaking when we left. Sometimes we brought the children back with us. That was always such a happy time.

Nigel had moved into Carole's, his new partner's home. Carole had two little boys of her own. It was extremely hard for Bill and me to accept this new situation. We had always commiserated with friends and their family break-ups and now we were in that position ourselves.

Maria started divorce proceedings and eventually gained custody of the boys after a lengthy court battle, as Nigel had applied for custody too. It was the most turbulent time. Maria's solicitor seemed to send daily epistles requiring an answer; all at a great financial cost. Nigel was unable to get legal aid as Maria was granted it first. It was a very traumatic and bitter time.

Eventually Maria moved back to Hemel, and we were able to be more supportive to her and our grandsons. We were overjoyed and to this day I share in their lives with joy and love.

Several years later Maria gave birth to a beautiful daughter. I received an urgent telephone call from Maria saying she was in labour and would I take her to the hospital and stay with her. I am so proud to say I helped to deliver the baby and cut her cord. This has given me such a special bond with my beautiful Alanna.

Maria eventually married a sturdy Scott named Jim McGraw. Nigel and Carole have been together for thirty years. Carole's sons and my four grandsons all have families of their own. I see them all frequently. Both the families mix and meet at various family functions and there are no issues from the past.

During this time life went on as usual for our Hanover family. Bill and I celebrated our fortieth wedding anniversary. The celebrations started from morning coffee time and went on all day. The residents presented us with a china figurine and a bouquet of red roses. It was so generous of them. Our own family party started in the early evening, although most of the residents came back to join us. It was certainly a day to remember.

I was approaching sixty and retirement. We needed to decide about our future. Our children had moved on with their lives. I had got to the stage of realising that the years were advancing at a rapid rate, and I could not defer planning my retirement. We owned the house in Horsecroft Road plus the cottage in Norfolk and were fortunate enough to have money in the bank. The options were many and that added to my confusion.

Our friends Eileen and Ernie had already retired, and the company had no intention to replace them. All the housing schemes were being adapted to an alarm call system. We missed them very much.

We received a telephone call from Ernie asking if he and Eileen could come to see us. He said it was urgent. When they arrived, they asked us if they could have first refusal on the cottage, should we decided to sell it.

Their request motivated Bill and me. We lay in bed that night and were still awake at 3 a.m. discussing our future. We decided on a price which Eileen and Ernie later agreed upon and the deal was done. We four celebrated with a meal out. Our solicitor did all the paperwork for both sides. All we had to do was remove our personal clothing and belongings.

I had to use up some leave before my departure from Hanover Gardens. We decided to spend a few days in Chepstow with my sister

Bette and her husband David before the four of us went on to Sidmouth, for a five-day break. Every night Bill and I lay in bed making decisions only to overturn them the next morning. One thing we both agreed was that we loved Chepstow and would quite like to retire there. There is no better place than Wales for sheer beauty.

We took home the local papers to peruse what was on the housing market. We found a four-bedroom house, the same size as my sister's. It was located on the same estate but not too close.

I took a day off work to view it. Bette and David were away, visiting their daughter in the Outer Hebrides. We left at 5.30 in the morning and arrived at the agency in time to see them unlocking the shop. We viewed the house and realised that it needed improvements. However, despite that, it was what we wanted, and we made an offer. It was accepted within the hour. My sister and brother-in-law were shocked upon their return home to find out that we now were the prospective owners of a property in Chepstow.

My retirement was finalised. Hanover Association asked me if I was leaving the area immediately. When I informed them that it would not be for quite some time, they offered me a job as a part time representative. The role entailed interviewing prospective tenants to assess the urgency of their needs. People's needs were rated on a point system. I loved the role and keeping my links to the company. I managed to keep that job for a year whilst we were upgrading the house in Chepstow. We ourselves continued to live in the house in Horsecroft Road.

We got used to travelling to and from Chepstow. The extended weekend visits provided time for D.I.Y. projects. We did all the home improvements ourselves except for the bathroom refit. Our dear friends Eileen and Ernie were always lending us a helping hand. We bought a range of kitchen units which Bill and Ernie spent a week installing. Ernie had the experience and Bill worked as the labourer. The finished kitchen looked very professional.

We enjoyed a lot of weekends in Chepstow with many of our friends and family. In was a very enjoyable and relaxing period after so many stresses.

Bill's two aunts accompanied by husbands plus a widowed aunt spent a week with us every year. We enjoyed having them stay. The visit started off with fun and laughter and continued for the whole week. Chores were shared and every couple contributed to the food and petrol. I smile at the memories of those wonderful times. It was a good thing that we had those times of tranquillity as they were interspersed with extreme stress.

CHAPTER TWENTY-TWO

An urgent telephone call from South Africa changed life's pattern for a short while. Alan had had extensive heart surgery. He was making a good recovery and wanted to be discharged. However, the hospital would only allow this if he had a carer with nursing experience. He asked me if I could fulfil this position if he paid for all my expenses for a month. Of course, I had Bill's blessing and off I went. I arrived to find Alan looking so much better than I had expected. I had only been in the house for fifteen minutes when I was shown the cocktail of drugs and times to administer them. The nurse left immediately. After that, my brother was completely out of hand and took liberties.

I drove him to the city to visit his company bosses. After that he went out most days on his own, socialising at the bowls club or visiting various friends' homes. I soon realised that I would be best using my time at home. I suggested getting my return flight booked. "No, you have to be here for my check-ups at the clinic." The rest of my time in Cape Town was spent reading many books to fill the days until my return home.

It was with great relief that I found myself on the internal flight to Joburg. As it was only an hour or so to Jan Smuts, the name of the airport at the time, I tried to take a seat nearest the front of the plane. I was fortunate, the first row only had one occupant, a gentleman. He made me very welcome and placed my flight bag in the overhead locker and even asked me if I wanted the window seat to be more visible to my family who were waving me off. It was obvious from his casual dress of shorts and shirt, that he was not an ongoing passenger. Within seconds, whilst the plane was taxiing into position on the runway, the gentleman saw to me being securely belted and enquired if I would like a cold drink. Such dedication to my welfare was astounding in such a short space of time.

His name was Arnold-de-Witt. He was the conductor of the

Johannesburg Philharmonic Orchestra. He told me that being a conductor was his pleasure. For a living he owned a manufacturing company in Durban. All this conversation took place within ten minutes of being in the air. He naturally asked me about my background too. On hearing that I did not know the city of Joey, as the locals call it, he made a proposal. "Please defer your on-going flight and let me show you the city at night." For the rest of that short flight, he tried his best to get me to stay overnight.

"My husband wouldn't like that."

"Why not? He can check me out and your brother can investigate me. I am a very responsible person and very well thought of in South Africa."

The speed of this flirtation was almost unbelievable. We arrived at the airport, and he indicated that I should stay aboard until the last passenger departed. He carried my very heavy flight bag. It all felt bizarre. I walked beside this man whom I had not even met two hours beforehand. He was at least five inches shorter than me. His pleading for me to stay was persistent.

"I cannot let you go. I must learn so much more about you." I gave him my brother's telephone number. "My brother will tell you everything that you want to know about me." We arrived in the central area of the airport. He turned and looked at my face. "You are not going to stay, are you?" We were standing by the Cartier carousel with its sparkling gems, and he pleaded with me to choose something to remember him by. I understandably refused. With tears pouring down his face he said, "You will always remember me. May I give you a goodbye hug?" He was right. I have not forgotten him. Alan checked up on him and he was the person he had claimed to be. I must be honest; I wish I had chosen a gift from the showcase.

I seem to attract passengers in adjoining seats who like to talk with me. I am sure I could write another book on the people I have met on my journeys. This next tale happened to me on another flight from Johannesburg.

I went to check in, for my onward flight to Heathrow but my baggage could not be found. This holdup made me the last person to board the plane. In front of me in the queue was a very tall gentleman of around six feet four. He turned around to wave to someone who was seeing him off. I turned to look and saw a very pretty, young lady waving with two little children, who looked like twins. I waited for confirmation that my luggage had been found and was onboard before making my way to the departure gate. As I walked along the aisle of the aircraft, I could see by people's expressions that I was not popular for delaying the flight by ten minutes or so. The plane was packed, and I was told that there was a seat to the left in row 26. As the cabin crew were anxious to take off, I said to the hostess, "I can find my seat myself, thank you." I reached row 26 and there was the tall gentleman who had stood in front of me at the check-in. I smiled at him.

"Good evening." I did not receive a smile back.

"I think you have made a mistake. I am a frequent flyer, and I am always allowed two seats when available." The hostess could see that I had not taken my seat, and the other passengers had already belted up for take-off. She swiftly joined us. "I am so sorry Mr Phillips, but the flight is full, and we cannot give you your usual concession."

He stood up and sighed heavily. "You can have the window seat."

I replied very sharply, "You choose the one you want. I am indifferent so long as I get back to Heathrow." He wanted the aisle seat to stretch his long legs.

As always on a flight it takes a while to remove your coat, sort out your hand luggage whilst deciding upon the essentials needed for the journey. I had sorted myself out and got comfortable when the hostess asked if we wanted cool drinks. My companion turned and repeated her enquiry, as a caring husband would.

Ralph Phillips was a businessman from Johannesburg who lived on a farm outside the city. As the journey progressed, I learned so much about his life. I had already seen his wife and two small children waving goodbye to him. He was a remarkably interesting man. I heard about his love of tennis, which he played to a high standard. I suppose when you have your own tennis court and can play every day you would soon become an accomplished player. By the first two hours of the journey, I knew much about his family and his business life and the fact that he came to England at least twice a year. On this trip he was alighting at Frankfurt to continue to America. He was thirty-eight and intended to retire when he was forty.

He paid me great attention and supervised the drinks and meals offered by the cabin crew. He turned to me and said, "I want to know everything about you when the crew stop giving us service."

"Well, it won't take all night. I lead a very ordinary life."

"I can't wait to hear. I am very intuitive and feel the interesting vibes that surround you."

'How do you follow that?' Now the ball was in my court. It was evident to him that I was married.

"I am a mother of three children and have a wonderful husband and live in Hertfordshire."

"Where in Hertfordshire?"

"Now that would be telling."

Ralph went on to ask me my age, which I thought a bit cheeky and laughed. We established that I was twelve years his senior. It did not matter to me either way whether he knew my age or not.

It was time for the lights in the cabin to be dimmed. We both nodded off for a short time. I then awoke when Ralph was attempting to place his pillow under my head to make me more comfortable. I have never been sure whether that was a ruse to wake me up or not but wake up I did, and he requested iced drinks for us, and the conversation resumed. Every word was said in a whisper as the people surrounding us were asleep.

We were about an hour from his destination when he asked me to meet him in London for a meal. I declined.

"I don't think my husband would like that."

"Bring him too." His next request was for me to give him both my address and telephone number. I had no intention of doing so.

"I travel miles and miles on aircraft and have never met anyone who interests me so much."

"And how many ladies have you said that to?"

As he left the aircraft, he waved back to me several times. The last wave was accompanied by a blown kiss.

I spread myself out in the vacant seat and nodded off. I was so tired.

The aeroplane started its descent to Heathrow. It was time to buckle up for the landing. Fortunately, I was one of the first to leave the plane and reach the conveyor belt in the luggage hall. It did me no good. I was still looking for my case when everybody had retrieved theirs. I was furious and very tired when they came to say it had been lost.

Poor Bill was concerned and wondered whether I had got on the wrong flight. He made enquiries as to my whereabouts but was not told about the lost luggage. I was relieved to finally get home, even though I was minus my suitcase.

The next day I reported its loss to the travel agents and was paid out instantly. I enjoyed replacing my clothes. A while afterwards my case was delivered to me. It had been found at Frankfurt. I confessed that I had already spent the compensation and was informed that that was my good fortune.

One morning, a few months later I received a telephone call. I answered then heard a familiar voice. "I know this might sound crazy, but did you travel home from South Africa in March?"

"Good morning, Ralph."

Ralph Phillips had remembered that I said I lived in Hertfordshire. He was working through all the Durrants listed in the phone book. We had a lovely conversation which ended with a request for Bill and me to dine with him at his hotel. Bill already knew the whole story, so the invitation was easy to relate to him. However hard I tried I could not get Bill to accept. "You must go Jane. I really don't mind." I left it for a couple of days before I telephoned to accept the invitation.

I got a taxi from Euston and Ralph was waiting in the hotel foyer for me. We had a very enjoyable meal and then walked through Hyde Park. I found it strange that we had met up as though we were old friends. He was surprised when I told him that we were going to emigrate to South Africa.

"I will telephone you every time I visit the UK, just to see how you are doing."

He called many times and when we had a date to emigrate, I promised to let him know when we were housed and settled in Durban.

I kept my promise and gave our South African telephone number to Ralph. My next call from him was to tell me that he was in Durban for three days as he had just bought a new factory and beach house. He asked if Bill and I could meet with him. As before Bill could not be convinced to join me.

I collected Ralph from his hotel on the sea front and I drove to where his beach house was. I only viewed it from the road. A gardener was working on the front garden. It was delightful. Ralph then turned to me, "Jane, you told me on the plane that you wanted to write a book about one of your patients. Now you have somewhere peaceful to write it. I will always let you know when I want to use the house with my family. This will only be once a year if that."

I discussed what Ralph had said to me with Bill and we concluded that it was all so improbable, however true.

A footnote to this story.

To my daughters I have to say, "No he wasn't the one who gave me my pearl and diamond earrings."

180

CHAPTER TWENTY-THREE

Life changed for me with permanent retirement. I had orders from Bill that I should not seek any further employment and that we should relax for the remaining years left to us. He was right. We now had all our grandchildren living close by in Hemel.

We spent quite a lot of time in Chepstow although had not progressed to moving there permanently. We both loved Chepstow with a passion. When there we spent each day visiting the surrounding countryside. We were accompanied for most of these visits by my sister and brother-in-law. David could always find the unexpected route which had breath-taking scenery. He had gained his knowledge of the countryside from a young boy and his love and pride for his beloved Wales shone out like a beacon. I thought that we should have bought a small touring caravan, but Bill did not want the hassle of towing one. I'm not sure I would have been brave enough either.

Travelling backwards and forwards from Chepstow to Boxmoor, plus the upkeep of two properties was taking its toll and depleting our income. We decided to sell one of the two houses. I said to Bill, "Let's take a vote on it." I voted to stay in Chepstow and Bill chose Boxmoor. It was stalemate so we decided to place the final decision in the lap of the gods and put both houses on the market at the same time. This seemed the fairest thing to both of us.

We returned to Boxmoor the following weekend and placed the property with the agents we had bought it from. We informed them that we did not want a board outside in case we changed our minds.

The house was viewed that weekend before it was advertised, or a brochure printed. At nine a.m. the next morning the estate agent telephoned to inform us that we had had an offer, ten thousand pounds short of the asking price. This was unbelievably quick, but Bill made the decision to accept it. We found out much later that some skulduggery had taken place. The estate agent was a friend of the purchaser and she had informed her friend that we were selling two houses and she was sure she could get the house cheaper. We found out about this from my sister Eileen. She was waiting in the queue in a fish and chip shop and got chatting to a woman who related how lucky her friend was to know the estate agent and get such a good deal on her house. I was furious when Eileen told me and wanted to sue. Bill was adamant that it was done and dusted, and he couldn't face any litigation.

Mike Green, our solicitor and friend, advised us to seek the advice of a financial expert. We did and he concluded that with the rising prices in the housing market we should sell Chepstow and pool the two amounts to buy another house.

The house in Chepstow sold. Bill came with me to view about six houses and then decided enough was enough. I was left to view properties on my own. I was despondent. I thought we had enough money to enable us to get a reasonable property, but it was not as straight forward as I thought.

I had heard that a new estate was being built in Hemel on a site in Fields End, so I decided to take a look. It was a dreadful day with torrential rain. The site was just one big sea of mud. Billboards lead me to the clerk of the works office. I thought I was going to see images of houses but no, it was just a planning map on the wall. It was hard to visualise a completed house. I enquired about the properties for sale. The patient clerk walked to his desk and unrolled a plan showing plots for sale as well as ones sold. Some properties were more than we could afford, others under our budget or not to our liking. He then produced a second map and informed me that the houses would not be ready for at least six months. The houses were to be built in a cul-de-sac.

The plan showed large, detached houses with one smaller house in between, also detached. It was in a perfect position with a double drive. I felt it would be just what we wanted. The clerk of works offered me a cup of tea then showed me the range of units, sanitary ware, flooring etc. that we would be able to choose. We finally stood on the cardboard path outside whilst he pointed out the plot of mud that would be our home if we chose to go ahead. I thought it was a good site, even in the pouring rain.

I went straight home and dragged Bill out to view the plot. We only had twenty-four hours before the developers required a deposit to secure that specific plot. Bill said little. "If you think it's right Jane, we will go for it." What a responsibility on my shoulders.

Having a house built was something new to us. Each week we

went to see what progress had been made. The day the windows went in, we were ecstatic, as we could anticipate a moving day approaching. Our house sale in Horsecroft Road was ready for completion. Bill's Aunt Vera said we could move in with her until our new house was ready, so long as I did the cooking. Our furniture went into storage. We stayed with Vera for the two months prior to possession. We were incredibly grateful for her kindness.

We moved to Hollyhock Close feeling such joy and the anticipation of another new beginning. The first home that we had witnessed being built for us. We had come a long way from our rented two rooms when we married. We had climbed the property ladder slowly.

As everything was new, we concentrated on the garden. Money was much tighter, and we had to prioritise. The house was surrounded by brick paths which proved to be a bonus. I bought fairly cheap pots and filled them with colourful plants. Bill's first consideration was to lay lawns, front and back. Bit by bit trellises and a corner arbour were built which I covered with heavily perfumed roses. Conifers lined the neighbouring fences. Our last task was to create a large pond. Bill was not fit enough to do the digging, so Nigel offered to excavate it. I am surprised that he survived as he started it on one of the hottest days of the year. We had to erect a gazebo over him such was the heat. He would not give in and stop until it was completely dug out.

Establishing a pond is a slow process. Vera was very experienced with garden ponds, and we relied upon her advice. It took months to come into fruition. Finally, the day came for us to purchase fish. Vera was with us and was so fussy about their condition. They had to be perfect carrying no blemishes. She knew her stuff when it came to fish, tropical or cold-water ones. I spent a lot of time in the garden. It gave me so much please. It was my little bit of paradise on earth.

Our children were all getting on with their lives. Each of them had good jobs and their own families were growing up fast. Emma our golden cocker spaniel was getting older and grumpier by the day. We had to force her out of her basket for walks. From a puppy she had been a difficult dog and didn't like being handled, unlike our previous dogs who were springers spaniels with wonderful temperaments. We never replaced her and to this day I feel a little incomplete without a dog in my life.

Bill started becoming tired quite frequently and would not go to the doctor. He lost his balance several times. He would tell a fib and say to me that he slipped. I was so worried that I sought advice from the surgery. An appointment was made with the doctor, and he confirmed that Bill had had a further heart attack without knowing. From then on Bill was well monitored by the surgery with frequent visits.

Our lives slowed down, but we managed to continue to enjoy occasional trips out, however, Bill stopped driving. Fortunately, he was of a very contented disposition and could watch hours of television in-between frequent naps. He suffered with oedema in both legs which limited his walking. He looked forward to the children's visits which were frequent. Melanie habitually came after she had left work. She sat with her dad and watched Countdown on the TV. They were fiercely competitive and would vie with each other to see who was the fastest completing the conundrum or the number games. My job was to make the tea.

Bill's health seemed to be failing. I made an appointment to see his G.P. to discuss my fears. I came out of the surgery stunned. I was told that he might only have two years left. I thought long and hard about telling the children and concluded that they loved him so much, their distress would reveal itself. He was surrounded by love and had everything he wished for.

We both discussed our forth coming Golden Wedding Anniversary. I rather fancied a cruise. Bill wanted a party. "I want to invite everybody who came to our wedding and every neighbour that has lived beside us." It was a surprise to me, as out of the two of us, I was the party person. I looked across at him and realised he was frail. I also appreciated that during our marriage Bill had always said, "D*o what you want.*" This request was a first. So, a party it was.

My goodness, it was all systems go. Melanie, Andrea and Nigel got together, and plans were hatched for it to be the party of a lifetime. It was an exciting time, everybody seemed to be wishing us well. Our next-door neighbour promised the gift of a large traditional cake, in whatever design we wanted. His friend made cakes for the aristocracy, how could we better that. The top tier had two golden hearts at an angle with our names on, the second tier had three smaller hearts with the names of our children. The base had much smaller hearts with the names of our grandsons. It was so poignant. It was a joy to look at and represented our married life.

Nigel was the compère. Melanie decorated the hall and all the tables; Andrea organised the band and sourced the sheet music for the song 'Temptation.' Bill volunteered to sing this song to me, in public, when we stayed at Butlins Holiday Camp when I was sixteen. He sang it again that evening, accompanied by the organist. There were tears in many people's eyes. Our children were a good team and made the evening an unforgettable experience. We got to bed at 4 a.m., very tired but on an extreme high. Visitors and feeding them spilled over into the next day.

It took us a week to recover. We were so grateful to our children for their hard work and support. The event was recorded on video and has been watched many times over the years. It is one of my most precious possessions. Several months after the celebration, Bill was sitting in his chair reliving the experience. He said, "Do you know Jane, that was the best evening of my life. Everyone who loves us was there." How right he was.

Unfortunately, Bill's legs were becoming more of a problem; the oedema was causing us great concern. One night, on going to bed, Bill said, "I think I have caught this flu that's going around." In the morning I could see he needed a doctor. I telephoned the surgery and requested a home visit. By good fortune Nigel called in to visit and was able to help me. The doctor arrived within ten minutes and immediately ordered an ambulance. Bill was instantly admitted to the cardiac unit where he died hours later at 1.10 a.m. on New Year's Eve 1998. His death was caused by the septicaemia, not as expected, a further cardiac arrest. All his family were with him, and he was aware of them. He was such a loving husband and devoted father and grandad. We were all devastated.

So many people attended his funeral service to pay their last respects, which was a great tribute to him. Letters and condolence cards arrived for weeks afterwards. Bill was such an unassuming person and would not have guessed how much he had influenced people for the better during his lifetime. I too learned so much from him.

CHAPTER TWENTY-FOUR

It was so unreal to me that Bill had died. Life would never be the same. We had been together since I was a young girl. How could it be that I was now a pensioner who had to bear the loss and be solely responsible for decisions. It was a hard period. I put on a brave face. Everyone thought I was coping but going through the front door when there was no one to say hello, was the worst. Grief takes its own time, and no one can grieve for you.

Several months later I was surprised to receive a telephone call from a lady called Christine who was the chairperson of Abbeyfield House in Potten End. I did not know her or anything about Abbeyfield. Apparently, someone had recommended me to her. The home was looking for a nurse-carer to visit every morning, to assist any resident who found dressing and bathing difficult. I was informed that the residents would pay me directly. I was extremely interested and went for an informal interview.

I was sixty-eight but got the job. Getting up early in the morning was no problem and I was usually finished by ten thirty, which gave me the rest of the day to myself. My ties with the guild were still strong and I was now available in a way that I had not been before. I also kept my interest in the Derby and Joan club in Apsley. It was nice to think that I was continuing the work that my parents had started. It involved organising various outings and sometimes a coach trip to Belgium. Running the Darby and Joan club wasn't all work. It gave me much pleasure and I was constantly rewarded by masses of smiles.

I liked the Abbeyfield job and the people I worked for. When I arrived, I met the postman and collected the mail. I then posted it through everyone's letterboxes. On one such day I noticed that Kathy's letter was addressed to the Honourable K. Nelson. I saw her a short time afterwards and said, "Oh, Kathy, I see you are an 'honourable.' I must address you differently." This was all said in jest with us both smiling.

186

"Well," she replied, "it's only because my son is the present Lord Nelson. His uncles were without heirs and the title has passed to him." What a lovely caring lady she was.

I really enjoyed working but at the same time felt that I could take on a more demanding job. After a year, I gave in my notice to the residents and placed an advertisement in the Lady magazine. 'Carer with nursing experience looking for a live-in position.'

It wasn't long before the telephone started to ring nonstop. Some of the enquiries really astounded me. Some peoples' demands were so unrealistic. Several callers suggested no set hours with the salary being that of the Disability Living Allowance that their dependent relative was receiving. It was a different world of caring from the one I was used to. I was disgusted by the expectations of some families. I almost considered abandoning my intentions to seek residential work.

A telephone call one evening renewed my enthusiasm. It was a request from a gentleman who lived in the Isle of Man. He wanted a fulltime carer for his disabled wife. He informed me that he employed a cook and a cleaner, so I knew that I would not have to embrace any domestic chores. Sam Knight came across as a remarkably confident individual. He asked me what salary I was expecting, which I was taken aback by, as I did not have a figure in mind. A salary for a live-in job with no set hours was not something I had contemplated. I plucked a figure out of the air. "I would expect two hundred and fifty pounds a month plus my board."

"I was thinking more of a hundred and fifty pounds as I would have to pay your air fare on your time off." Little did he know how new I was to this game.

"I would only consider moving from the mainland for the figure I suggested."

"Very well. I like the sound of you. Please book your ticket to fly over for an interview and I will reimburse you. If I like you and my wife does then the money is not a problem."

I put down the telephone and sat laughing in a nervous way and said out loud, "What do you think Bill?"

I now had the task of telling my children that their mother was going to fly to the Isle of Man for an interview. To anyone who said, "That's a bit dicey." I replied, "The job was advertised in the Lady magazine and all their advertisements are vetted." Which was true but a little foolish, as no one can vet people responding to advertisements. However, a ticket was purchased, and a flight arranged. The flight cost around eighty pounds. I was to stay overnight and return the following morning. In hindsight, I realise how risky this was. I wrongly thought that a gentleman employing staff was an assurance of character. This is certainly not so. I was trusting and naïve.

Armed with a return ticket and my overnight bag I boarded the flight. It was so strange to go through customs without the usual palaver of passports. The small plane flew through a lot of turbulence over the Iris Sea, but within the hour we were touching down at Ronaldsway. I could feel myself getting more anxious by the minute. *'Here I am, miles from home. What am I doing?'*

I knew Mr Knight was not going to be at the airport. He had informed me he would send a hire car. A gentleman was holding up a board with my name on. I spotted him immediately. He was a pleasant chauffeur and once we were under way we started conversing. It was pouring with rain and everywhere looked dismal. The driver asked, "Are you the new nurse for Mrs Knight?" He seemed a little concerned.

It took less that ten minutes to arrive at the Knights' house, which was a converted chapel. Whilst I was wondering whether I should offer the driver the fare or at least a tip he said, "It's all been taken care of. I'm going to give you my card and if you want me for anything, just ring me. It doesn't matter if it is during the night." This made me feel a little concerned as I knew there were no night flights available on the island. I took his card and thanked him. Finally, he declared, "I do mean it, you seem such a nice lady." I wanted to turn and run. I could see he wasn't too happy dropping me off. He put my overnight bag in the porch and waited for the door to open before he drove off. It was the original door of the chapel, and everything looked somewhat sinister.

I expected a charming gentleman to receive me at the door. It was not so. Joan, the cook, opened the door and Mr Knight made an entrance from the sitting room. Mrs Knight was nowhere to be seen. Mr Knight told me that he had requested tea and cake. "Will that be all right with you, as we will be having dinner later?"

I looked around the large room. It was very modestly furnished but had several wall cabinets filled with beautiful silver. Tea was brought in on stylish tray with fine bone china and a silver teapot. I was introduced to the housekeeper who greeted me warmly.

After the pleasantries, the interview began. I could see that Mr Knight was incredibly nervous from the outset. Being aware of that, made all my nerves fade away and I began to feel that I was interviewing him. I explained that I wasn't an S.R.N., state registered nurse. He was happy with this and stated that a formal qualification was not required. He continued by declaring that my salary was a little more than he usually paid but he was sure I was well worth it. I sensed that the interview was going well and that he was going to employ me. I requested that I should like to meet his wife and find out how she felt about the prospect of me caring for her.

Mr Knight was around six foot three and stick thin. Agnes, his wife, was short and rotund, a tiny round dumpling of a woman. She glanced at me quickly then dropped her gaze.

I was shown a bedroom on the ground floor which was quite large with a bathroom opposite. This was my accommodation for the night and would be permanent if I accepted the position. Two large dogs completed the household. I am a dog lover so that was delightful from my point of view. I was offered the job and asked if I could start as soon as possible.

Once I had accepted, the Knights seemed to relax. I was amused to observe earlier, that whilst I was being interviewed, the housekeeper was listening to every word by the kitchen door. This was an indication for the future. I did not sleep very well as my brain was whirling. I had decided to take the job but kept reflecting on whether it was the right decision. I eventually concluded that it was.

As I watched the turbulent Irish Sea below the plane, the realism of what I was about to do hit home. I really didn't know anything about this man, other than what he had told me. I then thought about his staff who had been with him for many years and finally reflected on my observations of him with Agnes, his wife of many years. He seemed genuinely concerned about her. This helped to allay some doubts.

It was time to face the family with my decision. I accepted that I would encounter some opposition from all three children. Nigel had arranged to collect me from Luton Airport but was nowhere to be seen so I left the terminal. Sure, enough he was there trying to find a parking space. On the drive home I informed him of my decision. "Are you sure it is safe Mum?" As I related what had happened to him and explained that there were other staff at the house, he felt reassured. "You must do what you want to do Mum. Now is your time. If it doesn't suit you, you can leave. It isn't that far away." I felt much more confident by the time we reached home. Melanie visited not long after Nigel had dropped me off. She too was anxious to hear all the news and swiftly formed the opinion that I should, 'go for it.' She went on to say that if I was in any trouble, I could contact my nephew and his wife who lived on the island in Castletown, not far from the Knights' residence. I had not considered that. Andrea also listened to the story of my interview and had similar thoughts to her brother and sister.

My flight was booked. There was much to organise although it was much easier than when we left for South Africa. The Isle of Man was only a short hop away and I had already requested that I return home for a week at the end of every month. My flights were paid for on top of my salary. During the month I was on the island I worked every weekend.

I had a special reason for seeking a job, I had a financial goal. Although I had a little savings I only had enough to maintain my house and pay the bills. I had already bought a small car and was determined that my next goal was to fund a conservatory. At five thousand plus pounds this was a challenge. Most of my friends thought I was mad. I didn't feel any fear. It was only after my return that I realised how dangerous it could have been.

I left Luton Airport with butterflies in my stomach which I did my best to diminish. Because I felt apprehensive the journey seemed so short. We took off, were offered a beverage and then it was time to land. This was when my nerves took the better of me. *'Why was I doing this and why didn't somebody stop me?'* I told myself off and resumed my air of confidence.

I had expected my boss to pick me up, however a taxi had been arranged. We soon arrived at the house and the driver banged on the heavy wooden door. Once again it was opened by the cook. Mr Knight stood in the background. I had forgotten just how tall and thin he was. I received a handshake from him and a reluctant grin from the cook before being shown to my bedroom. I was informed that the meal was ready when I was. After I shut my bedroom door I thought, *'This is it my girl. Now it's up to you to make something of it.'*

My bedroom felt very cold and unfriendly. It had the original chapel windows which were without curtains or blinds. The furniture suite was made of walnut with a matching bedhead. It took me about five minutes to unpack my clothes and I sat in the only chair in the room awaiting a summons. The cook called out that the meal was ready. I checked on how I looked in the mirror and decided I was presentable. I didn't want to refresh my make-up as I didn't know how that would go down.

I walked into the room. The Knights were seated at the table awaiting my presence. I went towards Mrs Knight with my outstretched hand. She accepted it but Mr Knight interrupted the gesture, "There is no need for that." I think he meant it in a friendly way and wanted things to be less formal. The Knights sat at each end of the table, looking at each other without speaking. I was placed in the middle. Conversation was tricky as they didn't know anything about me as yet. The meal was brought in by the housekeeper. Both Mr and Mrs Knight had child sized portions. I was expecting mine to be the same but fortunately it was more generous. After we had finished the dessert both Mr Knight and I were asked if we wanted tea or coffee, but Mrs Knight was completely ignored. I waited until we had finished the meal, left the table then visited the housekeeper in the kitchen. I asked why Mrs Knight hadn't been asked which beverage she wanted.

"Oh, it's no good asking her, she always says no."

"Mrs Knight pays both our wages and out of respect you must ask her every time. If she says no, then that is her decision."

I wanted the cook to appreciate that the Knights were my employers and always came first.

Mrs Knight was my sole responsibility. Within a week she and I had a good routine worked out, although it did not come easily. Showering her was a rigmarole. I was called every name the sun. Agnes, as I now called her, had a vocabulary which included every swear word known to humanity. This pantomime happened every morning for about a month. The swearing gradually diminished, and she became a much nicer person. I sat her on the edge of the bed one morning and said, "Agnes if you want me to stay, you really must be more respectful to me. If not, I will have to leave." I discovered that she had had a succession of carers and every one of them had left after giving a month's notice and in some cases without notice. Now I knew why the taxi driver had given me his card.

My routine with Agnes gave me plenty of time for other chores. I felt I needed to earn my salary. I sorted and updated all her underclothing and cleared out old dresses. I felt so sad when I found numerous attractive dresses with matching bags and shoes stored away in one of the wardrobes. There were fur coats and capes to accompany all these beautiful clothes. The glamourous outfits were from their days of cruising. The Knights had been around the world first class, three times. Now she was reduced to being washed and dressed. It endeared me to her.

Agnes started to speak openly to me. She related wonderful stories of their travels. There was so much more to this lady than the people surrounding her knew. I loved listening to her tales. In front of other people, she was this quiet lady that never spoke, unless asked a question. To me she was a wonderful storyteller. I could see her blossom before my very eyes. Our relationship enriched us both. I now think of her as my lovely Agnes.

Mr Knight was a different kettle of fish. He was rude and very abrupt at times, and it took me quite a few weeks to suss him out. Over time, I did find his after dinner tales very revealing and entertaining. All his wealth had come from amusement parks and arcades. Evidently everybody knew him in Blackpool. Sam Knight had been a very tough cookie in his younger days, and no one dared cross him. He was immensely proud of his past reputation although I had a gut feeling that he still had a hold over several people and organisations. He dabbled in promoting boxing and wrestling. He once told me that Travellers made good bare-knuckle fighters and that this was very profitable for him. I heard fantastic stories about his arcades and various cafes that he owned. What a film it would have made.

I had only been at the house for two days when Mr Knight announced very abruptly, "I want you to drive me to Castletown this afternoon to the bank." I had seen two very rusty cars parked in front of the chapel. I couldn't believe that he drove either of them. He chose the old Mercedes. I thought it would collapse before we left the grounds. It was parked so tight to the chapel wall that only one person, and a slim one at that, could get inside.

"You had better get it out. If I hit the wall it will fall to pieces."

"You must be a bloody awful driver if you can't reverse out of there."

However, he complied. "I never drive faster than fifteen to twenty miles an hour and all the islanders know me when I am on the road."

'I bet they do.' I was shaking with nerves as he was bullying me the whole time. We arrived at a small petrol station. There was a car in front of us, so I waited for the driver to start to fill up. Mr Knight shouted at the man to let us in first as he lived on the bloody island and wasn't a tourist. I was mortified. After paying for the petrol, he got back in the car and threw money over my head. Some went on to my lap, the other on the floor between the pedals. "That's your first month's salary." It was two hundred and fifty pounds. I was appalled at his lack of finesse. Gathering it up as best I could we made off. *'He's mad or very nearly. I will have to leave.'*

192

On reflection I decided that I would have to make the best of it and persevere. I got to know my employer very quickly, but my aim was not to let him know me.

The rusty old Mercedes was so well known, wherever I drove everyone knew the car. I asked for it to be cleaned as I was ashamed to drive it. Mr Knight called in a handy man to do the chore. When he arrived, the man said to me, "If I clean it, it will just collapse. I just take the money and laugh."

I took over the responsibility of the weekly shop and drove to one of the local supermarkets to get whatever I wanted. I had stopped the tradesmen that called to the chapel, as the Knights were eating like sparrows and the bills, in my opinion, were far too high. I was truly fortunate. The whole time I worked for the Knights I didn't have to buy anything, not even my tissues.

I could go out every day if I chose to. Agnes went to bed every afternoon from one to four o'clock. I could go shopping or anywhere I liked so long as I told them I would be out of the building. Life was settling down to a routine of my choice. Everything fitted around Agnes. We had a silent bond between us.

Mr Knight asked to speak to me in private. I was invited to sit at the table opposite him. Before we started Mr Knight rose from the table and walked across the room to close all the doors. '*He's going to sack me.*'

With a very straight, if not angry looking, face he began. "I have to get this off my chest. I want to know the truth. Why do you call everybody by their Christian names but not me? What have I bloody done that has upset you? Your manner to me is always very cool but with other people you are all smiles and very tender. You don't show me anything."

This was not what I was expecting. I took a quick deep breath struggling to come up with a suitable answer. "Mr Knight. I …"

He interrupted me sharply. "Listen to you now. You are almost telling me off and for what?"

All in seconds I realised it was true, I did speak to him in a cool manner. "I am so sorry. I hadn't realised that. I don't call you by your first name because I respect you as my employer and it is a matter of respecting your position."

"Well, I don't like it. From this moment you must call me Sam. I realise why you are doing it but as I don't like it. You will use Sam when you talk to me. Go on say it. It isn't hard."

I felt like a naughty schoolgirl and said the dreaded word, "Sam." For the next few days, he pretended that he didn't hear me so that I had to call out his name. Gradually things calmed down and I found I was able to call him by his first name without any aggravation.

I looked forward to my week's leave every month. After my second week home. Melanie asked me if my grandson and his wife, Lee and Jennie, could stay in my home in Hollyhock Close. They were awaiting a flat to become available for them to buy. I agreed that they could stay until completion on their flat.

My week at home always went by so quickly. I used to catch up with my friends and attend church. It felt like a holiday. I loved my house; living in the strange atmosphere of the chapel made me appreciate my home even more.

My return visit to the island altered. Sam was always at Ronaldsway airport to greet me, wearing his best suit. There were never more than thirty to forty people on the flight and due to his height, he was easily detected and yet if Sam felt he was not prominent enough he would elbow other people out of the way and yell out, "Jane I'm here," which was totally unnecessary.

When we entered the chapel shouts of, "Jane is home," echoed around the hallway. On one occasion I saw the cook raise her eyes and pull a face to the cleaner. This made me smile but it didn't do my relationship with them any favours. They had told me already that they laughed at Sam taking an hour to change and make himself presentable, every time he left for the airport. I only know that those journeys were the only time the car smelt pleasant.

I knew that I had to handle the situation with Sam sensitively. I cared for Agnes, and I didn't want her to get hurt by any inappropriate behaviour from Sam. I asked Sam to buy bolts for my bedroom and bathroom doors.

"There has never been bolts on those doors before and we have had several lots of staff stay in those rooms."

"I don't care how they felt Sam. I don't wish to take a bath without any security."

He bought the bolts virtually straight away, the smallest bolts possible, but it took a couple of weeks of me nagging him to secure them to the doors. He was such a character. I should have been paid extra for having to keep one step ahead of him.

Winter on the Isle of Man was unbelievable. The house was right next to the sea. The noise from the crashing waves was alarming. It felt

194

as though we on onboard a ship. When I went out in the car, I had to use all my strength to pull the door to. Sometimes the waves would spray onto the car as I drove along the seafront. I found it quite fearful. The household used to laugh at me and call me a townie.

Sam became a much nicer person. He didn't swear as much, and he minded his manners far more. Agnes was getting frailer but was much more animated. I often looked across the room at her and she would purse her lips and blow me a kiss. That memory fills me with tears. On one occasion I was sitting by the roaring fire, sewing one of Agnes dresses. Sam and Agnes were sitting on the sofa, and he was holding her hand. He looked across and said, "Isn't life perfect." This jolted me into thinking. *'This domestic scene is what he wants and thinks he has got for the rest of his days. They are getting too fond of me, and I have allowed myself to get close to them. I will have to seriously think on. I will make a decision when I am next home on leave.'*

My next weekend home came around quickly. I checked my bank statement and accessed the Isle of Man account. I had reached my goal of five thousand pounds, the sum I needed to build a conservatory. It did not fill me with the joy that I would have expected. I decided that when I returned to the island, I would hand in my notice. I knew Agnes and Sam would be stressed and that I would have to live with that for a month. I wanted to tell Agnes myself that I was leaving. It would be so hard, as she had become much more than a patient.

My return trip to the island was far from pleasant as I was overwhelmingly anxious. Sam was at the airport as usual; he took my bag and we walked to the car. Instead of turning on the engine he said, "I want to talk to you." I was nervous as I had prepared my announcement. "Agnes has become much more poorly and needs the doctor daily."

I was surprised. "Let's get home quickly."

I rushed to Agnes's bedside and cuddled her. She really didn't look much different to when I left her, but it was the unseen illness within. She bucked up the next day. When I showered her, my concern at her weight loss, must have shown on my face. "Don't worry about me darling. I shall get better now." I couldn't drop a bombshell now. My announcement was going to have to be put on hold.

Life resumed at its leisurely pace. The doctor's visits to Agnes were less frequent and I presumed her health was back on track. I was wrong. Sam called me during the night. He had tried to help Agnes onto the commode, and she had fallen. Sam could not get her back into bed.

I tried without success. She was calling out and yelling, but unfortunately, Agnes used to call out in a similar fashion if she didn't want to do anything. I made a quick judgement that the doctor should be called. He came and requested an ambulance to take Agnes to a private clinic, in the full knowledge that Sam had plenty of money to fund it.

Sam and I visited Agnes daily. The clinic was not far from the house. Sam asked the cook to delay the midday meal until the evenings. This presented no problem. However, after several days of this routine he changed his mind and told the cook, "I am taking Jane to a hotel to dine." He had no qualms about this, but I felt ill at ease.

We used to walk into the hotel, and everybody would acknowledge him. He would then walk to the bar and call over, "Nurse what would you like to drink?" He knew full well that I only ever had lemonade and lime or water, but he had to show off. I eventually told him off. "I will wait in the car unless you stop doing this."

"I like to wind people up. I know there will be gossip all over the island that I have a young girlfriend." I was not impressed and found the whole situation tacky.

Agnes was looking good, and I thought she would only be in the clinic for two weeks at the most. The days were long and endless. I missed one weekend at home and wondered whether I should stay on the island for the second. In the end the decision was taken out of my hands. Agnes died.

I felt such sadness. I knew she had had a peaceful death, but I really felt I had lost a favourite person. Agnes had a quiet funeral. I decided to stay on a little longer to help Sam. It was not because legal papers and such like needed sorting out. I knew he would miss his daily contact with Agnes much more than he realised. They had been married for over sixty years.

I let a couple of days pass before I cleared out Agnes's clothes. I still had not given in my notice. "I need to talk to you Sam."

"I also want to talk to you Jane, and I intend to do it first, as I pay your salary." I looked at him in a disgusted way.

"I am only using your own words back at you." It was the first and only time that Sam made me laugh. It was true.

I went to bed that night thinking that I no longer needed to worry about breaking the news of my leaving. My terms of employment were specifically related to caring for Agnes. I had no idea what Sam wanted to discuss with me, but it didn't matter. My mind was made up.

The next day Sam told the cook that she could go home after lunch. The cleaner left around this time too. We had the house to ourselves and there was no need for closed doors. I chose to sit at the dining table in case Sam sat next to me on the sofa.

Sam started by saying, "Whatever I am about to say, please will you not interrupt or answer. Wait until I have finished."

I laughed. "It might be a hard job, but I will try."

"I don't want you to laugh. Just absorb what I am saying. You have known me quite a while. Would you say I am a man who keeps his word?"

I answered him truthfully, "Yes."

"I don't want you to leave."

"I have no function here, now that Agnes has gone."

"Will you not interrupt! That is what you think. Well, you do have a function. You can marry me. I know I am a lot older than you but as you know I have all my marbles. You told Agnes that you would have loved to cruise around the world. Well, you can. I have been around it five times first class, but I would love to take you. It is another world. You wouldn't have to worry about clothes, only go out and buy the best."

I was speechless. My brain was all over the place.

"I overheard you say to Agnes that you would never marry again. Perhaps the right man has never asked you. I will continue to ask you until you say yes. I know I am uneducated, but I am respected by all who come into contact with me. I will buy your house from you, and you can give your children their share. We will keep the house as our English home. You can change the staff if you wish and do anything to the chapel to make it into your home. Please consider what I have said. I know from your conversations at different times that you have always worked hard. Well now is your chance to change all that. I know what you will answer if you answer me without thinking. It will be no."

By now I was shaking. '*I must be dreaming. This doesn't happen in real life.*'

Sam was right about one thing. My answer was no. He didn't want to accept my answer and kept bombarding me with more pleas.

"You can transform this place into a beautiful home, buy anything without worrying about the cost. Look how the dogs love you. Harvey is a funny dog but as soon as I saw you make a fuss of him, I was jealous. Just give yourself time to think. Maybe you want to talk it over with your children?"

Melanie had met Sam earlier that year. She was staying for the

197

half term break with her cousins who lived on the island. She visited us for afternoon tea. She thought both the chapel and Sam were menacing. On leaving she whispered to me, "Mother get out of this place. It feels evil and Dad would be horrified."

I knew what Melanie's reaction would be and I didn't need to discuss it with my other children because I knew I would never marry Sam.

I stayed at the chapel just long enough for me to sort myself out. I used to go for long walks on the golf course and replay the conversations in my head. I returned one afternoon to overhear a wonderful piece of gossip coming from the kitchen.

"Do you think she will stay and marry him?"

"I know he is loaded but she is much younger. She owns her own house on the mainland, has got a nice car plus family. If she says 'yes' I will tell her that he calls her his piece of class to everybody who will listen. That would stop her."

My life on the Isle of Man ended. I did a bad thing when I left. I gave Sam the impression that I was thinking of returning as his housekeeper. The thought had crossed my mind. On the way to the airport, he asked me once more to marry him.

"I expect you wouldn't want to share my bed."

"Of course."

When we parked and leaned into the boot to retrieve my luggage, he brushed his lips against my cheek. That certainly confirmed all my thoughts. I would have been owned by him and I doubted that he would have kept his word.

I came home to stay, much to my family's relief. Lee and Jennie moved to their flat a couple of weeks later. My telephone call to Sam informing him that I would not be returning wasn't pleasant. He could not believe that anybody could turn him down. He was so arrogant and confident that he was a good catch. There wasn't enough money in the world to ensnare me. A poor man would have stood a better chance.

I got many telephone calls from Sam. He always said the same thing. "Please speak to me."

I too always replied with the same words. "I am sorry Sam, but I will have to change my telephone number if you continue to call me."

"You will never have an opportunity like this again in your lifetime."

"Bye Sam."

I tried to put the Isle of Man experience behind me. I wanted to now organise a conservatory to be built. I had certainly earned the money and gained a lot of experiences along the way, some of which I could have done without.

CHAPTER TWENTY-FIVE

On completion of the conservatory, I flew out to Cyprus to join my sister-in-law. It was my second visit. My first visit was a couple of months after Bill died. Jean and Bob planned it all. They wanted me to have an uplifting holiday to recover from Bill's death. I enjoyed it more the second time.

I went for long walks every morning whilst Jean sat or read. I loved the place and its relaxed way of life. I was fond of the Cypriot people who were so friendly. I thought I could live in Cyprus. I returned home and this notion stayed with me.

After six months I asked Jean if she wanted me to book again, however Bob and she had other plans, so I booked myself in to the same hotel for the following February. I could not wait for the cold winter to pass.

With no commitments I was able to help some of the charities that the Guild supported. My team of ladies always turned up to the Wednesday market stall to fund-raise for the local hospice. In time the manager of the market extended our space and we had four tables in the most prestigious spot. From the moment we set up until the end of the day we did not stop laughing. From behind the stall, I witnessed the best of the British public, always giving and very generous in spirit. They were incredibly good, happy times.

My next holiday to Cyprus came around quickly. I knew things would be different for me without my sister-in-law but after the Isle of Man I felt prepared for anything that might be thrown my way.

I felt quite thrilled when I arrived at the hotel and was given a warm welcome by Charlotte, the front of house manager. She had booked me into my usual room. I arose the following day with a smile on my face. It was a beautiful day and the start of my two weeks of bliss. The crystal-clear sea looked enchanting as I walked along the promenade to Paphos harbour. *'I do love this place.'*

I walked much further than I intended, totally absorbed in my thoughts. As I passed the jeweller's shop, Eleni, the owner, came out and gave me a hug. She had remembered me from previous visits. Both she and her husband eventually became dear friends.

On my way back to lunch at the hotel, I browsed in all the estate agents' windows. I was astonished at the property prices. By the time I sat down to eat my brain was working out house prices and where the new builds were situated. After lunch I lay on the bed with my book which was abandoned within minutes. I went down to reception, picked up some property brochures, and made enquiries to a member of staff as to where she thought was the best place to live. She thought Peyia was the up-and-coming place. I returned to my room with a cold shandy, lay back on the bed and viewed the property papers. *'I am going to look at some properties tomorrow.'*

After my evening meal I walked into Paphos and looked in the windows of the smaller property developers. I noticed some new builds in the Maispa office, so I walked in and requested details of the villas and plans of the area. I was such a rookie. I had only looked at plans once before for the house in Hollyhock Close, but I had Bill to guide me. I was awake until the early hours with plans scattered all over the bed. Surprisingly, I was not nervous about the venture I was contemplating. Perhaps I should have been, but I knew I could discuss things with my children on my return.

The next morning the young agent, Martin Enderli, turned up at the hotel to take me to whichever sites I wished to view. We looked at so many. He told me weeks later that he could not believe how knowledgeable I was about sites and new buildings. I told him that I had nothing but common sense to assist me. Bill and I used to visit the site of our new house in Hemel, at each stage of the build and we used to speak with the builders. I must have retained more knowledge and know how than I realised.

Martin picked me up from the hotel most mornings. We must have visited dozens of newly built houses plus numerous plots. I used to go back to the hotel tired out. After my bath I used to pick up my book and take it onto the balcony, accompanied with a drink, before going down to dinner. I never read more than two pages before retrieving the dozens of property brochures and perusing them instead, such was my enthusiasm.

Whilst I was waiting for Martin, I decided I would like to investigate the new plots in Peyia. Peyia was situated along the coast

201

from Paphos between Coral Bay and Agios Georgious. It was a delightful ride with acres of banana trees lining either side of the road. I was shown an available plot allocated for a bungalow, but it was further out of Peyia than I thought.

We arrived at the next site and my first impression was a good one. The plots were opposite three properties already occupied but the real attraction was that they were being built at the foot of a mountain. Goats with bells on their collars were running up and down with their shepherd whistling to them. I walked onto the plot which was a generous enough space for my needs. I felt a little tinge of excitement until I realised that views of the sea would be impossible with it being single storey. There were other houses in the road. Martin showed me another, but I wasn't interested because of all the passing cars entering the cul-de-sac. "Well, we can forget Peyia," I said out loud. We drove out of the site in the opposite direction. I noticed a property on a corner plot, the last Maispa house on the site.

"Martin has that been sold?"

"I am sorry, I think it has but I will check at the office when I return."

I returned to my hotel room shattered with my brain addled from all the information I had to retain. I took my usual therapeutic bath and soaked in my expensive oil. I felt I had earned it.

Martin telephoned later to say that someone was interested in the property I had enquired about, but as yet, hadn't returned to the developer to pay a deposit. He went on to tell me that he had somewhere else in mind that he knew I would fall in love with it.

Martin collected me the following morning. He was full of apologies as he knew that the Peyia villa met all my requirements. We travelled along some country lanes that I hadn't been down before. Unexpectedly we arrived at the villa I was interested in. Mr Maise, the developer, had told Martin that as the other interested party hadn't paid any money or telephoned his office, I could have first refusal. I was overjoyed and couldn't believe my luck.

It was only partially built but I could see that this was my dream house. Everything now seemed a possibility rather than a pipe dream. *'My children will never believe what their mother is intending to do.'* Martin was euphoric too. He had become a friend, not simply an agent.

I now had all the documents I needed with respect to the sale. There were only three days of my holiday remaining. I spread them out on one of the beds so I could study them. I found my first query on the first page. I made a note of that and added several more. I completed reading the paperwork in the early hours of the morning. I had a list of questions I needed answering and I wanted to see the boss, not just anybody.

When I awoke the next morning, I realised it was a Saturday and the owner of the company would not be there. I telephoned the office requesting an appointment with Mr Maise at nine o'clock on Monday. It could not be later as I was catching the afternoon flight. The staff didn't think this possible, as the boss only showed up a couple of times a week. Mr Maise owned a lot of property all over Cyprus and was extraordinarily rich. It didn't occur to me that I was a very small fish in a very large pond coupled with the fact that many Cypriot men rarely talk business with women. Their place is not in a man's world.

I got to the office at 8.30 a.m. on Monday morning. Nobody was around. I waited until a young lady arrived. I apologised for being early and told her I was happy to wait for Mr Maise to arrive.

"Mr Maise won't come in today. We only see him occasionally."

"He will come as he hasn't answered my telephone call and that wouldn't be good business."

Whilst talking to the receptionist I could see the shadow of a person watching me through the frosted window. I surmised Mr Maise was surreptitiously weighing me up. He kept me for a full ten minutes and then called me in. "This is very unusual. Whatever do you want to see me for? I don't usually see clients." I related that I had read all the paperwork about the house. "Well, I am sure it in order."

"Yes, but I have one big problem. I have read that I must put down £2,000 pounds instantly to retain the house and a further £2,000 in two months."

"Yes. They are the usual rules."

"I know but I haven't got any spare money. I have a beautiful new house in England that will sell as soon as it goes onto the market. The English market is booming at present."

He laughed. "What makes you think I would consider that?"

"Because I give you, my word. I am sure you will have made a judgement about me by now."

He stood up and shook my hand. "How could I turn down such an interesting English lady? The house in Peyia will be yours as soon as I get the first £2,000. I will not sell it to anyone else in the meantime."

I walked away feeling on top of the world for at least a minute and then the shock of my commitment hit me. I made a quick return to the hotel to do my packing. *'What will the children think?'* After those thoughts I reasoned with myself. *'This is the first time in my life that I am doing something that I want to do, and I am not accountable to anyone.'*

I suddenly became aware of the enormity of the task ahead with no husband to guide me. I wondered what the reactions from my children would be. I didn't think that the family would think their mother crazy, but they would be concerned about the distance between us and how I would cope. I felt so sure that I could survive, and I knew that if it proved to be a mistake, I alone would have to resolve any consequences from my decision.

The flight home was filled with thoughts about this colossal undertaking. I wasn't having second thoughts, only positive ones. I didn't have to smile when I saw Andrea at the arrival lounge as my face was alight with anticipation. We saw each other immediately and our hug was tighter than usual. Stanstead Airport wasn't the airport of my choice but the only available flight at the time. As the journey home was longer than the usual drive, I suggested that we ate lunch before departing.

We sat down and pored over the menu. After the waitress took our order, I bent down to my flight bag and retrieved a large file. I passed it over to Andrea. "Have a look at this. I am buying this property and its being built from scratch." After the shock of my words, she opened it and could see the plans and various pages that contained my requirements for tiles, wall colours etc. The marble for the staircase was from a particular quarry so there was nothing to deliberate there. I watched Andrea's face and could see it was almost too much to take in.

"It looks wonderful Mum. So long as you are sure that you will be able to cope with being all that distance away from us. We all have phones and can Skype."

Our journey home was nonstop discussion about my future and the decisions I still had to make. I appreciated Andrea saying, "Mum you have spent all your life caring for people, now it is your time to do something for yourself." It gave me strength. Melanie and Nigel's reactions were the same.

I proceeded with the sale of my house. As predicted the house sold to the first viewer. I had to let it go for two thousand pounds less than I wanted but time was of the essence. As soon as the agent confirmed that the purchaser was anxious to proceed with the sale, I contacted the developer. Mr Maise told me that he was delighted to be able to reserve the villa and confirmed that it could not be sold to any other person. Phew! I was home but not quite dry.

I remember sitting in my conservatory with all the villa documents laying on the floor around me. I found the situation totally absurd and couldn't believe that I had proceeded with this enormous undertaking on my own. I often spoke out loud to Bill. "Bill if this isn't right for me, I know you will find a way to stop it."

I decided to ship a lot of my furniture to Cyprus. I needed to take as much as I could, as I didn't want to have to buy anything for my new home. I knew I would have to purchase the white goods. Charity shops were bombarded with things I'd hoarded. I vowed that my new home would not harbour any unnecessary items. In fact, I was aided by the building itself, as it didn't have a loft.

Friends and family wished me well. Many remarked that they could not do what I was doing and quite a few people said they couldn't understand my reasoning, as I was so closely involved with my children. Yes, I loved my family, but I only saw Cyprus as a short flight away. Should I have moved to Cornwall the journey time would have been the same. Others asked what would happen when I was old and could not travel. I answered that I was only in my early seventies, but people would have to visit me and have a holiday at the same time. That's how positive I was about the whole adventure.

The shipping removal van appeared to nearly fill the close. The packers took no time at all, and I was surprised how small my home contents seemed in such a large container. My little Starlet car could have easily fitted into the available free space, but it was too late to have the shipping manifesto altered. I watched the removal lorry leave the close with a fast-beating heart. My departure to another country was almost upon me. I knew I had done a similar thing before, but the difference was, Bill and Nigel were by my side.

I went back into my empty house with very mixed feelings. I hoped I was doing the right thing. I picked up my clothes and suitcases and drove to Adeyfield, which was to be my home for the next few months or until I was able to take possession of my new house in Peyia. Adeyfield was not in my plans or a place that I knew very well but now it was featuring in my life.

CHAPTER TWENTY-SIX

A Christmas party for supporters and fund raisers of the hospice was held annually. I had always been responsible for the catering but this year I wasn't able to, due to my imminent departure to Cyprus. This meant I was seated at a table with Jocelyn Harris, my friend of many years. Seated around tables throughout the hall were many of my friends from church. It was a delight for me to have so many of my friends in one place. I knew this would probably be the last time, I would see them altogether.

Unexpectedly Edwina Smith, the chairperson, came up to our table. "Would you do me a favour? I have a man who has just turned up. He doesn't have a ticket and doesn't know anybody. He comes to our bereavement class and seems sort of lost. Jane, you are one of the counsellors and you'll know how to handle him."

I thought, *This is the first time I have sat down as a guest at the Christmas gathering. I hope this doesn't take me away from the party.'*

I had two vacant seats to the side of me. I looked across and saw a very anxious gentleman watching Edwina's every move. Of course, I said I would look after him for the evening and introduce him to others. Jocy wasn't too happy. "It's a cheek. It's your night off."

Edwina brought him over and introduced him. "Jane, this is Ron Parbery."

I shook his hand. "You have a very nice surname." He sat down on the furthest chair, leaving a space between us. Although there were other guests sitting opposite us, he spent the whole evening telling me his life story. He only stopped for the speeches.

"Can I take you out for a coffee sometime?"

"Counsellors do not go out with clients."

"But you told me that you have retired from the job. Can I have your phone number in case I can get you to change your mind?"

At the end of the night, we made our way towards the exit and

Ron stayed glued to my side. He then put my coat around my shoulders.

"I will walk you to your car. Where have you parked?"

Jocy answered for me. "She knows where it is."

I laughed. "We will be fine, thank you."

However, he followed us and held the car door open for me. As we left, he called out, "I will telephone you."

I couldn't stop laughing and the more I laughed the crosser Jocy got. She later declared that he had ruined our evening. I told her not to be concerned as I wouldn't be seeing him again. In any case, I certainly wasn't interested.

Ron constantly telephoned with offers of help with my packing. After a short time, he offered to take me out for a meal. I could choose wherever I wanted to go, even to London should I know a special restaurant. He really tried hard to win me round. I eventually gave in, and Ron booked a table at a local restaurant. During the meal I made it clear that complications in my personal life were the last thing I needed. My plans were made for a completely new life in Cyprus. My children were all used to the idea and were looking forward to their future holidays. I was not looking for a relationship with anybody. The conversation ended with Ron saying, "Can I be your friend whilst you are still here?" I did not see any problem with that as it was only for a few months.

The house sale completed much faster than usual and I had to decide where to live for my last three months. Ron owned his own house at the edge of town. He offered me the option of moving in with him without any strings attached. After much thought I decided that if I could take my own bed and bedding it would be fine. I also insisted that I pay the bills during my stay as Ron had said he would not take any rent.

I remember standing in the bedroom that first night and I felt lonely and afraid of the future. Ron kindly ran me a hot bath. I lowered myself into the bubbles and stayed there until the water became cold.

I usually arose early, made tea then took Ron a cup. Afterwards he got ready for work. Ron was employed to drive children with disabilities to and from school. I soon became settled in Ron's home, knowing that it was only for the remaining time I had left in England. I helped him around the house by adding a woman's touch and we both worked on the garden.

Ron wanted me to meet his family, but I could not see the point in that. I felt it would put the relationship into a different category. However, I ended up doing just that. It was Christmas. I met his only daughter Linda, her husband Gary, and their two children. They made me welcome, but I felt the need to explain to them that I would soon be moving away. After a couple of weeks Ron asked if I would like you to meet his youngest son.

"He is a builder and has done rather well for himself."

"Ron, there is no point to this. I won't be seeing them again after I leave England."

"Please meet them. They will be upset that you have met Linda and not them."

I agreed and a date was set. I was made very welcome, but I thought, *'They think this is a relationship. What has Ron told them?'* We talked of my future in Cyprus without their father's name being mentioned. On our way home I asked Ron if he had led his family to believe that we had some sort of relationship which he denied. A fib of course.

Around this time, I made time to visit my sister and brother-in-law in Chepstow. At some point during the weekend, the conversation was steered towards Ron. Bette and David were very disturbed about me living in his house. My sister challenged me, "You say you have no relationship with this man and yet you are staying in his house. Do you expect us to believe that you are not sleeping with him?"

"I am not sleeping with him but if I was, that is my business. I am not sixteen. I am able to make my own decisions."

I returned to Hemel and received a letter from my sister a few days later. She told me that she thought my behaviour was appalling. She and David totally disapproved and told me that I had made myself look cheap. Bill would turn in his grave. What was I thinking of? I was a pensioner acting like a teenager. After the anger had subsided, I started to laugh and decided to let sleeping dogs lie. It was the end of the matter and was only resurrected years later with much laughter at the old-fashioned attitude to morals.

Finally, it was time for my departure. It was August and I knew the weather would be extremely hot in Cyprus. Aunt Vera had asked if she could come with me for a month's holiday and help me with the move. Andrea was going to follow two weeks afterwards.

Ron was in such a distraught state and said he could not live without me. My living at his house had showed him that I was the one he wanted to spend the rest of his life with. I was consumed with guilt and felt I should not have stayed and allowed him to see the relaxed, private me. The fact that Ron was petrified of flying made things easier for me as I didn't have to extend an invitation to him. We agreed that he was free to telephone me when he felt down and that I would stay at his house when I visited England. My bedroom would remain as I left it with the promise that no one else would be allowed to stay in it. I felt I was going away in the nick of time. The last thing I wanted was a serious relationship.

It seemed a long journey to Gatwick airport and the flight itself seemed to go on forever. I think it was because I was in such an anxious state. We arrived in tremendous heat. It was as hot as Durban in the summer. Martin, the agent, was there to greet us and drove us to the flat we had rented for a month. We needed accommodation whilst we awaited the shipping containers from the docks.

Martin was incredibly helpful in assisting me with all the paperwork required by the customs authority. We made several journeys to Limassol docks before the container could be released.

I needed to hire a car until I bought my own. I soon realised what a difference it made not having Bill at my side. Vera, being elderly, had no idea about how I felt about all the decisions I had to make. She was on holiday. I put off purchasing a car until Andrea arrived as I knew she would assist me. It was such a hectic time. We always seemed to be in offices of some kind, organising this, that and the other. We were extremely grateful that they were air conditioned as the intense heat zapped our stamina.

Suddenly everything came together. The shipper's delivery was imminent. Martin came up trumps and enlisted four Scots he knew to assist in the unpacking, plus his wife. Customs officers from Limassol followed the container. They asked me to sign a declaration that I was not bringing in anything I should not and then proceeded to break open the seal that had been secured at Hollyhock Close. One of the officers said, "I can see that you wouldn't have any illicit alcohol in there or drugs." This made me smile. There were no drugs, but Bill's stock of alcoholic spirits was packed alongside the kitchen equipment.

We found one of my cane chairs and sat Vera in it, where she could observe all that was going on without feeling she was in the way.

What a day. Boxes were constantly flying out of the bedroom windows after they had been unpacked. The helpers worked their socks off. My neighbours later told me that they had never seen anything like it. The team were worth every penny I paid them.

We sat down that night as though we had lived in the villa for months. Even my clothes from the container had been hung in their wardrobes. After a sit down to catch our breath and take stock we returned to the flat with the intention of returning to the villa for good in the morning. I had paid a month's rent in advance, but I didn't care. I owned a beautiful villa, and I did not have a debt in the world.

Unfortunately, during our first night we discovered a foul smell and noise coming from the air conditioning unit in Vera's bedroom. It was faulty and had to be replaced the following day. That was the only hiccup that we had.

After breakfast we viewed the garden for the first time. The swimming pool looked inviting and was such a beautiful blue, matching the sky but the rest left a lot to be desired. As the house was the last to be built, the garden had been used for dumping unwanted rubble. Behind the boundary wall was a drop of six feet onto a plot of barren land. I knew where the stones would be heading.

I stood on the balcony of my bedroom and looked across at the mountain with its goat herd, *'I cannot believe I am living in this haven.'* I felt so much more confident about my future. Yes, jobs needed to be organised, but it was all possible with time. Andrea's arrival was approaching. I valued her opinion and knew she would confirm the various tasks that needed attending to and in what order to execute them. I realised I would need the help of a couple of workmen plus a plan, come design for the garden. The prospect was exhilarating. However, whatever we decided between us I knew it was far too hot to perform any tasks outside. Vera and I were greatly affected by the heat. How grateful I was, that I had decided not to penny pinch and have air conditioning installed.

Andrea's plane had already landed when we arrived at the airport. My excitement was that of a small child expecting a special present. I drove home on the coast road so that she could get her first glimpse of Paphos waterfront and its harbour.

When we arrived home, I immediately gave her a tour of the villa. Andrea was pleased with her bedroom and that she had a balcony to view the distant sea and hills. It was an incredibly special time. After a good meal and a few cold drinks on the verandah it was time to retire to bed. We three slept well that night.

After breakfast, the next morning Andrea said, "You have to remember Mum, I only have two weeks and I want to get all your little jobs done." Making good was her first job. Martin had already put up the curtain rails, but Andrea had noticed they were already pulling out of the plaster. The number of tasks that she accomplished in those two weeks was unbelievable. We went into Paphos shops daily, sometimes twice a day, for DIY supplies. Before I moved, I had given away what I considered mundane things. We did not have one screw, nail or hook. How crazy was that.

The heat was getting to Andrea, but she would not stop. She appreciated that when she returned home, I wouldn't have anybody to help me with these essential jobs. In between the tasks, heat permitting, I drove us to various beautiful locations, all within half an hour's drive of the villa.

Apart from driving along the south coast there were always mountains to ascend, the first was behind my villa, followed by several more. It was a very picturesque drive. At first the mountainous terrain seemed a bit hairy to negotiate. Later I found it exhilarating and was able to revel in the distant views. On the other side of the mountain range, we discovered the villages of Lachi and Polis with their wonderful beaches and crystal-clear coastal waters. We used to walk along to the quiet harbour with its delightful boats bobbing up and down at their moorings. It became familiar to me over the years, but I never lost my delight in seeing it.

Andrea's second week was as hot as the previous one, unbearable. She has never been able to cope with heat but despite this she persevered and proceeded to clear the garden in the evenings by throwing the builders' discarded stones and rocks over the boundary wall. After hours there were still hundreds left to deal with in the following days. We revived ourselves afterwards by cooling off in the pool.

Despite thirty degrees plus, Vera could not be tempted into the pool, not even for a paddle on the steps in the shallow end. Andrea eventually cajoled her into dangling her feet over the edge of the pool, but only up to her ankles and with her nylon tights still firmly in place.

Martin hosted a large dinner party before Andrea departed, all three of us were invited. It was in Paphos, near to his home. When we arrived, everyone was already seated. I instantly recognised faces. Martin had invited everybody who had helped with my move. After we had eaten, he made a speech and announced that he had just received his commission from selling my villa and thought he would share the proceeds with the people that had helped. I could not believe it when he said it was the equivalent of £2,000. It seemed a fortune to me at the time. However, that generous gesture said a lot about Martin's kind nature. I am still in touch with Martin.

Andrea's departure came all too soon, and tears flowed. I knew how much I would miss her.

Vera had been with me for four weeks and I escorted her back to the UK. I felt it too soon to return as I had only been away a month. I had no need to visit friends and family.

Ron collected us up from the airport. He broke down and cried when he saw me. My short stay was at his house. Fortunately, I still had my Starlet which gave me the freedom to go where I wanted when I wanted. Ron kept telling me that he did not want me to leave him. What a predicament, this now had become something I had to deal with. Ron told me that his house was not his to sell, as it belonged to his son. That news rather surprised me, but I realised that I couldn't get involved with Ron's life. It was up to him to make his own decisions. I had sorted myself out and made enormous decisions with respect to my future. I had spent all my middle years looking after both sets of parents and tried to be the best parent I could after Bill died. I really could ill afford to use up my emotions on a man whom I really had not known for long.

I made the decision to remove all my possessions from Ron's house before I returned to Cyprus. He pleaded with me to leave my clothes as he knew that meant he would see me every visit. It was a difficult time. Ron was such a lovely caring man without a mean bone in his body. Hurting someone of that nature is more than hard. I finally agreed to leave my clothes and always consider that I had a home in England.

Ron was petrified of flying and although he said he would love to come out to visit me for the following Christmas he wondered how it would be feasible, unless by land or sea. After I arrived home Ron mentioned in one of his daily telephone calls that someone had helped him research the trip. It could be done but would take two days. They had apparently done something similar in order to take their animals to Cyprus.

Days later Ron's thoughts had taken a different tack. He informed me that he had booked a flight with a return ticket for a month later. I was more than surprised. "How do you know that I haven't accepted an invitation for Christmas with my Cypriot friends? Elleni, who owned the jewellers in Paphos, had in fact asked me but I had declined as I thought I might be having family out from England. Ron replied, "That's all right, I will stay in the villa."

"How will you cope with flying?"

"Anything to be with you. If the plane crashes that will be fate."

Needless to say, the plane didn't crash, and some wonderful people befriended him and extended their kindness for the entire journey, right through to me greeting him in the arrivals lounge. I could not believe the weight of his baggage. Various people had asked him to bring their Christmas presents. I do not know how he charmed the stewards at the weigh in. Ron's innocence always made people want to help him.

Ron's month went by very quickly. During the last week he was so despondent and said, "I am not going back." That was not an option.

He cried at the airport which started me off. His parting words were, "You see, you are going to miss me otherwise you wouldn't cry. I will telephone you every day for the rest of my life." People behind, in the check-in queue, were looking concerned and saying things like, "Isn't it sad when old people have to part." Ron's shoulders were still shaking as he ambled out of sight with someone's support.

I was left not only in tears but with concerns. I was fearful that my whole future would be jeopardised should I even consider a relationship. *'I have been a carer for my whole life, now it is my time. I don't need new responsibilities.'*

I returned from the airport with a determination that I would forge ahead with the plans I had made.

CHAPTER TWENTY-SEVEN

During the first few months of occupation, the villa was targeted by many unemployed tradesmen. One of the business cards posted through the door was from a builder who had his own labourer. He showed me various credentials, but I was savvy enough to know they could be fraudulent. I interviewed him and he came across as genuine.

He accepted my plans for the garden but had some creative ideas of his own to improve upon my design. Before the landscaping could start, I needed the villa's boundaries to be fenced. This task was a marathon, especially in the intense heat. The trellis panels needed varnishing which proved to be a nightmare as the varnish dried too quickly. After the completion of the hard landscaping, irrigation system and electrics, I organised various nurseries to deliver plants and trees. I was determined to have fruit trees. Having my own orange, lemon and limes trees was a novelty. I was very conscious of overseeing the whole project.

I had budgeted around £10,000 for the entire garden but I kept adding to the plans. Every night I would go through the day's work and expenditure. It was quite tough on the nerves, having nobody to share and discuss this with. I adopted the attitude of in for a penny in for a pound. A long time afterwards when my neighbours had become friends, they told me that I was the focus of daily discussions. They had concluded that I must be wealthy as I had a team of people moving me in, followed by gardeners and tradesmen galore.

Swimming pool maintenance was another area that I knew nothing about. I had a pump house with all the mechanisms in, plus chemicals for one month left by the installers. I had to find my own pool maintenance men. I recognise now that I did quite well for a retired lady in her seventies. At the time I did not realise all the pitfalls that could have befallen me.

I could not wait for the garden to mature. I aspired to picking my

214

own grapefruit for breakfast. It came to pass eventually.

Finally, I was now in the delightful position to have visitors to stay. The first were obviously my children followed by friends. All those who came were enthralled. The verandah was such an asset and was used for breakfast. I sat there at the start of every day. I made my plans there and when I had guests the day's activities were organised from there.

When I came to the end of my spending spree, I made a budget for bills and housekeeping plus my annual visits back to England. I felt I had things under control.

I made many friends and resumed my church membership. My future looked quite rosy. I felt my dream had come true.

My garden was a joy. It really had met all my expectations. I was impatient for all the trees and shrubs to grow. Some of us gardeners expect miracles in a short space of time.

I became very friendly with a Cypriot nurseryman, who was very generous with his advice. Yanni visited the villa to see if I had planted the trees and shrubs correctly. This was the start of a very precious friendship. Yanni remained my friend for all the years I was in Cyprus. He looked after me, proffering advice on all matters Cypriot. I took family to meet him. He lived in Polis. Yanni always greeted us with drinks. He would then leave us for five or ten minutes whilst he drove to the bakery that specialised in local produce. He always returned with delicious Cypriot treats. I have such lovely memories of a truly kind gentleman. All the Cypriot people that I met were kind. I was often invited to their homes and made welcome by their families. Yanni would watch over me if he thought I was getting chatted up. "Watch out Janie you are a very good catch." Our friendship could not be defined by any words. He would say, "Janie you are my English mother." I really was too young to be his mother and too old to be a girlfriend. Great friends is the only description that fits.

Yanni always found an excuse to have a family get together. Long, old wooden tables would be dragged into his courtyard with the oldest assortment of seats imaginable. Some were in better condition than others. It was a question of first come first served. Usually by the time I arrived the wine had been flowing for some time. It did not matter that I only drank soft drinks, I was offered wine for the whole evening. Every time a guest wanted a drink the host filled the entire table's glasses. I don't recall anybody ever saying no. Singing would start as the guests became more convivial and it grew louder by the minute. I was invited to many Cypriot celebrations and was always welcomed and respected. Most Cypriots speak English but when they reverted to Greek another guest would always start a conversation in English with me and often translated the Greek conversation.

I hold a deep affection for the Cypriot people and will never forget the hospitality they extended to me. It was warm and caring. I knew that if ever I was in any sort of trouble or threatened in any way my Cypriot friends would have come to my aid.

My life was idyllic with weather to match. Friends surrounded me and my church family played an important part of my life. My neighbours always invited me to their barbecues, and I reciprocated. I often sat and listened to the chatter surrounding me and reflected on how good life was. My visitors were always reluctant to return home, their two weeks was never sufficient time for them. I really relished every moment of their stay.

Although the villa was large, I did not find it hard to maintain. The dust was my only bugbear. Every surface would be dusted clean and within an hour it was back again. At certain times during the year sandstorms blew in from the Sahara. They really were invasive. You could write in the debris deposited on the balconies. That was my only grievance about the country I had chosen to live in. Balanced against the joys of my everyday life, it was nothing.

Ron telephoned me every day despite me telling him it was too expensive. Andrea would always Skype. This new technology was such a thrill. It was wonderful to see each other. On one occasion I answered a Skype call completely forgetting I could be seen with my hair rollers in place and no makeup on. Melanie telephoned me often and always updated me with news of my grandsons. Nigel did the same. Modern communication made the world seem much smaller. It would be better still today because all the children, even the little ones, can use the modern technology.

Visitors arrived on a regular basis. I got to know all the villages that surrounded Paphos and made many trips to the Troodos Mountains. On one occasion I booked a stay in a beautiful mountain hotel for Melanie and Ken and me. It was a pleasurable visit. The architecture and history were a bonus. There were magnificent wooden carvings remaining from centuries before. We spoke to the owner who was so proud of his heritage. The hotel had their own stream and provided fresh trout for breakfast or the evening meal. Surrounding the hotel were narrow streets with nooks and crannies and alleyways, a sight that took your breath away. Most of the stone houses were adorned with carved wooden balconies. It was enchanting. The first time I was taken there I was spellbound. On subsequent visits the magic remained.

Each January I booked my ticket home to the U.K. for the summer months. Late June onwards was far too hot to bear. Although the house was air-conditioned the heat outside was intolerable. Air tickets were always expensive because of the high demand. However, it was a joy to return home to see all my family and friends.

I was fortunate that I had an arrangement with Ron and was able to stay at his house for as long as I wanted. Usually, I would be home for a couple of weeks before taking myself off to Chepstow. Much to my amazement, my sister suggested that Ron should come too. I was hesitant. Bette spoke to Ron over the phone as she wanted the invitation to come from her. I was far from sure, but Ron was over the moon. He saw this as a positive sign, family approval. I think Bette really wanted to see if Ron was a suitable candidate for her sister. I dreaded the visit as they held Bill in such high affection.

The weekend passed much better than I expected. Ron felt incredibly happy and thought Bette and David were a delightful couple. I reminded him on the way home that the visit did not signify how I saw our relationship. "You are going to expect more of me than I am prepared to give. I definitely don't wish to remarry. I have a wonderful life in Cyprus, and I don't wish to change things." We finished the last hour of the journey without our usual chit chat and banter.

CHAPTER TWENTY-EIGHT

Ron felt he was now an experienced flyer and asked if he could return to Cyprus again in a couple of months. This would give him time to save for his ticket.

I had only been back in Peyia for a couple of weeks when Ron phoned and told me he had exciting news. He had booked his ticket. I was astounded and a little irritated as he had presumed that I did not have any other visitors staying. He gave his standard answer, "That's all right. I can always sleep on the settee."

I felt refreshed from my holiday, seeing my family had been uplifting and I looked forward to seeing them again in Cyprus for their holidays. Life carried on with me doing the rounds of friends and enjoying the idyllic lifestyle. Ron and I talked on the phone every day. His excitement about his forth coming visit was palpable. He kept asking me if I wanted anything special brought out and said that my children had already given him various packages to bring. His fervour was infectious, and I found myself looking forward to his arrival.

Ron arrived at the airport like an experienced traveller. He was weighed down with luggage, made even heavier by all the extras he was transporting. I think that day was the first time I felt really relaxed, as though I was in the presence of an old friend.

As the second week of Ron's holiday approached, he asked me if he could extend his holiday. I said he could, but he would have to change his ticket and there would be a financial penalty.

"I don't care. I will just buy a single when I go home."

"But if you do that you will lose your money."

"That doesn't matter. Being with you for a longer time is worth every penny." Money did not come into the equation. I accepted that.

Many weeks flew by, and life was remarkably comfortable. I enjoyed Ron's company and he was immensely popular amongst my neighbours and friends. He proved to be a truly kind and caring man.

Ron never redeemed his ticket, never went back to the UK, and never informed the Cypriot authorities. He was in fact, an illegal immigrant and lived with me for six years.

During this period, we travelled home every summer. I really ponder to this day and cannot think why the authorities did not pursue him, but I am very thankful that they didn't.

Ron said he felt re-born and everyday was his Christmas. We were fortunate for the first couple of years and were able to stay in the house in Adeyfield. Things took a different turn when we heard that Ron's son wanted to put the house on the market. We were concerned and wondered where we would stay when we came home. Gary, Ron's son had the answer. He planned to convert some space and a garage into an apartment for us within the grounds of his property in Bourne End. Problem solved.

However, it was a massive re-think and adjustment for me. My cherished stability was shaken. Ron was in a state of distress as he thought I would sever my relationship with him. It was too late for that to happen as I had become so fond of him. I could not let this man out of my life now.

We made the best out of the situation. Every time we went through customs on our various trips home, I expected the heavy hand of the law to descend on Ron's shoulder. Ron was not concerned and did not worry about it. He never felt the apprehension that I sensed on every trip.

My children and friends accepted Ron as my other half. Ron asked me many times to marry him, but I was happy with things as they were. In days gone by it was frowned upon if you lived with a man and were unmarried but times had changed. All my friends knew of our relationship and accepted the situation. We had a very loving and caring relationship over the many years we were together.

Ronnie's health was giving me cause for concern. I could not put my finger on it, but I could see he was deteriorating before my eyes. He kept saying, "You are fussing about nothing. I am fine." We had already bought our air tickets for our annual trip home and as soon as we got to the apartment in Hemel, I telephoned for an appointment to see his doctor. We got one for the next day.

Ron asked me to go into the examination room with him, but I declined. The doctor knew Barbara, Ron's wife, very well and I did not feel like explaining myself. I sat in reception. When Ron returned, he walked down the corridor looking punch-drunk.

"Dr Nodder has just told me I have cancer."

We found this unbelievable as Ron had had no tests, not even a blood test and yet the doctor had diagnosed cancer plus a heart defect and told Ron his time was limited. We both sat in the car in a state of shock.

All my years of working in the surgery had not prepared me for this. What a blow. I drove back to Bourne End in a stupor. It was beyond comprehension. We broke the news to Gary and his wife Lorraine, immediately. Then later told Tony, Ron's other son. We all found it incredulous, especially as he had not had any tests.

We later discovered that the tumour was so large it was evident to the GP during his cursory examination.

After the devastating news I guessed that time was short for Ronnie. We cancelled our tickets home and decided to make the most of the time left to us.

We drove down to Bournemouth where Ron's daughter and family lived. Linda's husband had a terminal illness and only a short time to live. We did not want to burden her with this added prognosis of her dad's.

Ron did not accept the doctor's conclusion and kept saying, "I am sure they have made a mistake." A couple of x-rays confirmed the doctor's prognosis. The cancer had spread and was far too invasive for any treatment. Ron kept smoking his roll-up cigarettes until the end, despite being told that all the veins and arteries to his heart were blocked from smoking. What a hard price he had to pay.

Ronnie was admitted to the hospice in Watford and had his eightieth birthday the following day with all his family around him. He spent the next day with me and his family reminiscing. Ron then went into a deep sleep and did not wake up again. He died in the early hours most peacefully with me by his side. He was a lovely man and a joy to live with.

CHAPTER TWENTY-NINE

I continued to live in the apartment at Bourne End for several years after Ron's demise. In 2013 my grandson Adam and his partner Karina chose to get married in Cyprus. A lot of the family flew out to Paphos for the wedding. It was ironic that we could not stay in my villa and had to rent accommodation. After Ron was diagnosed, we had asked some friends who were renting in Peyia if they were interested in renting the villa. They were very keen and were there for some years. Visiting my old home before flying back home after the wedding, made me nostalgic and I debated whether to return to Cyprus or not.

I knew it would be different. I was now in my eighties, and I wondered if I could manage the large house. Like everywhere the expense of maintaining the property had increased greatly. Me returning meant that I would have to give my tenants notice. It really was a soul-searching decision, but I concluded that I should return to my home with the view to eventually selling it.

We had lived at the apartment in Bourne End paying a peppercorn rent towards the heating, but Gary now needed to rent it out. Once a date was set for my return, I organised shippers and emptied the apartment.

I knew returning to Cyprus was going to be extremely hard. I would be dealing with everything by myself. I understood I had a hard task ahead of me. I discussed my concerns with the family and my son-in-law Ken came up with an incredible proposal. He volunteered to return with me and stay for a month to do all the jobs that needed attention. It was an unbelievably kind offer and Melanie whole heartedly supported his decision. The tickets for my return to Cyprus were booked. At the same time, I wrote a letter giving notice to my tenants. I also telephoned them to warn them of the impending letter. I am afraid it was a bitter blow to them. They were good tenants, but I just could not continue financially and needed to sell. The villa was vacated just

221

before our arrival. We arrived home and found everywhere clean making it was easy to move back in.

I explored the estate agents at the first opportunity and placed the villa with one in Coral Bay. I was there during a lunch time, and the boss was out of the office which meant I didn't sign any papers which proved to be fortuitous. A couple of weeks later I was told of a Russian estate agent in Paphos. I was impressed by their agency and how they marketed properties. I decided to cancel the Coral Bay agent and proceed with them.

Ken soon started on the various jobs that needed doing. He began with the re-varnishing of the cane furniture on the verandah. What a trial that was. It was still extremely hot, and he had to paint accordingly. Ken loves the sun and alternated between sunbathing and getting jobs done. Gradually all the tasks got completed. I could not have done it without him. Melanie decided to fly out for the last week of Ken's visit and then Andrea joined us, followed shortly afterwards by Nigel. I spent thirteen years in Cyprus, and this was the only time all three of my children were there at the same time. We had a fabulous long weekend all together.

Melanie stayed on and helped with all the household bits and pieces that need doing and Andrea was there to assist with the arrival of my shipping. The family's support eased me back into my Cypriot life again. I felt truly blessed and looked after.

The family all departed at different times. The last journey from the airport home to Peyia was different. I knew that I was now on my own. I spent the whole journey telling myself not to cry, but it was to no avail. I cried aplenty.

The next morning, I woke up to a noticeably quiet villa and decided to go to Agios Georgios. If you want tranquillity this is the place to be. I took a book, bought a coffee and looked at the wonder that was the harbour with its bobbing fishing boats, awaiting their next trips out. The cloudless azure sky, the crystal-clear seawater with a wonderful view of the Akamas mountains. It was a wonderful sight, despite having seen it so many times before. I told myself what a lucky woman I was to have all this beauty within reach of my home. My neighbour would walk there in the early morning, between six thirty and seven o'clock and return running. He did try to convince me to join him one morning, but I knew it would be too much for me.

It was now a question of waiting for prospective buyers to arrive. I thought the villa would sell quickly but it didn't. Weeks turned into months. There were the usual time wasters having days out viewing properties, people offering sums ridiculously lower than the asking prices. Eventually a German couple requested a second viewing. They lived in an apartment and did not need to sell their property. It looked promising and I wondered if they would make an offer. I was disappointed when I heard nothing. However, the husband returned a couple of weeks later and made an offer which I said I would think about. It was July and time for my usual holiday back in England. Things were quite different as I had not got a home to return to. Arrangements were made for me to stay with Andrea, Hilary and Ally in Berkhamsted. I was looking forward to the break and seeing the family. Andrea and Hilary had arranged to collect me from the airport.

My mind was in a turmoil. *'Maybe I could have a sale, nothing was guaranteed, there is still so much ahead of me.'*

I had been feeling under par for a few weeks, but I put it all down to the stress of selling my home.

CHAPTER THIRTY

It was a week prior to my leaving when I started to feel quite ill. Any movement caused breathlessness. I wasn't sure whether it was anxiety stemming from the probable sale of the villa or my trip home to England. I made an appointment at a private clinic for a check-up and the doctor concluded that my blood pressure was low but could not find anything else wrong. He assured me that I would be okay to fly. I didn't feel relieved or convinced when I left the clinic. Several days passed and I still felt unwell. It didn't matter what I did the situation didn't improve. Even to walk the slight slope of my drive was difficult. Two days before my departure I was invited by my neighbours for an afternoon drink to say our goodbyes. I was not well enough to return home by foot, even though they lived behind my garden boundary. I had to ask Tony, my host, to take me those few yards in his car. He was greatly concerned.

Once home I rested then with great determination and effort packed my suitcase. I knew at that stage that I would not be able to lift it down the staircase. The next morning, I drove to the clinic to seek advice once again from their doctor. He was not available, working at another clinic in Coral Bay. The receptionist telephoned him, and he agreed to fit me in to his schedule. My friend Joan came with me.

The doctor took my blood pressure again and confirmed that I would be able to fly. I was surprised and thankful that I had asked for assisted passage for the flight home.

On arriving back at the villa, I was relieved that I had packed my case. I checked all my flight documents in readiness for the journey the next day and stayed sitting in the same armchair for hours, only getting up to refill my water jug. It was in the evening that my body started to react differently. I knew I was having a heart problem. I had witnessed my father's heart attacks on two occasions and knew the signs only too well. I called out, "God you will have to help me as there is only you and I." I expected to die. I didn't want a neighbour to find me on the floor or in my chair, so after an hour or so had passed, I decided to try and negotiate the stairs. How stupid was that. At a snail's pace I traversed the spiral staircase to the top and reached my bedroom. I slid onto the top of the bed and was astounded to see the light of the new day. Come what may, I knew that I would try and make the trip home. I just could not tell anyone how ill I was.

Brian and Joan, my lovely friends, collected me from home to take me to Paphos airport. I confessed that I wasn't feeling too good and asked them to take me right into the terminal building. I only managed to walk through the doors. "Brian I will have to have a wheelchair. I cannot walk any further." When I said my goodbyes to them, I really felt that it was for the last time. On boarding the aircraft, the hostess said, "There is your seat. It is number eleven." It seemed a mile away. I literally fell into it and the kind passenger in the adjacent seat helped me by taking my handbag and placing it under the seat. He realised that I was extremely ill. It was an incredibly anxious journey. I was so relieved when I saw Andrea and Hilary waiting for me in the Arrivals lounge with a wheelchair.

Andrea was extremely concerned and as soon as we got home took my blood pressure. She telephoned the surgery, reported my condition and requested an immediate appointment. I was given an ECG and the doctor asked Andrea if she could drive me straight to the cardiac unit at Watford hospital, as this would be quicker than waiting for an ambulance. I remember looking at Andrea's face whilst she was driving, the stress was very apparent. I felt so apprehensive for her, as her own health was far from good.

I was in good hands at the cardiac unit and felt the better for it. During that night I arrested but thankfully pulled through. I was monitored the following day and night and the cardiac team concluded that I needed to have a pacemaker fitted.

I consider that I was extremely fortunate being in a country with experienced heart consultants whose skills came free with the National Health Service. I would most certainly have died without their expertise which was given so graciously.

I returned to the care and hospitality of Hilary, Andrea and Ally. I was now faced with the fact that I could no longer live alone in Cyprus. Fortunately, I had been on the council's housing list for around four years. I had renewed my application after Ron died.

I applied to the housing department to be rehomed. A housing officer visited me in at Andrea's home in Berkhamsted and my medical conditions were considered a priority. Before too long I received an offer to be rehomed in sheltered accommodation in Gossoms End. A date was made to view the property.

As the door of the flat was opened, I was immediately struck by how small it was. The living room was a similar size to my hall in Cyprus and the bright orange carpet didn't help. I drew in a deep breath and looked at my daughter's face consumed with anxiety and stress. I knew instantly that I would accept it, however I perceived it.

Papers were signed and my small abode has been my haven for the past two years. I am safe, warm and protected.

Nigel ferried me around to various furniture stores. I was grateful to have both his arm to steady me and his opinion on my choices. Andrea advised on the soft furnishing. Workman came to fit the curtains and tracks. Melanie arranged to stay with me for two weeks to see me settled in and keep an eye on my health. How fortunate was this old lady?

Melanie returned to Devon and reality set in for me. This was now my future. I used to sit in my chair and appraise the situation. I was fortunate to be alive, also fortunate to have loving children. My church friends have always been a great support and remain so to this day. I had given my car to Andrea who always returned it to me whenever I visited from Cyprus. It was now mine permanently.

After discussions with my children, I made the decision to finalise the sale of my villa in Cyprus. The purchasers had offered far less than I was hoping for, but time was ticking, and I decided to cut my losses.

Melanie returned with me to vacate the property. I had sold the villa fully furnished and only needed to remove the last of my personal possessions. We rose early on the day of departure, changed the sheets and towels, re-made the beds and hung fresh towels in the bathroom. We left the villa pristine ready for the new owners to slip into their beds on their arrival. Although I felt sad when we shut the door for the last time, I hoped that the new owners would take care of both the garden and home as I had done.

The new owners e-mailed me with their thanks and delight at their new home. They have contacted me several times with pictures of the villa. It is still as I left it and has not been changed in anyway. Last Christmas I received pictures of them sitting down at the table with my linen Christmas tablecloth, plates and cutlery. They were raising their glasses to the camera. I am so pleased that my furnishings and possessions have provided further joy for other people in Cyprus. The love I left in the villa has been enriched by the joy of the new owners and their children.

I am now prepared and ready for the life that I that nearly lost.

My parents did their best as they saw it.
My marriage was surrounded by enduring love.
My children light up my life each and every day.
Their children and my great grandchildren make every heartbeat count.
I am blessed with caring friends.
I am loved.
I have it all.
Thank you to everybody that touches my life now and encourages me on my final journey.

EPILOGUE

I am now living in the delightful town of Tring. My ground floor flat looks out on attractive grounds with lawns and mature trees, and I spend a lot of time watching the birds and the squirrels' antics.

I have now reached the age of ninety-one. In 2020 my family organised a party to celebrate my milestone birthday, but like so many events, it had to be cancelled because the entire country was placed in 'lockdown.' The coronavirus Covid 19 was declared a pandemic. I've seen nothing like it before in my lifetime. There have been, so far, over four and a half million deaths worldwide and we are still living with it. How lucky we are to live in a caring country and have the wonderful NHS.

I've slowed down physically although I still drive. Melanie and Ken still live in Devon but the rest of my ever-expanding family live locally within Dacorum. My six lovely grandsons have given me ten beautiful great grandchildren.

Lightning Source UK Ltd.
Milton Keynes UK
UKHW012305250422
402032UK00001B/13